Words and Concepts that Are and Are Not Conducive to Enlightenment

I0429608

Understanding Principles Fundamental to Integral Deep Listening

Joseph Dillard

Integral Deep Listening Press
Berlin, 2016
ISBN-13: 978-1530350124
ISBN-10: 1530350123

Also by Joseph Dillard

Dreamworking:
How to Use Your Dreams for Creative Problem Solving
Transformational Dreamwork:
Toward an Integral Approach to Deep Listening
Waking Up: How to Use Integral Deep Listening to Transform
Your Life
Seven Octaves of Enlightenment: Integral Deep Listening
Pranayama
Healing Integral 1: Toward a Global Re-Alignment
Healing Integral 2: Transformations for the Future
Integral Deep Listening Interviewing Techniques
Integral Deep Listening Practitioner
Integral Deep Listening and Healing
Integral Deep Listening and Meditation
Dream Sociometry
Understanding the Dream Sociogram
Integral Deep Listening: Awakening Your Life Compass
Transcending Your Monkey Mind:
The Five Trees and Meditation
Ending Nightmares for Good
Integral Deep Listening Case Studies
Light from Heaven: Deep Listening to Near Death Experiences.
Words and Concepts that Are and Are Not Conducive to
Enlightenment:
Understanding Principles Fundamental to Integral Deep Listening
Dream Yoga: Der weg der Träume

Table of Contents

Forward

Like Icarus, you are going to have to learn to fly on your own if you want to approach the higher regions of enlightenment. The words and concepts you take for granted are like feathers that will melt away as you ascend. More refined feathers will take you higher, but in time, even they can no longer define you or support you in your further ascent. But how do you know which you need to keep and which ones are weighing you down or will cause you to plummet?

Buddha believed that some questions about reality, as well as some activities, such as asceticism and living a worldly existence, are "not conducive to enlightenment." However, he said that there are seven sets of qualities that *are* conducive to enlightenment.[1] Integral Deep Listening (IDL) shows that enlightenment is a never-ending process of lucidity, clarity and waking up. Could it possibly be that something as important as spirituality is not conducive to your enlightenment? Could spiritual concepts such as soul, Self, God, karma, reincarnation, positive thinking or love be blocking you from the enlightenment you seek? *Words and Concepts that Are and Are Not Conducive to Enlightenment* has something to challenge, irritate or piss off everyone. There are very few sacred cows here that are not sent to the slaughterhouse and ground into Happy Meals.   Far from being an exercise in malicious torment of devout seekers, its intent is to help you examine your own assumptions so you can get out of your own way. What beliefs have you outgrown and are now blocking your growth? What assumptions do you want to keep, after having examined them closely to find out if they still do indeed support   your   enlightenment?

---

[1] These are: 1) Four establishments of mindfulness (body, feelings, mental states, mental qualities; 2) Four right exertions (for the preventing of unskillful states to arise, the abandoning of the already arisen unskillful states, the arising of skillful states, the sustaining and increasing of arisen skillful states; 3) Four bases of power (will, energy, consciousness, examination; 4) Five faculties (conviction, energy, mindfulness, unification, wisdom; 5) Five powers (conviction, energy, mindfulness, unification, wisdom; 6) Seven factors of Enlightenment (mindfulness, investigation, energy, joy, tranquility, unification, equanimity; 7) Noble Eightfold Path (right understanding, right intention, right speech, right action, right livelihood, right energy, right Mindfulness, right unification.

1: What Is Enlightenment?

So, why aren't you enlightened? You've read the books, you've gone to workshops, you've learned and practiced meditation. Let's look at the standard answers to this question and show why they are non-answers. We will then look at how your barriers to enlightenment probably lie in what your understanding of enlightenment is and is not. Finally, we will look at what it takes to become enlightened and how Integral Deep Listening (IDL) supports that process.

Why Most Explanations for Why You Stay Stuck Won't Work for You

It is simple to look at the standard reasons we are given, or we give ourselves, for our lack of enlightenment, and then discover why they are inadequate. You may have been told or believe you are not enlightened because you either haven't used the right approach or because you just haven't meditated or prayed appropriately or enough. You are visualizing Avalokiteshvara when you need to be visualizing Manjusri. You are doing hatha yoga when you need to be doing kundalini. You are attempting to open the wrong chakra, or open them in the wrong order, or using agni yoga instead of bhakti yoga to open them. You are following channelings from the White Brotherhood instead of following Jesus. You are following Jesus instead of finding your totem animal and going on your vision quest. You are not doing Reiki enough or doing Tarot instead of I Ching or kabbala. You are wasting all your time in that spiritual mumbo-jumbo instead of becoming a rational scientist or secular humanist. So if you're not enlightened it's all your fault.

The "right" approach always ends up being whatever I, the master, the authority, tell you to do; if you aren't using my preferred method you are using the wrong approach and that is why you are not enlightened. However, because most, if not all approaches and teachers operate from this set of assumptions, the only reasonable conclusion is that searching for the *right* approach to enlightenment is a fool's errand. There is no one "right" approach. If there were, it would consistently produce enlightened individuals. Where are such people? Where are such approaches? What we find when we look for enlightened masters are people who are awake in some ways and brain dead in others; none of them are perfect. We find approaches that will help you wake-up in different ways, depending on your own aptitudes, interests, and needs. Do they produce enlightened individuals? Go take a close look at those making such claims and draw your own conclusions.

This also means that no, it is not true that every approach is the "right" approach or that any and all roads lead to enlightenment. This is the bland, fuzzy thinking and excuse-making of the egalitarian and pluralistic world view often associated with late personal levels of development. We are all one big, happy family, and who are we to say that Christ love is better than Wicca or that Scientology will not make you enlightened? All is in divine order, so whatever you do is right!

If you have practiced some approach like Transcendental Meditation for years and still cannot levitate (a claim it makes) and are not enlightened (another claim it makes), is it because you haven't used TM enough or done it correctly? Such conclusions can easily be tested: out of the hundreds of thousands of practitioners of TM you would find some who can levitate and who are enlightened in a way that stands out among humans, yes? If you do an investigation, you may find some TMer's who can "hop" a bit when they are meditating, and you will find some who have high brain coherence and who experience states of bliss from time to time. These gains may indeed be impressive, and convince you that you can benefit from practicing TM, but are these people enlightened?

In order to know, you have to be able to look at the entirety of their lives, not just who they present themselves to be in public. When you do so, or when you talk to those who know them best, you will find that they are as human as you are, meaning they have plenty of characteristics that are imperfect and do not fit into your definition of what it means to be enlightened. You can in similar fashion test the claims made by Christianity, Tibetan Buddhism, Zen, and contemporary enlightened "masters." Note that contemporary "masters," like Andrew Cohen, are most easily shown to be unenlightened. The farther back in time the easier it is to construct a history around a person that conforms to your definition of enlightenment. For example, believers and invested scholars have been playing this game with Jesus for centuries. Buddha's appeal rests on the idealism of the mythology surrounding him, mythology that grew up in the hundreds of years before an account of his life was ever written down.

Enlightenment claims are effective for those who want to believe and who therefore do not ask too many questions. In fact, a preliminary demand of most spiritual paths is that you suspend disbelief and doubt and have "faith." You accept whatever you are told as true. You are asked to suspend your adult ability to think and reason and instead regress into simple childlike belief. Is regression a path to enlightenment? Is moving toward undifferentiated unconsciousness a path to clear, lucid wakefulness?

IDL offers a path to greater wakefulness, but that is quite different from making claims that you will become enlightened if you use it. It assumes that life itself spent millions of years evolving creatures with frontal lobes and capable of rationality for good reason. These developments represent a major evolutionary step toward greater wakefulness. Those who believe that enlightenment involves suspending thinking, questioning, and reasoning take on the burden of proof. It is they that need to show how regression to pre-rational, childlike states of awareness produce greater states of wakefulness or enlightenment than does belief combined with thinking, questioning, and reasoning.

Notice that IDL is not saying "reason is better than belief" or that "adulthood is better than childhood." Instead, it is saying, "You need to combine and integrate the strengths of both childhood and adulthood, belief and reason if you want to transcend both." Notice that this approach embraces rather than rejects belief. It notes that scientific humanism, skepticism, and atheism are systems of belief and that belief is not optional; only our ability to delude ourselves into thinking we do not have beliefs is optional.

We can also gain clarity by asking, "What are the psychological benefits of making claims that we are enlightened and can teach it to others?" Notice that those who make such claims invariably shift responsibility from the teacher, master, teaching, "path," yoga, religion and themselves onto you, the student. Your lack of progress is never because of any limitations of the teacher or the approach; they are enlightened. You just haven't said the right mantra, done the practices in the right order, or haven't done enough of them. You lack dedication, devotion, patience, and perseverance. You need to redouble your efforts and have more faith.

I first encountered this sanctimonious groupthink in the psychology of enlightenment when I was about twenty-one. I traveled to Escondido, California, land of fruits and nuts, to become enlightened studying "Agni Yoga," or "The Light Work" under one Russell Paul Schofeld, self-appointed spiritual master and chiropractor, who had some impressive telepathic gifts. Ralph Metzner was my teacher. He was one of the psychedelic-testing trinity of ex-Harvard psychologists, including Timothy Leary and Richard Alpert, later to become Ram Dass. I experienced Agni Yoga as brainwashing of an impressive sort. It gave me nightmares. Wavering, I was told by Schofeld in a "dream" that if I would only hold out to Agni Yoga lesson number thirty-two all would become clear. By that time, I would probably have become so enmeshed in the cultural groupthink of this cult that I would have not only been blind to its limitations but incapable of objective judgment or individual decision-making, both characteristics associated with enlightenment. Don't we need more of them, not less? I had worked for dreams for years already at that stage in my life, and this "dream" felt like Schofeld himself, attempting to persuade me where I was most vulnerable, as he knew of my respect for my dreams. I concluded this was a case of psychic invasion.

Clearly, there are people and organizations out there that will take advantage of any misunderstanding of enlightenment that you have. Because no one is born with such an understanding, we have to learn what enlightenment is and is not. "One of the world's greatest problems is the impossibility of any person searching for the truth on any subject when they believe they already have it." –Dave Wilbur

What Enlightenment Is Not

What is this clear state of consciousness that, in some ways, is the destination of transformation? Setting enlightenment as your goal ensures that you won't get there! This is because enlightenment transcends and includes all dualities, including that between the seeker and that which is being sought. Any positive statement of what being awake is will be at some point found to be limited, inadequate and outgrown. Any negative statement of what being awake is *not* will not adequately communicate the fullness of life. Any injunctive process, or yoga, risks confusing structure for the life that gives it meaning.

As a term, enlightenment is also inherently ambiguous. Is the speaker referring to a final destination, a path, a state of mind, or an evolving context?

While enlightenment is usually associated with the following characteristics, by themselves they are unreliable indicators of the enlightenment of the individual expressing them. Here's why:

Psychic Ability: Great psychics can be, and often have proven to be, morally depraved.

Oneness with Nature: Mountains, dogs, and infants are one with nature. Are they enlightened?

Oneness with God: Lakes, cats, and infants are one with God; they are not enlightened.

Love: From the perspective of the moneylenders in the temple, was Jesus being loving? Love is a highly subjective measurement. Very loving people can still make huge mistakes or be very foolish. Love is one value among several, including fearless confidence, wisdom, acceptance, inner peace, and witnessing that need to be cultivated and balanced. To reduce any of these to the others, (for example to say that all these are varieties of love), is to impair your development.

4

Long Life: Historically, enlightened people don't seem to live any longer than most other people.

Good Health: Enlightened people can and sometimes do suffer from physical health problems.

Resurrection from the Dead: Most enlightened masters live normal life spans. Few, if any, resurrect.

Ecstasy and Bliss: These are signs of spiritual opening. While they do maintain a state of mental clarity and purity, enlightened masters don't walk around in a state of constant ecstasy or bliss. They have work to do.

Mystical Experiences: Saul on the road to Damascus, saw Jesus, was knocked off his horse and made blind by His Light. It so changed him he started a religion, called "Christianity." Was Saul enlightened?

Near Death Experiences: Read any of the many accounts of near death experiences that are out there. Contact and get to know some near death experiencers. Draw your own conclusions.

Ability to Lucid Dream: Children and criminals have reported the ability to lucid dream. Are they enlightened?

Wakefulness in all States: If you are awake when you are deeply asleep does that mean you are enlightened, loving, or balanced? If you are awake in a dream does that mean that your decisions in your dream are wise? Are you awake right now? Just like when you are dreaming, might you merely think you are awake? How do you know if you are awake right now or not?

Trustworthiness: People are not alive to live up to your expectations. Because you will tend to put a Master on a pedestal, he or she will almost inevitably disappoint you.

The End of Pain: There is an important difference between pain and suffering. While misery is optional, heightened sensitivity, which is often experienced as pain, is a byproduct of evolution. The more you evolve the more sensitivity that you will have to both pleasure and pain. Ecclesiastes puts it like this: "In much wisdom is much grief; and he that increases knowledge increases sorrow."

The End of Limitation: What is freedom but the end of limitation? But this is only one side of the coin of enlightenment. The other side is increasing responsibility. In Mahayana Buddhism this is expressed in the Bodhisattva vow: "May I attain Buddhahood for the benefit of all sentient beings."

The End of Evolution: Is enlightenment the perfect end of all growth or is it about learning a way to look at your life that keeps you from getting in the way of your future development?

One of the worst forms of grandiosity you can have is to think you're enlightened and then to proceed to inflict your brilliance on others.

What ARE Characteristics of Enlightenment?

• Ability to witness – to continually watch yourself go by.

• Ability to stay out of drama in the three realms of interpersonal relationships, thinking, and dreaming.

• Increasing perspectives that transcend and include your body, emotions, mind, soul, and others.

• Becoming increasingly aware and awake in waking, dream sleep and deep sleep.

• Constant awareness that waking life shares the reality and many of the characteristics of dreaming — without thereby discounting waking life.

• Balance between doing and being, between affirming and letting go.

• Constant thankfulness.

• A sense of great, overflowing, constant abundance.

• Cosmic humor: not taking so seriously the fact that you take things so seriously!

• Not taking things personally, because there is no real or lasting self to get defensive.

• Polyperspectival: able to look at life from a multitude of perspectives – and at the same time.

• Knowing that life is not about you; it is about life waking up to itself in and through you

• Balanced in the six core qualities: confidence, empathy, wisdom, acceptance, inner peace, and witnessing.

• Enjoyment of life.

• Embracing the extraordinary nature of the ordinary, the sacred in the secular.

• Has evolved to late personal or above on all major developmental lines.

• This means that the enlightened are intelligent, morally worthy of respect, emotionally healthy and maintain mutually respectful relationships with all others, based on high order empathy. It does not mean that they are necessarily physically coordinated, charismatic, or mathematical or musical prodigies.

• A willingness to make mistakes, fail, accept responsibility for them, and move on.

• High-order empathy: the ability to take the role of all others, in dreams and after death, and know your life from their perspective.

• Thinks it's ridiculous that people view them as enlightened!

• Dedication to service to all sentient beings in all dimensions.

• Outstanding patience, perseverance, and determination.

• Good luck; life flows!

• Extraordinary mental focus.

• Challenging to be around. You would feel challenged to be more and do more. This could cause you to feel unaccepted and self-critical, but that would be your own projection.

• Inspiring. Such a person will awaken the best in you, but that may also trigger your fears of failure, rejection, and abandonment!

While "enlightenment" is often used to refer to the pinnacle of development, it is clear that enlightened masters are not perfect in all lines of development. Upon closer examination, we find that enlightenment often refers to the completion or fulfillment of one line of development, the self line, or your sense of who you are. When enlightened your self-sense becomes another tool, like your hand, a transparent concept that no longer defines your identity. Enlightenment then is no longer about "you" waking up. Instead, it is seen to be about life waking up, in and through its dreaming, of which you are one dream character.

Think of enlightenment of a never-ending process of waking up. Just as there are levels of dream lucidity, escape from life illusion, and suffering, so there are levels of enlightenment.

What Does It Take to Become Enlightened?

"It's not a matter of what is true that counts but a matter of what is perceived to be true." –Henry Kissinger

Enlightenment is an ongoing, never-ending process of awakening. Life evolves, and as it does broader contexts into which you can awaken are created. The context of the enlightenment of Buddha or Jesus was limited by the social, cultural, psychological, and behavioral assumptions of the times in which they lived. A butterfly has capabilities for enlightenment that did not exist for it as a caterpillar because its context has been radically expanded. Because you live in a subsequent time with broader contexts, you have the potential of becoming enlightened in ways that they could not, because current possibilities had not yet emerged.

Consequently, approach enlightenment as an integral, ongoing process. It is more important that you balance several fundamental competencies than it is for you to be outstanding in any one. For example, is it better for you to become an outstanding lucid dreamer or for you to be balanced on your self, moral, cognitive, and empathetic lines? Which is better, for you to become balanced among confidence, empathy, wisdom, acceptance, inner peace, and witnessing, or for you to be the most loving person around? If you have deficits in any one of those six core qualities of awakening, aren't your efforts at being loving going to be limited? This is the purpose of developing an integral life practice, or a yoga that is made out of several yogas designed to develop key physical, emotional, interpersonal, psychological, and spiritual competencies. IDL recommends that you do not trust your own judgment or those of others in choosing these practices. Instead, it recommends that you choose as best you can and then interview various dream characters and personifications of life issues, using IDL interviewing, in order to benefit from internal sources of objectivity regarding your goals and practices. *Then* choose as best as you can! Use IDL interviewing to monitor your progress and stay in touch with what emerging potentials are trying to be born within you. Use it to access recommendations about how to best nurture their development, and so speed up your entire process of awakening.

Such a path is not dependent on your blind faith and belief in the path others think is best for you. Instead, you learn from others while aligning your priorities with those of life, priorities that are attempting to emerge into expression through you. This way, your path partakes of, but is independent of, your belief systems, mythologies and practices, while directed by a yoga of listening to yourself, others, and life itself in an integral way.

Expanding Your Sense of Self

Who you think you are and are not determines how you relate to others and the world. For example, if you think you are a member of a family, professional group, religion, or nation, you will identify with those perspectives and tend to exclude or come into conflict with those individuals and ideas that lie outside your self-definition. The broader and more inclusive your self-definition the less likely you are to come into conflict with others and with life. Self-definitions are stories we tell ourselves to validate our world view. They are arbitrary, like dreams, and have no basis in fact. Consequently, any story that we tell ourselves about who we are needs to be approached with a fair amount of humor. The more serious and "important" the story is, the more humor is in order. IDL powerfully expands your sense of who you are by teaching you to regularly set aside your habitual self-definitions in order to experience the expansion, freedom, relaxation, openness, receptivity, and clarity that results. You discover that the more you thin and broaden your sense of who you are the easier life gets because you get out of your own way.

So Why Are You Not Enlightened?

"Most of the greatest evils that man has inflicted upon man have come through people feeling quite certain about something which, in fact, was false" –Bertrand Russell

IDL assumes that enlightenment is a never-ending developmental process that is supported by an integral model and a competent methodology to guide your integral life practice or yoga. If you think you are already enlightened because you had a mystical experience or have met the True Guru, or believe in your religious tradition or current yoga, you will disagree with this conclusion, because you already have The

Answer. Because you are already a True Believer you have chosen to limit your possibilities for further enlightenment to those conclusions already drawn by some pre-packaged answer, thereby considerably reducing your ability to find and follow your life compass. You will continue to wake-up, just slower.

IDL also assumes that enlightenment is a product of a process of triangulation, in which both external and internal sources of objectivity are consulted and compared, using your own common sense. If your framework or context for making these comparisons is limited to some historical revelation or pre-cooked model of reality, such as one you derived from a mystical experience, your future journey to enlightenment will occur within those parameters or guidelines. The story you tell yourself about it and its meaning is like a repetitive dream; you keep dreaming it. IDL assumes that you are more likely to grow in enlightenment much more rapidly if you adopt an evolving set of guidelines, which is what occurs when you take on the yoga of interviewing emerging potentials on a regular basis and applying their recommendations in a way to test the method and develop trust in it. This is because the guidelines of IDL say that there is no one true story to tell yourself, just as there is no one right or true dream to dream all your life. If you practice deep listening to whatever dreams you are dreaming you will wake-up out of them. This is called enlightenment, of a developmental sort.

IDL encourages you to embrace the traditions, teachings, paths, practices and yogas that you are currently using and that you have found valuable. IDL is meant to help you get the most out of being a Buddhist, Christian, shaman, mystic, near death experiencer, atheist, humanist, demon worshipper, capitalist or addict. It says, "Do not give up what you are currently doing!" Instead, use it and build on it! This is how children learn to walk and talk. They don't give up crawling and baby talk; they outgrow them. If you look back at your life you will probably see things you fervently believed were true that are embarrassments to you now. Maybe it was that cult you joined, or those years you wasted in a dead end relationship or the unethical, soul-destroying work that you did for all those years. Maybe it was how you treated those you love the most. We all have had such experiences and we can either hold on to our regrets and embarrassment and beat ourselves up about them, or we can ignore, repress and forget them, or we can learn from them. When we choose to learn from them we place them in larger contexts, we outgrow them while respecting that what we were so sure was true, ultimate or real could be and should be outgrown. And so it is with your present reality. IDL is designed to provide you with your own unique way forward into ever-expanding enlightenment.

For more information about IDL: IntegralDeepListening.Com, DreamYoga.Com. Introductory texts on IDL include *Dream Yoga:*

Accessing Your Inner Compass and *Waking Up*. A free app for Android and Apple phones and tablets, "End Nightmares Forever!" You can connect with other students of IDL at "Friends of IDL" on Facebook. You can also learn how to become an IDL coach at IntegralDeepListening.Com

2: Who Needs Clarity and Credibility?

"Men occasionally stumble over the truth, but most of them pick themselves up and hurry off as if nothing ever happened."

Winston Churchill

Integral Deep Listening (IDL) encourages some common and comfortable usages while challenging others. Why?

Like Alice, in *Alice in Wonderland,* perhaps we might best begin by sitting at the feet of an enlightened master. Here is Alice's famous conversation with Humpty Dumpty:

"I don't know what you mean by 'glory'," Alice said.

Humpty Dumpty smiled contemptuously. "Of course you don't - till I tell you. I meant 'there's a nice knock-down argument for you!'"

"But 'glory' doesn't mean 'a nice knock-down argument'," Alice objected.

"When *I* use a word," Humpty Dumpty said, in rather a scornful tone, "it means just what I choose it to mean - neither more nor less."

"The question is," said Alice, "whether you *can* make words mean so many different things."

Humpty Dumpty is clearly using words in whatever way that he considers best and demanding that Alice accept the meanings that he gives them. Most of us aren't quite as extreme as Humpty Dumpty, but it is common for us to assume that our listeners know what we mean when we speak and forget that their varied life experiences have probably caused them to associate entirely different meanings to words than we have. If we don't care about that, we end up talking past each other,

11

insisting that we are clear when we are merely talking to ourselves and confusing or alienating our audience.

Words are not only important because they convey meaning. They are also important because they create the contexts that define your reality. How and what you think is determined by the words you use and the meanings you give them. Those words form concepts and those concepts together create the world view that determines what you see and cannot see, what you value and what you discard. Let me give you an example. We are used to imagining that meditation changes world views, but in my experience these two are relatively unrelated. You can be a champion meditator and still hold world views that are antithetical to human development. I was good friends with John, a very dedicated meditator whose background was in Hindu Vedanta and Tibetan Buddhist approaches to meditation. He went to meditation workshops regularly, some of them over a month long. He would meditate two to four hours a day, including in the middle of the night. John was also a stock trader, that is, a professional gambler. A committed libertarian, he did not believe in the minimum wage, taxes, or government regulations. He supported war and the apartheid policies of Israel. He believed in American exceptionalism. Why didn't all that meditation change his political views and his understanding of human rights? The problem was that John had adopted a vocabulary of words and concepts that created a world view that provided the context in which he meditated. Like John, the words and concepts you use are either supportive of your further awakening or you have outgrown them and need to let them go. Which ones are which? How can you know?

Regarding the concepts that you think are conducive to enlightenment, those choices reflect your own level of development. As you continue to grow, you may well find that those things which you now view as conducive to enlightenment are not, just as you have with words and concepts which you once believed supported enlightenment that now are seen to be hindrances.

What drove me to write this text was the yawning, widening gap between the words and concepts I grew up with and the view of life of emerging potentials, in the form of dream characters and the personifications of life issues, that I have learned to interview using IDL, and which I have done my best to ignore, misunderstand, or discount for years. I have slowly grown into appreciating intrinsic, relatively autonomous perspectives that are more simple, elegant, and intelligent than my own. In the process I have had to take a hard look at many words and assumptions that I have taken for granted most of my life. I make no claims that the conclusions I have reached are "right" or are suitable for you; we are all at different levels of development, and what we need at different stages is indeed different. However, most of us also need shocks to knock us out of the complacency of our present world view. That is what happens with many IDL interviews, and what I am attempting to encourage here.

IDL attempts to use words with clarity and objectivity, two qualities of waking up and enlightenment. It wants to use words that reflect not just an ability to think, but wisdom, and it wants those words to build both confidence and inner peace. At the same time, IDL is mindful that words and concepts can be used as weapons, and that clarity and objectivity need to be balanced with compassion and acceptance.

Words are tools that point to meanings, values, and uses. Choosing ones that point where you want to look is important if you want to find something. Choosing not to use words that are ambiguous or which are likely to lead others to make assumptions you do not share are not helpful. This is true particularly for words that have metaphysical referents, like "soul" and "spiritual," that point well beyond the sensory world and toward the realities of an enlightened life. Consequently, IDL recommends that you set definite meanings for the words you use when you want to communicate clearly and let your listener know what those meanings are, to avoid ambiguity and confusion.

Eliminating words from your vocabulary that can get in the way of your development and instead using those that are more likely to support your development is a smart thing to do. However, most people never question the meaning or clarity of the words they use, although they think they do. Instead they assume, like Humpty Dumpty, that their word usage is both clear and useful. Jews, Christians and Moslems, climate change deniers and new age fundamentalists typically do not question the words they use and the core concepts they represent, because they assume they are good, helpful, and "right." They validate who they are and the world view that matters for them. But if most everyone does the same, yet they use different different words and concepts, or the same ones, but with different meanings, what is the result? Either words and concepts do not matter, or most people are blind to the importance of the words they use and the impact of the concepts they signify.

A study by Stanford University and the University of Chicago published in *Current Anthropology* has shown how culture impacts how people experience spirituality. Christians generate different kinds of spiritual experiences than Buddhists because their cultural understandings of both mental events and bodily sensations are different. Both have different meanings in different spiritual traditions. One person may feel a damp coldness and believe that a demon is present. Another person may shake uncontrollably and attribute this to the Holy Spirit. A third feels a light, floating sensation and associates it with a meditative state. These conclusions are those of Tanya Luhrmann, an anthropology professor at Stanford University. Her research examines how the presence of a specific cultural name for a mental or bodily sensation may affect that sensation within a specific cultural and social setting. The research findings reveal the importance of local culture on spiritual perceptions. Americans were more likely than Thai to report cataplexy (loss of muscular function), adrenaline rushes, and overwhelming emotion as spiritual experiences, and they were more likely to report everyday encounters with demons,"

"...if a spiritual experience has a specific name in the local religion, then the physiological sensation that is understood to be the sign of that experience is more likely to be reported to the researchers. For example, the adrenaline rush of a "Holy Spirit" experience is inherent to the evangelical Christian belief system. For a Buddhist, such a sensation is understood to be contrary to spiritual goals." The research showed that different religions value different kinds of experiences. "Buddhism has no divinity, no omniscient presence. The goal for a Thai Buddhist is to detach and feel untethered from the cycle of suffering." "Thai subjects were more likely to use an idiom of "weight" to describe their feelings of lightness and calm, which is often connected with meditation. "A mind that is concentrated (as it should be in meditation) is a mind and body that is light." In contrast, evangelical spirituality in the United States is focused on encountering a specific being who touches followers through "presence." "Overwhelming emotions that feel uncontrolled become signs of that divine being because the controlling agency is attributed to God."

Luhrmann says that the way people think about spiritual experiences shape the spiritual experiences they remember and report. "Yet some bodies, either because of trauma or genetic inheritance, may be more likely to experience certain striking anomalous events often thought to be spiritual, like out-of-body experiences, or sleep paralysis, than others," she says. All of this points to the importance of the words and concepts that we use, as part of our cultural context, in framing what is conducive or not conducive to enlightenment.

Words and concepts are necessary, extremely powerful tools, but some humans would rather fight and die than give up their favorite ones. Just like milk, tomatoes, and dog food, words and concepts have a shelf life. However, instead of being measured in days, they are generally measured in decades and, if unquestioned, generations or even millennia, like "guilt" and "sin." You have probably noticed that some people are much better at abandoning outgrown words and concepts than others. Most of us only give up outgrown words and concepts when we are assimilated into a culture that doesn't use them. This most often happens in school, where we adopt the prevailing language of teachers and peers either in addition to or instead of that of our family of origin, and later in work environments, when we adopt whatever professional terms and buzz words are associated with productivity and status. The move away from scripted language generally feels lighter, freer, and less encumbered. Loaded words from our childhood can evoke strong feelings and regressive ways of thinking. When words and concepts, like things, come to the end of their useful shelf life it is time to recycle them, re-purpose them, or simply give them the pitch. However, most of us simply pigeonhole them when we move into new roles and life contexts. This means that they lie latent and unexamined, ready to frame communication when circumstances are right. This often happens with cross-cultural marriages or with people from different religious backgrounds. During the first stages of the relationship these differences are often ignored, avoided or are invisible. It is only when the relationship is stressed or new circumstances arise, such as when parents visit or decisions are to be made about what religion children should be raised in, that underlying assumptions, world views and the words and concepts that reflect them surface, creating confusion and conflict.

There is an old Hindu metaphor that provides a good way to think about how we use our words and concepts. In this story, a driver of a chariot controls its four horses with reins. If he does not use the reins, or uses a whip, or uses the reins wrongly, the horses may charge off the road and into a ditch, over a cliff, or simply stop and graze. In this metaphor, the chariot is your body, the horses are your emotions and the reins are the words and concepts that you use to convey your preferences to your horses. If you do not use your reins, or use them improperly, your horses may graze or take you into trouble. Horses generally do not need a whip or a lot of instruction with reins. Most of the time horses are to be trusted and given their head; they can see the road and they know they are to take it. But does that mean it makes sense to let go of the reins? This is what most people do, living their lives on automatic pilot, then finding themselves wondering what happened when they go nowhere or over rocks, taking a very bumpy road through life.

Our words and concepts are the reins we use to control our horses and guide our chariot. If they are not well chosen they will take us where we did not intend to go, and we will not know why.

Reducing Resistance to Clarity

Think of enlightenment as a two-fold process of moving away and moving toward. You are moving away from, or thinning, your identification with physical, mental, cultural, and social filters that are delusional and distort your ability to awaken. Mystical and near death states are examples of relatively non-filtered states of greater clarity. Both moving away from filtering and toward clarity are equally important. Filters are necessary to do work in the world; it is *identification* with the filters, or believing that your filters are real and accurately describe life, that is not necessary. IDL has specific and powerful processes designed to thin your identification with your filters. The first involves recognition of your familial and cultural life scripting, a necessary step if you are ever going to be free to choose another path for yourself. Rebelling against scripting is not freedom from it. The second approach IDL teaches to freeing you from the filters that keep you caught in your delusions involves recognition and reduction of drama in the three realms of waking relationships, cognition, and dreaming. Drama is karma, *dukkha,* and *samsara;* it is self-created misery, and misery, unlike pain, is optional. The third process involves eliminating your emotional, formal, and perceptual cognitive distortions. This is an approach associated with cognitive behavioral therapy and is based on the assumption that how you think determines how you feel. IDL expands on that by pointing out that how you perceive determines how you think. In addition, IDL teaches communication skills. These processes are explained in detail in *Waking Up.* Together, these are the major strategies that IDL uses to reduce major barriers to clarity.

Generating Clarity

The processes that IDL uses to actively generate wakefulness, clarity, and enlightenment are IDL interviewing, acting on recommendations provided by the interviewing process, incubation, meditation, and triangulation. A fun introduction to the interviewing process is provided by the free App for Android and Apple phones and tablets, *End Nightmares Forever!* Those learning to be IDL coaches, practitioners, or teachers learn to interview others as well as themselves using the IDL interviewing protocol. Empowering others, particularly children, by teaching them how to find and follow their life compass speeds the evolution of humanity. Because others represent aspects of ourselves, the act of interviewing others integrates those aspects more completely into an expanded sense of who we are. In the process, we learn not only from their interviewed emerging potentials but increase our ability to deeply listen. All of this powerfully supports enlightenment.

Acting on recommendations from interviews strengthens our confidence in the method and in ourselves. Because these recommendations represent priorities of emerging potentials, they represent shortcuts into the enlightened reality of our future selves.

Pre-sleep incubation sets intention for dreaming, deep sleep, and tomorrow, shifting dream scenarios away from drama and needless filtering toward the six core qualities of confidence, empathy, wisdom, acceptance, inner peace, and witnessing. Less reactive and regressive dreaming means that we awaken with better mood and greater clarity, which in turn supports waking choices away from addiction to habitual patterns and toward greater awakening.

Meditation: Because meditation is focused practice in strengthening intentionality and expanding clarity, it accelerates the entire process of awakening. IDL encourages both sitting and active meditation, for instance while one is driving, working, or even when arguing with others. It teaches the naming of the contents of awareness to interrupt train of thought and teach non-judgment. It also uses observation of breath to build the six core qualities in a balanced way.

Triangulation increases clarity by improving decision-making. It does so through the consultation of others, interviewed emerging potentials, and your own common sense. If we can't make good decisions or effectively solve the problems that arise on our path, how can we expect to become enlightened?

Balanced Development of Core Lines: Enlightenment requires balanced development over a number of important areas, particularly cognition, self, morality, and empathy. Here is some of what it means to become enlightened in each of these four critical areas.

Expanding Cognitive Development: Learning to reason, question, and recognize logical errors is a necessary prerequisite for any type of lasting enlightenment because how you think determines not only what you see but what sense you make of what you see. Therefore, the conclusions you draw about who you are, how to relate to others and the purpose of your life are determined by how you think. The clearer and more objective your thinking becomes, the healthier and beneficial the spontaneous expression of your emotions becomes. This is why Wilber's integral AQAL states that the cognitive line leads the development of the other lines. That does not mean thinking is more important than feeling but only that how you think generates the world view, contexts, and framing of reality in which other aspects of your consciousness evolve.

For example, if you have a near death or mystical experience, it is likely to be awe-inspiring and overwhelmingly emotional. Your level of cognitive development will determine what you perceive during the experience and therefore what you remember and are able to integrate into your life from it. This is made more obvious by looking at your responses in your dreams as well as comparing how children, adults, and people from different religions and cultures view the same experience. IDL presupposes an integral model or world view as a jumping off space for understanding life, what interviewed characters say, and how to apply their recommendations. This is Wilber's AQAL, or "all quadrant, all levels, all lines, all states, and all types" as well as his "integral life practice." IDL does not assume that this integral model is final or all-inclusive, but only that it provides a well-thought through, multiple-perspectival lens on development.

IDL strongly supports the development of cognition past personal levels into a broader, trans-rational world view. It does so notably by identification with apparently absurd and irrational dream characters and imaginary personifications of life issues such as toilet brushes and kangaroos. This is practice in *multiperspectivalism,* a core characteristic of transpersonal anything. Seemingly meaningless, silly, absurd and

17

imaginary characters are recognized as not being irrational at all and in fact, in the context of IDL interviewing, reflecting broader perspectives than our own. A small, undeveloped sense of self is associated with selfishness, narcissism, fear, defensiveness, and reactivity. The more inclusive your sense of self becomes the less you personalize what others say and what happens to you. You slowly realize that life is not about you; life is about life, and you are an instrument for it to awaken to itself.

IDL also supports development of the cognitive line by noting that both integration and transcendence are important. Integration creates the stable and balanced launch pad you require if you are to get launched into a higher, broader reality. Transcendence or transformation is important if you want to grow in your experience of what it means to be enlightened. These two styles of development can also be called hierarchy and heterarchy. Hierarchy says "Yes, Christ love is a more adequate expression of enlightenment than Scientology or Wicca." Heterarchy says, "What matters is caring about everyone and everything without exception." Both of these approaches are required; you don't have to reject one, but rather learn which to use based on what is required at the time. Together they create a growth dialectic that propel you toward enlightenment.

Adaptability at Different Levels of Development

All of the following words and concepts, both those conducive and not conducive to enlightenment, are cognitive distortions. They differ in their adaptability at different levels of development, their intrinsic value or destructiveness, and in their type. For example, the concept of gun ownership makes sense when you need to hunt for food. For sport, guns make sense for skeet shooting, but not so much for killing harmless animals for fun. In urban cultures, gun ownership makes almost no sense whatsoever, as statistics show that gun owners themselves and their family members are by far the most likely victims of gun violence. This is an example of not only a behavior - gun ownership - but a conceptualization about life and its values, that makes sense at early to mid pre-personal levels of development, but quickly loses both value and validity the more individuals and cultures evolve into personal stages.

IDL believes that every word and concept has an "expiration date," or a level of development by which it becomes invalid as a way to explain who you are and how life works. Some concepts are harder to outgrow and remain useful through the three personal levels of development and perhaps even a bit beyond, into multi-perspectivalism. These are those which IDL is here advocating as "conducive to enlightenment." Many common concepts, however, lose their usefulness much earlier, but are retained because they are habits. How can you tell the difference?

Some Ways of Determining the Usefulness of a Word or Concept

"Does It Have Intrinsic Worth or Am I Just Addicted?"

Compare addictions to coffee, alcohol, nicotine and breathing. While there is no doubt that you have a dependency on oxygen, most would not classify it as an addiction because it is both healthy and unavoidable, while addictions are normally defined as unhealthy and avoidable. This is not necessarily so. For instance, William Glasser, creator of Reality Therapy, explores positive addictions, activities that are good for you that produce addictive endorphin highs, like running and meditation. However, addiction generally implies that we are doing something it would be better if we did not, but is it ever better for us not to breathe? IDL teaches observation and amplification of the pauses after both inhalation and exhalation as a powerful way to cultivate luminosity, emptiness, clarity, objectivity and creativity in everyday life. However, *if* we were to view breathing as an addiction, it would certainly be categorized as an essential and highly adaptive one.

This becomes obvious when it is compared to coffee and certainly to alcohol or nicotine. For example, the adaptive advantages of smoking as a stress management tool for smokers is not to be under-estimated. Many will tell you smoking is the first, strongest, and most important stress management tool they have. While breathing is a totally justified dependency, nicotine comes close to being a completely unjustifiable one, in that its adaptive disadvantages so completely outweigh its many and strong adaptive advantages.

Smoking provides a clear example of how the adaptive value of some action can be almost completely different from its inherent destructiveness. Colonization is an example of a social-cultural concept that had high value for many societies for several centuries, but which is overwhelmingly destructive. The externalization of social and environmental costs is a fundamental principle that allows capitalism to work; because it makes money and creates jobs capitalism is highly addictive on socio-cultural macrocosmic levels of organization. This is another powerful example of how something, in this case a concept, that is inherently destructive can have such high adaptive value that it serves as an almost unbreakable addiction.

Is it a Cognitive Distortion?

Cognitive distortions are things we tell ourselves that we believe are true, but aren't. IDL differentiates three broad types or categories of cognitive distortion, emotional, rational and perceptual.

Emotional Cognitive Distortions

Emotional cognitive distortions are fundamental sources of both anxiety and depression, the two most common mental disorders. Varieties of anxiety and depression evolve as we do, becoming more sophisticated as we grow. However, whenever they are experienced, at whatever level of development we are on, they act as either agents of regression to prior levels of development or keep us fixated at our current level. The elimination of emotional cognitive disorders, as pioneered by Ellis, Beck, and Burns, has been shown to be an effective therapeutic intervention for both anxiety and depression. It is based on the idea that your thoughts create how you feel. Therefore, if you change how you think about your feelings, transforming irrational thoughts into rational ones, you will greatly reduce emotional disturbances of all sorts. Because identification with emotions is strongest at the mid-prepersonal level of development, identifying emotional cognitive distortions and substituting rational words and concepts for them, is most effective with people who are either functioning at mid-prepersonal or who have emotional fixations, in which parts of their personality still function at mid-prepersonal, even if they are Rhodes Scholars or Nobel Prize winners.[1]

Examples of emotional cognitive distortions include black and white thinking, over-generalization, jumping to conclusions, catastrophizing, fortune-telling, and personalization. Identifying and eliminating your emotional cognitive distortions is itself a powerful demonstration of how the words that you use and the concepts that they evoke are either conducive to enlightenment or keep you firmly chained to the back bench of Plato's cave. For example, it is impossible to use a number of common words, including "should," ought," "blame," "must," "always," "never" and "can't" without generating anxiety, depression or both. They are also

---

1 The references to prepersonal, personal, and transpersonal development that you find in this text are nods to the AQAL model of Ken Wilber. A familiarity of his developmental model is highly recommended as background for understanding the integral aspects of IDL.

signals that you are caught in the persecutor or victim role of the Drama Triangle. A description of each of the emotional cognitive distortions, including examples of their use and of substitute, rational statements, can be found in *Waking Up*, by this author. The best general introduction to the subject is *Feeling Good, The New Mood Therapy*, by David Burns.

Rational Cognitive Distortions

Rational cognitive distortions are also called formal or logical fallacies. These are logical errors in the rules of thinking. A very common example is a fallacy discussed above, the assumption that because Einstein is brilliant at physics that he must be an expert at ballet, called the "fallacy of attribution." It is also an example of the fallacy of arguing from authority, meaning that because someone respected as an authority said something that it must be true. The reverse of this is to assume that because a person is a criminal that they do not have strong positive attributes. Another common example of this fallacy is to assume that because we like someone that they must be a good person, or because we don't like some food that it must be bad for us. Other common rational fallacies are *ad hominem*, in which we attack the source rather than the argument, a form of changing the subject; "band wagon" is a basic fallacy of democracy, that popular ideas must therefore be right. It is commonly used to create unanimity in the media to support an irrational national commitment to war. A "straw man" argument is the fallacy of proving wrong a misinterpretation of what the other person was saying.

Rational cognitive distortions are almost always in the service of emotional cognitive distortions. For example, in arguments it is normal for someone to try to change the subject, generally from what they did to what *you* did or didn't do. Their motivation is typically an emotional response to a perceived threat, disguised as a principled argument. As discussed below, conspiracy theorists usually make the rational cognitive distortion of ignoring Occam's Razor, that is, refusing to favor the simplest explanation that covers the available information.

To use rational cognitive distortions you have to know how to think somewhat, and the better you are at thinking the more skillful you are likely to be at using them. Rational cognitive distortions can get very sophisticated, as in the rational manipulations used by high-functioning narcissistic personality disordered individuals or in the advertising of products and services in which we have a vested interest but which have little or no rational justification. Examples include the weapons and gambling industries, the oil and gas industries, nuclear power, capitalism, austerity and trickle-down economics, and the entirety of the global financial system. All of these are based on rational cognitive distortions that are supported by sophisticated arguments made by very intelligent people using statistical and empirical studies in peer-reviewed journals.

For example, the rational arguments that support the global gas and oil industry ignore the fact that dirty fuels create global warming that is driving many species extinct and creating multiple, massive disasters for humans. The rational arguments for generating revenues for schools from gambling ignore the high social costs to taxpayers of gambling. Austerity economics, globally used in justification of "trickle down" neoconservative plutocracy, is another common and pervasive example. News reports in the mainstream media is a continuous assault on rationality, supplying multiple case studies in the power and sophistication of rational cognitive distortions. Simply consider the premises on which almost any statement in the news is based. When you do, you will find that the rational cognitive distortions you encounter generally boil down to some personal, financial or security interest, which are forms of emotional cognitive distortion. You have to be rather good at handling the reins controlling your horses and chariot in order to recognize rational cognitive distortions and counteract them.

Perceptual Cognitive Distortions

Both emotional and rational cognitive distortions are in the service of the broadest of the three categories, perceptual cognitive distortions, or world views. These can be thought of as both personal and cultural mythologies, or systems of truth that are so pervasive that individuals and cultures cannot easily see beyond them. Even if they can, there are generally strong societal pressures to support prevailing, underlying myths. These generally justify exceptionalism and psychological geocentrism, themselves fundamental perceptual cognitive distortions.

Perceptual cognitive distortions are not optional; we all have them. They are rarely coherent or articulated because we are so subjectively enmeshed in them that we are unaware of the biases, prejudices and delusions that they contain. A perceptual cognitive distortion is a worldview that is justified as being "just the way the world is." The worldview of capitalism, in which the "invisible hand" of the market generates both social balance and general prosperity when each person works to maximize their personal profit, is an economic justification of a worldview based on selfishness. John Maynard Keynes, widely viewed as a highly influential economist, said "Capitalism is the extraordinary belief that the nastiest of men for the nastiest of motives will somehow work for the benefit of all."

Religion provides many examples of perceptual cognitive distortions. A word for "religion" did not exist in traditional China because religion was not differentiated from culture and life. Consequently, it was impossible for the Chinese to recognize how their religious words and concepts created massive, shared perceptual cognitive distortions called shamanistic folk culture, Confucianism, Taoism, and Chinese Buddhism.

22

Questioning someone's perceptual framework by calling it out as a perceptual cognitive distortion is dangerous business because our world views are our core, primary source of life meaning and self-identification. *We think we are our perceptual cognitive distortions.* If you question someone's livelihood as being a form of predatory capitalism they will feel you are attacking *them,* since they have made a commitment of great time, effort and status into their particular career choice. If you question someone's religious beliefs you run the risk of having them think you are attacking their core values and therefore *them.* Whatever your perceptual worldview or context is, it defines who you are, whether you recognize it or not, whether you want it to or not. However, which ones you have and the extent to which you allow them to define you are optional, but only if they are first recognized. This is a fundamental reason why this subject is important to IDL and why this text was written.

One of the most common and pervasive perceptual cognitive distortions and one that we shall discuss below, is geocentrism, in which the Earth is the center of the cosmos. Historically, it is associated with the Ptolemaic world view, but it is much more basic and older than that. It is pervasive because it is embedded in sensory awareness; every living organism on the planet assumes its truth on a biological level in one way or another, beginning with the importance of gravity. Therefore, there are strong physiological reasons to believe the perceptual cognitive distortion that the sun rises and sets. Circadian rhythms rely on it; culture and societies are built on the assumption of its reality.

Because our senses all validate the reality of the geocentric distortion, for most of history anyone who questioned its truth was obviously crazy. All one had to do is look up to know the truth. Geocentrism was so simple and obvious that every child has experienced it, and that is exactly the problem. Strong personal experience creates a world view or perceptual cognitive distortion that ignores both objectivity and contradictory information. Perceptual cognitive distortions like geocentrism are generally deeply engrained from early childhood. We do not remember a time when we did not have them. Therefore, they have been central to successful adaptation in our lives. If you question or change a perceptual cognitive distortion you call into question all the adaptive strategies that are built on it or around it. How could such an enterprise *not* be highly threatening?

To those at mid-personal and beyond in their level of development, learning to recognize and question the assumptions behind their perceptual cognitive distortions is an interesting exercise in intellectual curiosity, if nothing else. This is because from this level and the next couple of levels, identity is not defined by concepts, but by thinking about concepts. In fact, this is one way to roughly evaluate your level of development as you read this text. If you find that you have strong emotional reactions to what you read, it may be a symptom of a prepersonal level of development, meaning a strong over-identification with your emotions, or an emotional fixation, that is holding you back. If you find yourself thinking about intellectual reasons why some word or emotion is still adaptive for you and therefore necessary, you are probably at mid-personal or below. If you find yourself intellectually curious, you are probably at mid to late personal in your development. If you find yourself amused at discovering how enmeshed you are in some distortion in ways you hadn't realized, you are probably at late personal or multi-perspectival vision-logic.

However, if you find that you are likely perched on a higher branch of the developmental tree, remember that your fixations define you. It is not your strongest line of development, such as your intellect, that defines your overall level of development, but your *weakest*. That vulnerability acts on your overall development like wearing a pair of lead boots. Your favorite vulnerability may be an addiction or it may be a career in something that is unethical or heart-destroying that generates too much income and status for you to give up. It may be a relationship that offers you too much stability and security to leave. This is a common problem found with people who understand Wilber's AQAL model. Because their world view is multiperspectival and they understand the transpersonal with its three levels of experiential union and the non-dual beyond, they assume their overall development must have reached those heights as well. This is a rational cognitive distortion based on an emotional wish to be more evolved. For such people, integral AQAL serves as a perceptual cognitive distortion. Your level of development is not determined by your cognitive grasp of ideas but by the center of gravity of at least four major developmental lines: self, empathetic, ethical, *and* cognitive. You need to figure out which is your *weakest* major line and strengthen it if you want to move ahead. If you do not address it and instead minimize it, you will stay fixated at your present level of development.

Like Humpty Dumpty, it is selfish and elitist to define words in ways that work for us and expect everyone else to accept our definitions of them. This is particularly true when commonly used words are defined in ways that are unusual. While IDL does not claim to be right or to have the final say about any of the following words and concepts or their usages, evaluating these preferences is a helpful way to understanding why IDL is the way it is, why it works, and where it will take you.

IDL is an evolving integral life practice, and what makes sense today will probably not make so much sense tomorrow. So don't take any of these definitions too seriously; just suspend your disbelief and ask yourself, "What would be the result if I approached my world using this word in this way instead of the way I have been using it?" "How might it change my world if I stopped using certain words and conceptions that I take for granted and started using these recommended ones instead?" We will begin with the less threatening topic of this text: words and concepts that are conducive to enlightenment.

3: Some Words and Concepts that Are Conducive to Enlightenment

Clarity

If you are not clear about your purposes, meanings, beliefs, intentions, and preferences in your own thoughts, how can you expect to communicate them clearly to others? If you cannot communicate them clearly to others, how can you expect to have mutual understanding? It is impossible to be clear with others if you do not know what you want. How clear are you on your own goals? If you are clear, how do you know that your goals are reflective of those of your life compass? Clarity is like preparing land for a new garden or clearing ground for a new building. It creates space for new growth, but it doesn't create guarantees that what you will build will be of any value. For IDL, clarity is a core life process that is required for both balance and transformation but does not ensure either. It is associated with witnessing, luminosity, integration, and ontology, or the nature of the beingness of something.

Think about someone you know well and ask yourself, "What's important to them? Is it stated clearly or are their preferences simply conveyed non-verbally by what they do, their lifestyle and their reactions?" Most of us could be much clearer in expressing our preferences, beliefs and ideas. Our failure to do so is expensive. A good example is dating. The clearer people are about who they are, warts and all, as well as what they both want and do not want in a partner, the less time they waste dealing with people who have widely divergent or unrealistic expectations. They are doing both themselves and others a big favor by being clear. So why is it so common for people to tell others what they think they want to hear instead of providing clarity in the form of truths that others are going to discover soon enough anyway?

Clarity is not the most important thing for most of us. Fear of rejection is typically much more important. We want acceptance, relaxation, love, fun, and friendship, and if we have these things, who needs clarity? We hope that by the time people wake-up and realize we are not the product that was advertised that other reasons will keep them from returning the "product" and demanding a refund. This is the basic principle behind why people are not candid in their resumes, introductions, job interviews and writing. They skew what they write or say based on what they think their potential employer or partner is looking for, meaning that some traits and preferences that may affect acceptability are typically hidden. Employment and compatibility tests are designed to uncover these areas. The problem is that we all have assumptions and expectations about who others are, and when these clash, suddenly a crisis of clarity becomes unavoidable, and all the acceptance, relaxation, love, fun, and friendship in the world only shoves it back below the surface for a while. It won't make it go away. Therefore, a bit of clarity at the front end is preventive medicine for relationships and ventures of all sorts. This explains why relationships based on shared purpose, direction, or vision are more likely to last than those based on *eros,* erotic love, or even *philos,* or friendship. IDL does not believe that clarity is more important than things like acceptance, relaxation, sex, comfort, fun, love, and friendship, but it believes it is *as* important. Therefore, clarity is important regarding concepts IDL thinks are and are not conducive to enlightenment.

Clarity is directly related to *intention.* If your intentions are clear your actions are more likely to be clear as well. Remember, while we typically judge ourselves by our intentions, we judge others and others judge us primarily by our actions. Therefore, it is not enough to have clear intentions. Strive for focused, effective and clear action that reflects your intentions clearly. Do you just trust your intuition or do you have a methodology, like IDL, that allows you to access the goals of your life compass and compare them to your own? Clear goals protect you from depression by creating direction and therefore meaning in your life.

Credibility

While Pinocchio's credibility problem was obvious to all, in the real world, trustworthiness is not always so easy to detect. It is often built on illusion, of a patina of shinola. Wonderfulness is both hard to top or criticize. If someone is wonderful, for example a talented musician, physicist, or entrepreneur, aren't they automatically credible? Wonderfulness naturally causes us to suspend our disbelief, and some people and pursuits can then coast for years on that wonderfulness, with people fiercely defending it without any interest in credibility. The thinking, to the degree that there is any, is often, "This is so wonderful it *must* be true!" "This person is so wonderful what they say *must* be right!" We see this with people dazzled by actors, athletes, musicians, comedians, appearance, education or work experience. We see this in the "beautiful people" in high school who have so much status that they stop growing. Why should they change when they have all the status they want? Consequently, they stay stuck at levels of development that become increasingly maladaptive as time goes on. Because a person is strong in one area, like preaching or business, we assume they are strong in other areas, like morality or parenting. Why should we? Is there any correlation at all between those developmental lines and roles?

Credibility is associated with validity, truth claims, epistemology, and most importantly, what we do. People may initially trust you due to what you say, but in the long run you are likely to lose their trust if your actions conflict with what you say. The classic exception is if you become so wonderful in some area that people give you the benefit of the doubt in all sorts of other areas. Being wonderful, and thereby being able avoid protecting your credibility, is easiest if you have status, like a movie star, famous musician, or, on a local level, are a jock, cheerleader or just considered beautiful or handsome. If you have money in addition you can often buy both loyalty and the suspension of distrust; if you have looks, money and political power you have an almost invincible trifecta, in which you can do almost anything and keep a base of support, as for instance Reagan, Clinton, Bush II, and Obama achieved. This sort of lightening strikes few, and it is as often a curse as it is a blessing. Rather than blame these individuals we need to look at the power of groupthink and how we support it by both our actions and inaction.

Expecting people to trust you because you are wonderful, look or sound good asks people to listen to you, to be with you, for either partial or wrong reasons. The result is that you will end up surrounded by people who are not particularly supportive of your growth, because they want you to continue to reflect the image they were initially attracted to, and you may not know why you are encountering such resistance. In addition, most of us would like to ignore credibility and just assume that others will find us trustworthy because our intentions are good. However, people want and need reasons to trust you and what you say. To expect that they should or will trust you just because you are funny or talented in one area is naive, but this is in fact the way most relationships work. People will give respect to Donald Trump's statements on politics because he is a successful tycoon. We stay around people who make us laugh or feel good or who have some area of expertise that makes us feel like we are with a special person or with someone who will make us secure because of their particular expertise. Being wonderful, charismatic or talented and being credible are different things, unfortunately, and being both is much better than only being one. You will find that most people have an innate preference for one or the other and that the majority will give someone who is wonderful, or even simply notorious, the benefit of the doubt regarding credibility. This is how superficial people win popularity contests, plutocrats get away with stealing the world's wealth and how politicians get elected.

For most of us, it is relatively easy to lose the trust of others and blow our credibility. A simple and common example is keeping your word, which means learning not to over-commit yourself. From the standpoint of earning and keeping one's trust, fundamental to your credibility, it is far better to be non-committal than to make a commitment and not follow through. It is also true that many people think of trust and credibility in global terms. That is, if you are trustworthy in one important area, then you are either trustworthy in all areas or else other areas in which you are not trustworthy are ignored or overlooked. For example, some women will ignore or overlook pernicious forms of untrustworthiness in men if they are wealthy; employers routinely overlook unfairness in their place of work or predatory practices because their work gives them money and status. Instead, if we are hurt by someone once, in one area, we tend to insulate ourselves from further hurt by exiling the person completely from our lives. This is generally a loss for us, as that person represents a part of ourselves that we are disowning, as well as a loss for the other person. Out of our anger or fear we are punishing disproportionately.

Many citizens routinely overlook the criminality of their own government, holding politicians to more lax standards than they do themselves. The result is corruption, guaranteed. It is important to evaluate trust and credibility in different areas, recognizing that people, companies and governments that are untrustworthy in some areas may be extremely trustworthy and credible in others. This is why it is such a waste to imprison the vast majority of criminals. Society loses the benefit of their various strengths and competencies because of one area that is so grievous that society concludes that the individual simply cannot be trusted or worse, simply wants either revenge or to make an example of him or her for others. However, it is rarely the case that people who are untrustworthy in one area are therefore untrustworthy in all areas. We can see that with dogs. Because they may not be allowed near children does not mean that they cannot be excellent dogs in other situations. We need to remember to evaluate the credibility of each other in a similar way.

At the same time, it is important to remember that people, companies and governments that are trustworthy in some areas may be extremely untrustworthy in others. What generally happens is that once we decide to trust someone or some institution various rationalizations kick in to validate our decision. We end up ignoring or minimizing untrustworthy behavior that in time, though guilt by association, will undermine our own credibility in the eyes of others. What this means is that we must constantly monitor how and why we trust both others and ourselves. Are we too trusting? Are we not trusting enough?

Instead of emphasizing the communal, egalitarian embrace of cosmic love and light, credibility focuses on the mid-personal skill of asking questions and making discriminations. "How do I know this is good for me, besides the fact that it feels good and I like it?" "How do I know if it is likely to stand the test of time?" If people don't ask such questions about others, businesses, governments and paths to enlightenment, they should, because the road to waking up leads through reason, the rational, and the credible. To attempt to become enlightened without developing good criteria by which you determine if something or someone is credible, or to do so without developing credibility yourself, is naive.

Developing credibility is not easy, nor should it be. Many people assess the prevailing societal standards for credibility, rightly conclude that they don't meet them, and so go about creating their own standards for credibility and then surround themselves with people who accept them. I have witnessed this with many aspects of New Age thinking and pursuits, and I will take lucid dreaming as an example. There is a certain sector of interest out there that assumes that the capacity to lucid dream implies enlightenment. It doesn't, but if a person lacks normal measures of credibility, like a steady job and decent income that provide a modicum of social status, or have one or more addiction that they don't control, being able to say they lucid dream can supply an impressive patina of credibility in some circles. Because people get validation within their group they think they have credibility; it is all of those unwashed goats on the outside, in this case those who can't lucid dream, that lack credibility. This is how religions and all sorts of self-validating collectives get formed. Someone has an idea that makes them special. They find others that agree. Groupthink becomes an echo chamber that cuts out dissent and with it creativity. The result is that groups and businesses of all sorts start to fossilize almost as fast as they are created.

I can certainly relate to this. As a boy, I was uncoordinated and socially awkward, so I wasn't going to be accepted or valued based on either my sports or communication abilities. And of course, I considered myself ugly as well. My answer was to take refuge in areas that nobody knew about and, even if they did, were difficult if not impossible to validate, like dreams, meditation, the psychic, and all things holistic. Since nobody knew what I was talking about, since these were relatively new fields in the 1960's, how could they judge whether I was credible or not? If no standard of truth exists, how can one fail? While I went on to get my credibility card punched by society in some of the expected and appropriate ways, I have never put so much value or worth in credibility, as judged by society. For example, my professional work has been done under the aegis of my master's degree while my PhD, while much more relevant and personally satisfying, came from an alternative institution that does not enjoy accreditation. That was probably something of a mistake, because credibility is generally necessary to make money in order to eat or just to get people to listen to you. Your horizons are definitely going to be more limited when your credibility is not validated by society, and telling yourself that social criteria of credibility really aren't the important forms of validation generally doesn't get one very far. You will tend to bump up against barriers of income and power that can not only stop you from making your dreams come true but reduce your ability to help others to do the same.

Many people extend this hunt for credibility to using buzz words that make people feel good. When your goal is to get people to like you or to buy whatever services you are selling, you will probably do better if you use signal words that indicate that you are a member of the same cultural club. But what if the common language is confusing, misleading, and unhelpful? Do you use it anyway, because acceptance and apparent empathy are more important than clarity and usefulness? This is what is commonly done in politics, business and religion. IDL encourages you to not duck this issue; do whatever you can to build your credibility, but do it for the right reasons. Don't do it to be loved, accepted, or even respected. Do it because you respect the need of others to not only expect but demand that you have credibility in areas that are important to them. Honor that expectation. Don't expect people to just trust you because you're wonderful.

It is also not helpful to get hung up on establishing credibility, in an attempt to get other people to listen to you and respect you. Everyone expects you to try to prove how credible you are, by sounding scientific and being quantum everything, for instance. If instead of attempting to impress people you go out of your way to prove how non-credible you are, people will tend to relax out of credibility games and go into learning mode. Because they are so completely disarming, stupidity and ignorance are two excellent ways to develop your credibility. Psychological research has shown that doing or saying something that is stupid immediately builds connection, because everyone already knows that they are stupid and they are afraid you will discover just how stupid they really are. When you do or say something stupid it takes all the pressure off them. Similarly, asking questions is an excellent way to establish your ignorance, to be disarming and establish your credibility as someone interested in listening, all at once. Humor also works most of the time. These methods work particularly well if you have already given people reasons to trust you, such as some short biography. It is enough to establish conditions by which credibility can be determined and invite people to understand those conditions, see if they are satisfactory, and then to judge you and what you say and do by those conditions. This is basic to both the empirical method and yogas of all kinds. All along the educational path, encourage people to not believe you, to challenge you, to demand that you explain why they should believe you. Fundamentally, with IDL you can say, "Don't believe me. Do the method. Draw your own conclusions." The implication is that if people aren't willing to do the method themselves, then their criticisms of it lack credibility.

Wake-up Calls

Is experience best viewed as a series of wake-up calls? In IDL interviewing, no matter if the character is a dream angel or demon, cactus or toilet seat, it will tend to say that its function or purpose is to serve as a wake-up call. For example, if you have a dream of a knife-wielding criminal attacking you in the back seat of a taxi and you interview the knife, it will most likely say that it is there to get your attention, to jar you awake. This not only strongly implies that life has no problem threatening and scaring you in order to get your attention, but that

32

anything and everything serves this function if you will only take the time to interview it.

This is a radical idea, because it does not discriminate between human and non-human elements, between gods and devils or between the pure and the impure. From the perspective of life, all equally serve as conveyors of wake-up calls. The implication is that the basic agenda of life is to wake-up through you by having you evolve, expand and thin your identity by incorporating ever broader contexts and perspectives into your own.

Different interviewed dream characters and personifications of your waking life issues will emphasize waking up in different ways, according to their unique priorities and perspectives. However, what you will find if you do enough interviews is that there will be repetitive themes of areas in your life where you will get repeated wake-up calls. The implication is that if you focus your efforts on responding to those priorities, in the form of working on those associated recommendations that make sense to you, that you will be addressing the most important and broadest-based wake-up calls.

IDL does not therefore assume that all things and people *are* wake-up calls or that they see themselves as same. In fact, if you ask most people about their life purpose, few will say that they exist in order to serve as a wake-up call for others. It would also unfortunately be true that most people serve either to validate the *status quo* and prevailing groupthink or as examples of what not to do. Therefore, IDL does not impose upon others the assumption that their function is to serve as a wake-up call. Instead it asks, "What would be the result if I treated everything and everyone *as if* it were a wake-up call?" The result is a respectful, receptive stance toward everyone and everything, a stance that is more likely to teach us and thereby expand our awareness.

You are encouraged to experiment with taking this stance in your daily life and see what happens. Do your own interviews and see if you arrive at the same conclusion. Does interviewing enhance your ability to view life as one wake-up call after another?

Deep listening is an act of respect, and the cultivation of respect is a central activity of IDL. As such, respect implies neither agreement nor disagreement, but acknowledgement and a desire to place acceptance before judgment. This is different from many understandings of respect, which look for either courtesy or agreement. For instance, in Chinese Confucianism, courtesy is assumed to be respectful. Many parents, regardless of their culture. demand agreement from their children as a demonstration of respect. However, IDL believes you can be respectful without necessarily agreeing or being courteous. While abuse is best defined by the recipient, you get to define respect for yourself, in consultation with those around you. Ask others if they view you as respectful toward them, but feel no compunction to agree with their assessment or change your behavior as a result of their feedback. IDL encourages you to instead conform to consensus standards of respect expressed by your interviewed emerging potentials, as these are more likely to represent how respect is viewed by your life compass.

Deep Listening

Listening is perhaps it is the most fundamental and important measurement of respect. Respectful listening does not require agreement; you can strongly disagree and still be a good listener. All that is required is that you are able to demonstrate that you can accurately summarize what a person said. You get extra points if you can also accurately describe what the other person is feeling beneath their words.

Most people do not listen at all, much less listen deeply. Listening can be operationally defined as the ability to accurately paraphrase back what a person has said. If you can do so, to the reasonable satisfaction of the speaker, you can be said to be a good listener. If you cannot paraphrase adequately, you are not a good listener. Most people think they are good listeners but are not able to repeat back what others have said to them, because instead of listening they are thinking about what they are going to say next. It is only when we are held accountable, by actually having to paraphrase back what another has said, that we discover whether we are a good listener or not.

As important, vital and fundamental as these skills are, they are not *deep* listening. As defined by IDL, deep listening involves the extension of respect to all others, including imaginary elements such as dream characters and the personifications of important life issues. The reason this is as important as it is radical is that it breaks down dualisms of all sorts. Our normal distinctions between real and imaginary, sacred and profane, useful and useless, more evolved and less evolved, better and worse, good and bad, beautiful and ugly, desirable and undesirable are suspended. Because these distinctions are important and useful much of the time it does not follow that they are important and useful *all* of the time. On the contrary, if we do not create spaces in our lives where these dualisms no longer apply they take over our lives and crush the perception of non-dualism, except in extraordinary circumstances, such as under the influence of hallucinogens or during near death or mystical

35

experiences. The process that IDL uses for neutralizing this tyranny of dualisms may appear irrational or frivolous but it is not. Because the IDL interviewing protocol is based on a highly rational, well-thought out methodology that transcends the rational, it is a *transrational* process. This matters, because prerational processes create different consequences from rational processes and transrational processes create different outcomes from both prerational and rational ones. The problem is that until or unless one has developed to the place where they have experienced and can recognize the difference between these three, the psychologically geocentric conceit is that there is no higher, more developed level than the one that has been attained. This is called reductionism; higher, emerging potentials are assimilated into our current world view because we cannot conceive of one that is both broader and more effective than our own. What makes IDL transrational is that it includes but transcends both prerational and rational modes of consciousness. It does so by generating non-dual multi-perspectivalism through the interviewing process, as is evidenced by the thinning of the self and the development of significant levels of both witnessing and empathy. While cognition, morality, empathy and witnessing can be present as developed lines at any of the three personal levels of development, it is highly unlikely that all of them will be well developed at anything less than a transrational level of development. By definition, the self line does not transcend itself until the transpersonal.

It is important to make very, very clear that just because IDL is a transpersonal modality that affords opportunities for transrational experience there is no guarantee that those who use the process will develop into such levels, and it is much more likely that instead something much more important happens: people balance and integrate at the level of development that they currently occupy. The reason this is so important is that such balance and integration is a pre-requisite for healthy higher level development. If you attempt to storm the gates of heaven through blasting open chakras with drugs, breath work, asceticism or mystical experiences, you will not succeed in increasing your average level of development. You can only do so by supporting and integrating your lagging or fixated lines, whatever they may be. IDL has been shown to be an effective way to do so.

However, the effectiveness of this process is entirely dependent on learning to listen in a deep and integral way. This listening is deep because it is extraordinarily empathetic, in that it takes any and all perspectives without predisposition or prejudice and respectfully gives them voice, creating a depth of listening that is both rare and precious.

Intrasocial

When you make a commitment to practice deep listening in an integral way to dream spoons or dragons as well as to the personifications of your life issues, which may come in any form, you are not only taking an interdependent and multi-perspectival but an intrasocial approach to understanding yourself, others and life. If "social" refers to external, macrocosmic, "objective" and interpersonal relationships, then "intrasocial" refers to microcosmic, "subjective," and intrapersonal relationships. Objective and subjective are placed in quotes because our external world is a subjective delusion to the extent that it is a projection of our own world view, of which we are largely unaware. Our internal world is an objective reality to the extent that it is a "psychic fact," as it is when we dream or an authentic perspective that we take during an IDL interview, or experience during a "real" mystical or near death experience.

For IDL "intrasocial" does not imply self-aspects, subconscious or shadow. Intrasocial perspectives, roles and identities contain but are not limited to these categories. Dream characters, urges, feelings, dissociations and physiological processes may indeed be experienced as self-aspects, elements of the subconscious, sub-personalities or as shadow, but when interviewed they typically view themselves as autonomous. They support this stance with perspectives and strategies that include but transcend our own. Consequently, they cannot be reduced to sub-personalities of some larger self without ignoring or discounting those contributions which are not our own. They are neither completely subjective nor completely objective. They live in the same borderland as introjects from your culture, like your conscience, which you cannot reduce to either your own creation or a completely objective import. But rather than being derived from a social macrocosm they are part of an intrasocial macrocosm. It is a macrocosm because it is external in relationship to the self and Self.

When you consult such voices, you are acting democratically. That is, you are tabling, for the moment, your normal waking autocracy and totalitarianism in favor of considering if there might be benefit in seeking alternative relevant, embedded perspectives. You are considering the opinions not just of your constituency, but of your *sponsors.* They are alternative, in that they represent different viewpoints from your own in most but not all cases; they are relevant to the extent that when you operationalize their recommendations and apply them in your daily life you find that your life improves along some significant dimension. They are embedded in that they are invested in you and your life because they are components of some dream or the personifications of some waking life issue.

IDL does not seek consensus; it views such attempts as leading to stagnation, because different interviewed perspectives have different priorities that are legitimate. However, what can be done is to interview a cross-section or smattering of perspectives and look for patterns of agreement regarding where you are stuck and what you need to do about it. You can perform your own experiments and discover that these priorities are not infinite; they fall into categories or themes of wake-up calls. While each interviewed emerging potential has its own valid and unique perspective on how and where you are stuck as well as what to do about it, these are variations on a few broad underlying issues that are repeated. When you recognize and respond to those themes you are representing the broad majority of your intrasocial community while respectfully listening to the dissenters.

Examples of dissenters are the voices of addiction, which stomp and scream when they are deprived. These could be the nightmares or anxiety that arise when you stop smoking, drinking, leave a co-dependent relationship or swear off drama. These voices demand a restoration of comfortable dysfunctional equilibrium. When they are interviewed, it is generally discovered that they exist within contexts that take broader, more inclusive intrasocial perspectives offering respectful solutions that take into account the needs of the suddenly abandoned and acting out perspectives. For example, you will find this to be the case when you interview a variety of elements from a nightmarish dream. Generally, the act of interviewing itself, because it is a demonstration of respect, has a potent mollifying effect on fearful, demanding or regressive characters. Then, if you act on whatever recommendations that these "deprived" characters have that are acceptable to a broader consensus of interviewed perspectives, they tend to settle down. Clearly, this strategy implies that negotiation between different perspectives is often not only necessary, but highly effective, particularly when compared to imposing your authority in an act of discipline and will.

When you consult with and strengthen your intrasocial community you are creating something like an internal democracy based on respect. You are doing so without glorifying imaginary perspectives by assuming they are human or have the same needs as humans. Neither is true and such a perspective is both a dead end and does nothing to establish a healthy microcosm.

The more that you cultivate a healthy intrasocial community the more likely you are to rearrange your life so that your external, social and macrocosmic community will reflect interior, intrasocial and microcosmic culture and priorities. Some of this macrocosmic evolution will be deliberate; other aspects will seem almost magical; conflicts with people you always argued with stop or people and situations that always got on your nerves before not only no longer bother you, you find that you welcome them as wake-up calls to learn from. Such profound and important social changes are realistic to expect, but they will not come automatically or quickly. It took you years to establish your current equilibrium and it is not going to change quickly or radically just because you interview a few dream characters or life issues. IDL is a yoga, a transpersonal integral life practice that transforms your life from the inside out authentically but gradually, as any genuine yoga does.

"Emerging potential" is the name IDL gives to interviewed dream characters and personifications of life issues, as well as to these perspectives when you become them on subsequent occasions. To "become" them means to identify with them and to look out at the world from their point of view instead of your own. If they have no eyes, like a lamp post, you *experience* the world from their perspective, not yours. IDL does not encourage the suppression or repression of your identity, but merely its *suspension* in order to temporarily assume another perspective. You choose to do so during interviews because the perspective personifies a life issue that is important to you and that you want to resolve. You are encouraged to become the emerging potential later, after the interview, because it has either felt liberating, claims to be transformative, or has recommended that you suspend your disbelief and trust it as an experiment, in order to test its efficacy.

Therefore, emerging potentials are not things any more than a perspective is a thing. They are neither real nor imaginary, internal or external, just as these categories do not apply to qualities like tall or open. While we may say that we "have" a perspective, it is also true that *perspectives have us*. As a rule of thumb, those perspectives with which you have identified, and which become the core, habitual, assumed roles that comprise your sense of self, your social, cultural, and psychological identities, possess *you*. You don't have them, in that your identity is a subset of their existence and reality. Without those perspectives, your sense of self does not exist. They are the "glue" that hold you together. The possession of us by our perspectives can either be transformative or our undoing. IDL approaches the power and arbitrariness of perspectives as a third type of cognitive distortion, along with emotional and rational types, called perceptual cognitive distortions. Perspectives create delusional contexts which make waking up almost impossible. For example, we have seen how geocentrism is a perceptual cognitive distortion that validates a psychologically geocentric worldview. As long as geocentrism provided the assumed perceptual context for humans, evolving beyond psychological geocentrism was almost inconceivable.

Perspectives that lie outside of, or are different from your core, habitual, and assumed roles tend to be liberating when you empathize with them and look at your life from their point of view. This is because perceptual cognitive distortions include your sense of self, since they are extensions of your perceptual reality, and therefore "know" you, yet they *transcend* your sense of who you are in that they add their own unique, individual perspective with its own gradations of core qualities, to your own. This is why they are called *potentials*. They present possibilities for your identity that you can choose to either grow into or ignore. They are *emerging* because they are not yet who you are. You quickly forget them and fall back into your normal waking sleep walking existence. However, the more that you return to any one or to a variety of them, the more these potentials *emerge* and the more they are assimilated into a broader, more effective, less afraid, more inclusive and balanced, sense of self.

With enough of this, your sense of who you are becomes a joke, an example of cosmic humor, and your attachment to it a source of endless hilarity. You take on more of the sense of self possessed by the air you breathe, outer space, the spaces between notes in a song, sunshine, or a smile. But because life doesn't discriminate, your sense of self also becomes more like that possessed by a block of granite, spit, the smell of a skunk, and a decaying corpse. Life does not define itself by such things; why should you?

Multi-Perspectivalism

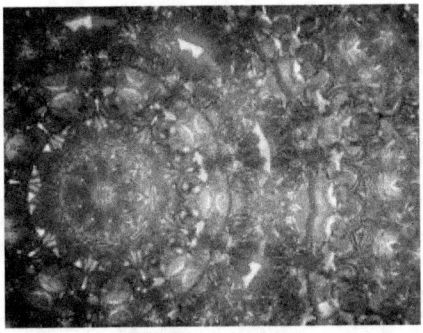

One measure of clarity, objectivity, wakefulness, and enlightenment is your ability to shift your perspective, or outlook on life. The ability to do so normally expands as we develop. Infants are locked into the perspectives given them by their senses and the needs of their sensory systems. When babies start to get in touch with their feelings they are learning to take the perspectives of their preferences, their likes and dislikes, and their emotions. They are able to observe their bodies, for example, when learning to walk. When children learn to ride bikes, they have the option of taking the perspective of their body, or the perspective of this or that feeling or preference, or the perspective of some linguistic conceptualization: "I'm losing my balance!" "Mom told me not to ride without a helmet." At about the same age, children start learning to take the roles of people that impress them: characters from movies or people who do things that seem fun or powerful: teaching, parenting, or fighting. This is the beginning of the formation of a social self that is observing a linguistic self that is observing an emotional self that is observing a physical or sensory self. Each developmental stage transcends yet includes the previous one, creating perceptual options or multi-perspectivalism within one identity or personality.

When children get older, they learn to take a perspective that questions the assumptions beneath their linguistic conceptualizations, "Is it useful that Mom told me to ignore bullies?" "What were Mom's motives for telling me not to do that?" This is the birth of reason, which provides a perspective that is more objective than the earlier ones that it contains.

Further along still, some people learn empathy, which not only involves taking the role of another person, but looks out at the world and at circumstances which are shared in order to see them from the perspective of the other person. "How would I view that situation if I were that bully?" "What does it mean to treat other people as I wish to be treated?" If a child doesn't want to share, instead of getting angry or having hurt feelings, empathy is reflected in the thought, "What would I be feeling or thinking if I were them?" This is an interpretation, to be sure, and there is no assurance it bears any resemblance to reality until it is verified by asking the person, but it is certainly a major step beyond the normal psychological geocentrism of humans. Empathy is an attempt to expand your identity beyond a separate self-sense to include the motivations and interests of others.

A further development in objectivity involves the ability to hold conflicting models or world views at the same time, for instance, capitalism, socialism, Christianity, Buddhism, Judaism, and Islam. It then becomes possible to look for patterns of agreement and attempt a grand synthesis, which is what Wilber's integral model intends. This is a type of conceptual multi-perspectivalism that Wilber calls "vision-logic," an intermediate developmental stage between late personal and transpersonal stages. Because Wilber's model is conceptual and emphasizes egalitarianism within a hierarchical structure, readers tend to overlook his strong emphasis on empathetic, communal and involutional aspects of multi-perspectivalism, including his strong advocacy for a devotional and interpersonal approach to the sacred. This non-recognition or misreading of Wilber by some is more likely to reflect the lack of integration of these two strands of multi-perspectivalism in most readers, since Wilber quite clearly understands and supports devotional and interpersonal approaches.

Many advocates of spiritual development are "blinded by the light" of oneness, meaning that differences, or the multiplicity of creation, are dreamlike and have relatively little reality, particularly when compared the Whole. At its worst this becomes a logical fallacy, in which these people unwittingly embrace distinction by saying in essence, "oneness yes, separation and distinction, no," blind to the fact that this belief is itself a distinction. They see themselves as pluralistic and egalitarian when in fact they repress distinction, separateness and hierarchy.

The rejoinder to the above question is, "Can you, after having had a mystical experience of oneness, experience the separation through the oneness?" Holograms are a good example, in that they do not deny or minimize the individuality of any specific place or entity. They depict the co-dependency of separateness and unity. The multiple facets of a diamond reflect the same principle. IDL, by teaching multi-perspectivalism, gives people direct experiences of the sacred within the profane, of the sacredness of multiplicity, distinction and separateness. Why do you think that so many people who have mystical experiences do not grow into a balanced appraisal of this fundamental issue? The initial overwhelm by awe-inspiring unity is completely understandable, but when that stance hardens into a dogma that still exists ten years later, one has to start asking, "Is this focus on unity supporting further development or has this person plateaued, sure they have found the key to universal knowledge?"

IDL agrees with Wilber that the broad variety of multi-perspectivalism that succeeds the late personal is a necessary but insufficient level of development for stabilization at any level of oneness that is generally called "transpersonal." The ability to look at issues, experiences and people, whether awake or dreaming, from multiple perspectives allows you to deepen and broaden the experience of oneness in all things. Anyone can have experiences of onenesses at any stage, but development into stable, ongoing life within the experience of oneness with nature, deity, the formless, or the non-dual requires high levels on the four core lines of cognition, self, empathy and morality. We have to learn how to think and make logical, rational distinctions regarding our beliefs and we must acquire both cognitive and empathetic multi-perspectivalism. Cognitive multi-perspectivalism is the ability to collect the views of various "wise blind men" who are reporting some part of the "elephant" of life and integrate them. Wilber's integral AQAL is an expression of the cognitive line evolved to vision-logic. Empathetic multi-perspectivalism is the ability to take the roles of others. Children can do so, in a rudimentary way, but empathy evolves just like morality and our sense of self. Few children or adults practice taking the roles of inanimate and imaginary objects, which breaks down dualisms of all sorts and teaches multi-perspectivalism on the post-personal level of vision-logic. Empathetic multi-perpectivalism without cognitive multi-perspectivalism will turn you into a polytheistic devotee; cognitive multi-perspectivalism without the empathetic will turn you into someone who replaces direct experience with concepts and abstractions. We need both. The development of these two core lines together tend to pull up both the self and ethical lines of development. This is because empathy expands the self and broadens decisions in ways that treat all others as if they were aspects of ourselves.

IDL is a representative of the next, rather radical step in this developmental progression. It may make anything - mushrooms, cake, monsters, chains, planets, deities, deceased relatives, - as the object of empathetic identification. The result is that a much broader expansion of perspective is made available to individuals, which speeds up the developmental process by breaking down all customary, habitual dualisms. As indicated above, it diminishes both the importance and the reality of basic determiners of reality for most people: real and imaginary, self and others, subjective and objective, sacred and profane, pure and dirty, good and bad, safe and dangerous, freedom and subjugation, pleasure and pain. The result is the cultivation of an identity that is based on qualities that transcend, yet include basic dualities that provide the structure of identity for most people. This represents a significant transcendence of core dualities and a useful embrace of oneness, in that it is tied to the understanding of everyday problems and dreams. It makes ongoing stabilization in awareness of oneness with nature, deity, formlessness or the non-dual much more realistic.

IDL emphasizes both the empathetic and cognitive strands of multi-perspectivalism. The empathetic, preferential, experiential face of multi-perspectivalism is expressed by actual identification with and response as this or that interviewed dream character or personification of a life issue. What is being emphasized is not conceptual understanding but *getting into and staying in role.* The more this is done, with sacred and secular, pure and disgusting, real and imaginary perspectives, the more advanced a multi-perspectival approach to empathy becomes. This is heightened when you identify with the attributes and values of a perspective that cause it to score higher than you do in one or more of the six core qualities.

The cognitive face of multi-perspectivalism is expressed by interpretations of the conceptual content of what interviewed characters say within an AQAL framework. Does it make sense? Is it practical? Can it be tested? How does it compare to your own conceptual emphasis? When you act on recommendations that arise out of an interview and evaluate the results, can they be validated by both external and internal sources of objectivity?

While IDL is not transpersonal *per se,* it is a transpersonal discipline for two reasons. First, it constructs the necessary pre-requisites for access of transpersonal states, largely through identifying with this or that perspective that personifies one or another definition of oneness. Secondly it constructs the necessary pre-requisites for stable, ongoing habitation of transpersonal states through following the recommendations of perspectives that are not only wiser, but more unified with life, than is the subject of the interview.

Life Compass

What could be more important than finding and following your life compass? If you were like me, your life was made unnecessarily difficult when you were growing up because you had no strong interior point of reference from which to evaluate the constant, often conflicting pressures from parents, teachers, peers, partners, and employers. IDL uses "life compass" to refer to a constantly available point of reference that you can rely on to steer you through the storms of your life. Your life compass is not really "yours" nor is it "inside you," which is why it is not called your "inner compass." It is constantly evolving as you do rather than standing as a fixed, eternal Truth or Reality. Because it speaks with its own voice within the context of your world view, yet independent from those of your parents or culture it is authentic. It is nurturing, in that its chief function is to provide you with wake-up calls that not only show you how you are your own worst enemy and provide suggestions about how to stop, but that also wake you up to life's emerging potentials that are attempting to take root in your consciousness and grow.

Traditionally, other terms, such as "soul," "Self," "God" (as indwelling, or immanent), "still, small voice," "intuition," the "divine" or the "sacred" have attempted to serve some or all of these important purposes. Each becomes less conducive to enlightenment in later developmental stages.

Terms like "soul" and "self" are psychologically geocentric in that they make life, growth, and enlightenment "all about you" and your freedom, bliss, and consciousness. You seek your nirvana, samadhi, and liberation. This is a shamanic, pre-personal perspective that is authentic, natural, and valid in the childhood of life. Terms like "God" point to a "something" or "someone" that is real, eternal, and all-inclusive. The experience of IDL, on the other hand, discloses contexts within contexts, called "holons," that continuously beckon us on, to be more than we are without implying a static, transcendent state, God or gods. Terms like "divine," "sacred," and "spirit" are problematic because they imply dualism and a reality that includes the non-divine, the profane, and that which is not spiritual: evil, sin, and abuse. Similarly, "life compass" is not your intuition or an "inner voice." These concepts imply a belief that you know what is true, right, or real, based on something akin to psychic ability. Have you ever met someone who bases their life on their intuition? They just "know," because their intuition tells them so, and because they know, it is their experience and their truth, which is not to be questioned or challenged because to do so is to question and challenge them. They take your questions as personal attacks! Appeals to intuition are often a way to say, "Don't question my belief about this; I know it is true and if you question it you are insulting me!" We see this mentality in True Believers of all kinds, but generally have a hard time seeing it in ourselves. In addition, tests of intuition have shown that it does not operate above and beyond chance or random variation. That does not mean that intuition cannot be accurate, just as random variation does not mean you cannot or will not win the lottery. Unlike appeals to intuition, IDL invites questioning, challenging, and testing. It invites disbelief and encourages personal verification.

Unlike many other terms for an internal source of guidance, such as "soul," "intuition," and "God," "life compass" has the advantage of not being a scripted part of the accepted family and cultural heritage that you grew up accepting. For IDL, your "life compass" exists only as a conceptual tool, a place holder, for the center of a constantly spinning vortex of potential that you uniquely access. This life compass has no ontological reality for IDL, because it is as distinct a "thing," "self," or "place." Instead, the term "life compass" is meant to point toward an experiential reality inferred by the confluence of multiple perspectives of many interviewed emerging potentials. An analogy would be to a hurricane or cyclone, which indeed has a center around which it forms and which gives it structure. However, notice that the center of a hurricane is empty. It can be so large that small planes can fly over the top and into the central "eye" or "life compass" of the hurricane.

The winds of storms have no identity. They are an impermanent, temporary, *ad hoc* collection of forces that manifest in a form that we call "hurricane" to differentiate it from "tree," sky," or "smile." However, like a smile, a hurricane is essentially a process, not a thing. Like a hurricane, a smile, and your life compass, you too are essentially a process, not a thing. This is a reality that becomes clear over multiple IDL interviews. You start to experience that your identity is no different than that of the imaginary mushrooms and skunks that you interview - *empty.*

The analogy of a diamond is another useful way to understand how IDL uses the concept of "life compass." This is because a diamond is clear and has no single, "right," or "perfect" way to view it. Its essence is to be a paradox of clarity and hardness, of harmonious stability and a riot of colors and facets.

The life compass is similar. It is clear, like the air within the eye of a hurricane, yet it is extraordinarily solid, durable, and stable. It is harmonious, like the light from a prism, or the proportions of the fibonacci curve that appear naturally in nature, and yet, upon close examination, it is a chaos of minor, individual imperfections. There is no such thing as a perfect diamond, or a perfect facet of a diamond; similarly, there is no perfection within a life compass, nor is it "your" life compass. It more appropriately is understood to belong to life, with "you" being a convenient figment of your imagination which, when taken as real, becomes your prison.[2] This is very similar to dreams, which we habitually refer to as "my dream," when a dream doesn't belong to the "dreamer," but to life and to itself and all the perspectives of the various elements that comprise it.

The concept of life compass grows out of direct experience with countless interviews of dream characters and the personifications of waking life issues of all sorts, using the IDL interviewing protocols. A consensus of perspectives, values, and recommendations emerges when you do enough of these interviews that points toward a shared reality that is prior to any form or particular value. This shared context derived from innumerable interviews provides you with a personal, experiential, and genuine definition of what your life compass is and is not.

"Life compass" points to a perspective that encompasses traditional distinctions, such as between the real and imaginary, the inner and the outer, the sacred and the profane. The more that you learn to look at your life from the perspective of your life compass, the less imprisoned you are by these dualisms. They continue to exist, but merely as tools that you use to communicate, not as autonomously existing realities. This is a basic reason why some common terms are found to no longer be so conducive to enlightenment, regardless of how useful and important they may have been at earlier stages of development.

Acting Ethically

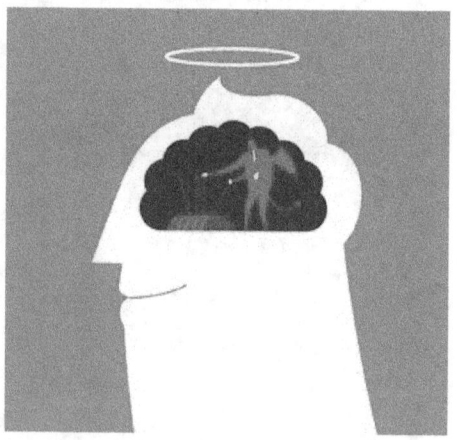

IDL views morality with skepticism and asks a number of questions about it. Why is morality important? Is morality something life does or something humans need in order to get along with each other? Is the

---

[2] An excellent description of how the delusion of self comes to be, how it works, and what is to be done about it can be found in *The Atman Project,* by Ken Wilber.

transcendence of morality a state of immorality, amorality, or simply a justification for not playing by the rules? Lawrence Kohlberg and others have done important work that demonstrate that there are developmental stages of morality and that these are both necessary and non-reversible. That is, once you awaken into a higher definition of morality there does not appear to be a regression to earlier, more limited definitions of what it means to be an ethical person.

As children, it is important to learn and internalize the ethical guidelines of society. These basically involve developing a conscience and following rules, such as the Golden Rule and the Ten Commandments. At this level of morality, you have internalized parental voices; you act morally because you should, not because it makes sense. That is the next step. You develop the ability to question the rules and follow those that are rational and make sense to you while discarding the rest. For example, you act morally because you experience that how you treat others is how you are treating those aspects of yourself that they represent. Because you do not want to damage yourself, or throw yourself into unnecessary conflict, you act ethically. This definition expands until it includes everything and everybody. Beyond this understanding lies ethical freedom, which is not to be confused with license. IDL deals with this delusion with triangulation. Both internal and external, subjective (dream characters and the personifications of life issues) and objective (authorities you respect) sources of objectivity are consulted when ethical challenges arise. The result is that your decision-making is informed but not controlled by public or social norms but neither is it controlled by your preferences or those by consensus recommendations of interviewed emerging potentials. However, each serves as a safeguard against self-delusion, with the goal being that a more balanced decision is the result, although it still is unlikely to please everybody.

IDL also supports the evolution of the moral line by providing repeated concrete experiences that confirm that how you treat all others is how you treat those aspects of yourself that they represent. It also provides repeated practice at high level empathy, a competency that reflects a high degree of moral development.

Evolving Empathy

The importance of empathy lies in its ability to expand and clarify your definition of who you are. While the line of development of your self-sense involves who you think you are, cognition how you think and reason, morality *why* you do what you do, empathy involves the evolution of your capacity to expand your sense of *who* you are. As a young child, you have empathy with physical sensations, then with your emotions. These are all self-centered forms of empathy, but they do involve an evolution of awareness toward greater objectivity. It is important to note that some people never evolve in empathy beyond these early stages, although they may be highly intelligent, charismatic, and successful. Empathy is not a requirement for success in school, bedding attractive partners, or making a lot of money. Successful people can appear to be highly empathetic but merely learn to appear so because it is a highly effective way to get people to do what they want. Think Donald Trump. Non-empathetic people are often troubled and even criminal, because an inability or unwillingness to empathize is self-centered, exploitative, and remorseless. Consequently, psychiatry is likely to label adults who are fixated in the development of empathy at early to mid-prepersonal levels as personality disordered, demonstrating sociopathy or narcissistic personality disorder.

Taking the roles of others is the next normal step in the development of empathy in childhood. It is a mechanical identification with the appearance and observable behavior of desirable roles, such as sports or military figures, super heroes, or helping professionals like teachers or doctors. This is an important step in the formulation in identity for children, but it involves little insight, reflection, or what is normally considered to be empathy. There is little to no awareness of the motivations of others, but more the parroting of things they say when they are performing exciting or interesting behaviors. This is all that is expected of good actors, although a good actor will also possess genuine empathy. Most people never develop empathy beyond this point; they call sympathy empathy and believe they are being empathetic when they are sure they know how other people feel.

However, the only way to know how another person feels is to ask them.

People who have evolved to the next level of empathy have learned to do so by checking out their assumptions of what others are feeling, thinking, or suppose by doing something radical: *they ask them.* This is a skill for enlightenment that is taught in IDL interviewing; you develop empathy by asking questions about what your interviewed character is experiencing. This involves the ability to suspend your assumptions about what others feel in order to hear from them what they are actually feeling. This radical idea involves not only listening to the motivations, intentions and feelings of others, but not interpreting them so that they fit into your world view. How many people can do that? How many people recognize this as a core characteristic of enlightenment? Even most trained therapists are certain they are empathetic when in fact what they often do is reframe their client's experience in terms of clinical models that they are familiar with. This is manipulative, and is a form of "empathy" that projects interpretations once the clinician believes they have established empathy and know not only what the client is thinking and feeling, but what they need.

The Golden Rule is a specialized and near-universal statement of empathy. In its earliest forms, it functions as a moral mandate to be internalized as conscience, it largely functions within the Drama Triangle as parental "shoulds" and "oughts" that create guilt and other forms of self-persecution when violated. IDL demonstrates, through taking the roles of other perspectives, that as we treat others we are treating those aspects of ourselves that they represent. As a consequence, the Golden Rule is followed not because one "should" or due to internalized social norms, but because it is common sense. Why would we want to hurt ourselves? This is a rational and late personal understanding of the Golden Rule. Beyond this is the actual taking of the role or perspectives of others and treating and viewing ourselves as they do. This is transpersonal multi-perspectivalism and a form of empathy that includes but transcends both moral injunction based on belief and rational understandings of the Golden Rule.

IDL is practice in empathy that minimizes interpretation, as we shall see. It does so by requiring the suspension of interpretations and personal filtering of information from the subject as best as possible, in addition to listening to their thoughts and feelings. The result is an authentic taking on of the perspective of the other and supporting them in evolving their own further integration. Because you are empathetic you support the enlightenment of the other; because you support the enlightenment of the other the part of yourself that they represent becomes more enlightened.

The next level of empathy is spontaneous and ongoing multi-perspectivalism, in which shifts of perspective naturally occur. Every interview that you do, whether for yourself or for another, strengthens your capacity for empathy. When you do an interview on yourself, or someone leads you through an interview, the requirement to stay in a novel role for an extended period of time in order to answer the various questions means that you expose yourself to an expanded state of empathy to a degree and extent that you are not otherwise likely to do in your waking life. When you interview someone else the development of empathy is supported in a somewhat different way. In order to keep them in role you have to recognize the difference between "their" voice, perspective, or world view and that of the interviewed character. This is an evolving competency. Non-empathetic or novice interviewers will not do a very good job at this, although the interview structure attempts to ensure that in most cases the results are at least adequate.

Doubt

"Do not believe in anything simply because you have heard it. Do not believe simply because it has been handed down for many generations. Do not believe in anything simply because it is spoken and rumored by many. Do not believe in anything simply because it is written in Holy Scriptures. Do not believe in anything merely on the authority of Teachers, elders or wise men."

This famous quote by Buddha indicates a major way Buddhism distinguishes itself from other world religions. It also explains what makes Buddhism as much a life philosophy as a religion. The ability to question one's beliefs and access permission to question and challenge the highest of authorities are marks of confidence, reason, and wisdom that do not exist on pre-personal levels of development or in those belief systems that are grounded in them. In contrast, such systems are threatened by challenges to their authority and respond to questions by appeal to scriptural authority and broadly accepted dogmas and mythologies rather than with reason.

We do not have to be affiliated with a particular religion to be dogmatically married to our view of life and the words that define it for us. Examples can be found in the scientific, religious, psychological, economical and political worlds. What are their key assumptions? Are they able to doubt their own premises? Do they question the foundations of their own belief systems?

Doubt is a gateway into conscious witnessing of your feelings and thoughts. The more you question your assumptions about the importance and reality of your body, your experience, your feelings, and your thoughts, the more your sense of self is objectified and separated from them. The result of such objectification is that you have full use of your thoughts and feelings, but without strong preferences that create barriers to your ability to choose the best or most appropriate one for the situation. Therefore, doubt itself becomes just one more tool rather than some core value or end in itself. Psychology has done human development significant damage by labeling this process as "dissociative." It is no more dissociative than empathy, and at least as important to development.

Doubt, in the sense of suspension of both belief and disbelief, both toward the beliefs of others and your own, is healthy. There is an old joke, "Don't believe everything you think." It would be closer to appropriate to say, "Don't believe *most of* what you think." The phenomenological approach of IDL requires the suspension of both belief and disbelief, with a preference for asking innocent, disarming questions and requesting more information: "That's interesting! Tell me more." "I haven't ever thought about it that way; how did you arrive at that conclusion?" "You seem to have a pretty strong belief about that. How did you come to know that was the truth?" This is helpful because many people so identify with their beliefs and opinions that when you question those assumptions they feel like you are not just questioning they beliefs but attacking *them*. You want to respect this natural tendency and do what you can to neutralize it without avoiding the challenge all together.

For IDL, doubt is not a permanent predisposition but merely a tool that you pick up and put down as needed. IDL interviewing uses doubt not only for the suspension of both belief and disbelief but in challenging and confronting interviewed emerging potentials: "Why do you say that, lamp post?" "I'm confused. Zebra, it sounds like you just contradicted yourself." "Why should we listen to you, sea turtle, when you are just the figment of my imagination?"

Questioning

"I cannot teach anyone anything. I can only make them think."

Socrates

There is a principle which is a bar against all information, which is proof against all argument, and which cannot fail to keep a man in everlasting ignorance. This principle is, contempt prior to examination."

Rev. William H. Poole

"Contempt prior to examination" either precludes questioning or creates questions designed to validate preconceived conclusions. The natural psychological geocentrism of humanity naturally creates this "contempt prior to examination" toward the perspectives of dream characters and the personifications of life issues. The phenomenological methodology employed by IDL is designed to counteract this pervasive prejudice. It does so by teaching, encouraging and supporting the suspension of beliefs, assumptions, preferences and prejudices of all sorts during the interviewing process. The problem is that many of our beliefs and prejudices exist out of our awareness; we do not realize that they exist and are functioning automatically, filtering out possibilities for healing, balancing and transformation. For example, the ability to differentiate reality from delusion and illusion is a fundamental competency necessary to maintain our sense of self. To surrender it can automatically generate a sense of threat to our self-sense. Another is our automatic distinguishing what is valuable from what is not. IDL questioning assumes and proceeds based on the suspension of such basic criteria for sanity and identity. The conclusion that it is foolish or could not be worthwhile can easily be a rationalization to protect a sense of self that senses attack.

Questioning can perform many purposes. Medical and psychological questioning is primarily diagnostic. Legal questioning is designed to ascertain the "facts." The questioning of the Socratic dialectic is designed to discover truth through the questioning of irrational assumptions. The questioning of a child, explorer or scientist is essentially to understand. IDL questioning is designed to amplify and disclose the perspective of the particular emerging potential that is being interviewed. You can only assume a perspective to the extent that it is defined and clear; IDL questioning clarifies perspectives so that they can be more effectively inhabited as a therapeutic strategy for expanding and thinning your sense of self. This is itself in the service of moving into the transpersonal, to make relative selflessness alive from multiple authentic perspectives.

While more traditional motivations for IDL questioning, such as curiosity, diagnosis or the discovery of truth play their part, the idea of questioning in order to assume the perspective of a dream villain or coffee pot is not a familiar use of questioning. This simple unfamiliarity, quite apart from any sense of threat, poses another barrier to the comfortable adoption of IDL for some. Children are more likely to find themselves comfortable because of their natural curiosity, enjoyment of fantasy role playing, and absence of the critical and rational filters of objectivity that normally arise in adolescence.

Interviewing

Interviewing is programmed, structured questioning. It has a pre-selected intent and is designed to collect information about one or more specific, identified issues. Integral Deep Listening grew out of interviewing strategies developed by J.L. Moreno, M.D., a contemporary of Freud's. His sociometric procedure asked children or adults their preferences regarding different topics, such as not only who they wanted to study math, play or work with but who they would *not* want to do these things with. This information was collected for groups and displayed in a diagram called a sociogram, which depicts group relationships - who is most and least liked or excluded. This information could then be used to re-organize the group for more efficient learning, work or play. Clearly, Moreno used interviewing in extremely creative and unusual ways for a specific end: improving group functioning.

With IDL, the purpose for interviewing dream characters and the personifications of life issues is similar in some ways and different in others. Its assumption is that answering questions requires us to take the role or perspective of the interviewed character, imaginary or not. This requires the surrendering of our identification with our current role or perspective on the one hand, and the practice and cultivation of empathy on the other. These are different purposes for interviewing than imagined by Moreno because they involve interviewing not social collectives, but *intrasocial* collectives, or multiple perspectives that are accessed by the same individual. The idea of interviewing *oneself* is unusual, because we often believe that we know our own mind, but it is not so unusual, as writers of fiction, who create dialogues among imaginary characters, routinely take the role, first of one and then the other as they create their literary figures. In a sense, these characters are being interviewed informally, with their dialogue and actions a reflection of the questions and concerns that the author has about who they are and their relationship to the world he is creating.

IDL also expands the normal assumptions of *what* can be interviewed. This is because there is no limit to what might appear in dreams and anyone or thing that can appear in a dream may be interviewed. When this concept is extended to waking life, the availability of perspectives that can be taken and interviewed is infinite.

IDL interviewing follows a specific formula designed to support getting into role, define or clarify that perspective, and to access specific recommendations that relate to life issues that are important to the questioner. Once this interviewing protocol is understood and learned then variations on it are encouraged, similar to musical improvisation after basic scales have been mastered.

IDL interviewing is also designed to be challenging. If an answer doesn't make sense, it is questioned. If an answer is confusing or impractical, that is pointed out to the character, with the expectation that no answer is to be accepted on face value just because an angel, guru or God said it.

Reason

"Personally, I would save my credulity for things for which there is evidence rather than believing everything until it is proved to be impossible."

Strange, The ScienceForum

It seems crazy to need to list reason as a concept conducive to enlightenment, but there are just too many people out there who think that enlightenment either doesn't require clear thinking or else believe reason is actually the enemy of it. Since both of these ideas are not only wrong but nonsense, an explanation of why reason is important to IDL is in order. Reason is mostly a matter of parking your preferences, beliefs, and emotions in order to think things through. It is based on the question, "Does this make sense?" It does not assume that sensory experience, feelings, beliefs or ideas are rational just because they are coherent within a given set of conditions. *Everything*, including nightmares, is coherent within a given set of conditions.

Reason guides what you say when it is important for you to make sense. When you want to have fun, tell a good story, or get someone to like you, reason is not so important. Consequently, reason is not always useful, nor is it everything. Doubt encourages the development of reasoning through the thinking through of assumptions and presuppositions. A common defense by people who do not like having their assumptions or beliefs questioned is to accuse the questioner of being cold, unemotional, unempathetic, unloving or, if the questioner is a child, a pesky nuisance. Even a little questioning and skepticism can evoke claims that someone has turned into Mr. Spock because reason feels relatively cold, calm, and lacking the fire and aliveness of impulse, drama, and emotion. This is because reason is relatively objective, observational and removed while emotions are relatively subjective, enmeshed and invested. Most of us can go a long, long way toward greater rationality and logic before we have to get concerned about turning into Mr. Spock. That reason and objectivity are incompatible with emotion is a perceptual delusion and is easily discovered to be untrue when you yourself cultivate your own ability to reason. While some people who are intellectuals and logical are relatively distant, there is no data to back up the stereotype that this is an inherent characteristic of those who think before they act or speak.

Most of the accomplishments of humanity are products of rational minds. The fact that much of the destruction in the world is also a product of rational minds does not diminish the accomplishments of the rational mind but only points to the reality that it requires adult supervision. Your rational mind by itself is not your life compass, the crown of creation or the terminus of the evolutionary arc of life. It is merely a necessary competency to master as a pre-requisite for accessing the trans-rational, which is where adult supervision resides. The problem is that the transpersonal and trans-rational both look like the pre-rational, in that both are experiential, with the result that they are commonly confused. However, the pre-rational self mistakes prejudices for thinking while the trans-rational is experienced by a trans-personal, multi-perspectival, transparent oneness that has rational capabilities.

What most people call thinking is mostly justifying their world view and rearranging their prejudices. "Reason" is revealed to be either an emotionally-driven statement of preferences or the following of some pre-learned, automatic script. This ranges from scripture-quoting and dogma recitation to work procedures and routine ways of handling customers, complaints or disagreements. Even though such responses may be rational, reasoning processes, their automatic or habitual nature implies that they are learned adaptations for dealing with particular repetitive, necessary life situations, like getting a refund or the steps for fixing a car.

Because anyone, including children and criminals, can access any and all transpersonal states, the naive conclude that reason is unnecessary for stable access of those states. But it is notoriously difficult to duplicate transcendent experiences. Why? Doing so requires a predictable developmental progression and an unavoidable part of that progression is learning how to think, which means to doubt oneself and to reason. Those who attempt to access the transpersonal without making reason their friend can access temporary states that are indeed transformational, but without the objectivity of reason to interpret these experiences and direct their expression, emotion, belief, groupthink and preferred mythologies take over. The results are at best harmlessly delusional, but sometimes they are frighteningly deranged, justifying killing, child abuse, warfare, enslavement torture in the name of pre-personal, irrational enlightenment. Those who have had such experiences may in fact have a huge following of adherents who believe they are incarnated masters, but is collusion in groupthink proof of enlightenment? Such people are posing as someone who is more highly developed than they are, and they themselves are the first victims of this delusion.

In integral developmental models, the attainment of transpersonal developmental levels requires previous stabilization in the rational. This means that learning to think is a pre-requisite to transpersonal stages of development. This is why children may access transpersonal states with near death, psychic, or mystical experiences, but are not at transpersonal levels of development. People have to learn to reason; you and I are not born with the ability to think, nor is learning how to think past a certain minimal level required to grow up, get a job, have a family, be talented, or make a lot of money. You will find many irrational people doing all these things.

While reason is invaluable, it should hardly be the only tool in your tool kit, nor always the first one that you reach for. Very rational and intelligent people, like Barak Obama, can still destroy themselves and countless others if they are unwilling or unable to question the premises of their perceptual cognitive distortions. This is why learning to think logically is a necessary but insufficient step in the process of waking up. Learning by doing is often more important. To avoid the disasters of highly rational actors who remain prisoners of groupthink, such as Obama, IDL encourages triangulation, which involves the checking of accepted cultural norms not only with common sense but with internal sources of objectivity such as interviewed emerging potentials.

Reason is cultivated by IDL in several ways. While suspending your beliefs, assumptions and rationality appears to be irrational, prepersonal and contrary to what is advocated here, it is done for highly rational reasons. Consequently, it is not a move into irrationality but rather *arationality*, or a space that temporarily suspends both irrationality and rationality in favor of deep listening. You will find that many interviewed dream characters and personifications of life issues are more rational than you are, in that they are more objective and separated from cultural scripting, groupthink, drama and emotional reactivity. Consequently, accessing and becoming them cultivates your ability to think clearly and to reason, because thinking is thereby objectified from your habitual motivational emotional impulses. The investigation of emotional, logical, and perceptual barriers to reason, called cognitive distortions, are discussed in *Waking Up*.

Empiricism

In the above picture, Jerry and his buddy have a theory that awaits empirical testing - hopefully by someone else! How do you test someone's claims of spirituality? Empiricism responds by asking,
"What are the steps to follow to test this theory or belief?"
"Am I following the steps (performing the experiment) correctly?"
"Are my results confirmed by those who have previously done the experiment?"
These are the three steps of scientific, interpretive and transpersonal yogas and integral life practices. They are hardly new. Buddha said, "Believe only after careful observation and analysis, when you find that it agrees with reason and is conducive to the good and benefit of one and all. Then accept it and live up to it." This statement indicates the primacy of both reason and empiricism for Buddhism.
Empiricism is validation through duplication. There are many things that are real and impressive but which cannot be duplicated, like faith healers that pull tumors out of bodies with their hands. I know of no instances of this skill set being passed on to students, but I know of a number of students who have tried to learn how and have failed. UFOs and collective hallucinations, like the account of the sun, as witnessed by thousands, bouncing around in the sky, in the famous Marion apparition of Fatima, are other examples of realities that do not rise to the standards of empiricism because they defy duplication. State openings, even when they are collective, tend to be one-of-a-kind events. Accounts of mystical and near death states validate the realities we have experiencing without requiring empiricism, reason, moral development or anything else.

When you get a Tarot reading, a Reiki treatment or throw the *I Ching* you may be impressed with the results. I have been.[3] However, have you ever noticed how validity diminishes with repetition? Experiments to demonstrate that Tarot or the *I Ching* operate above chance have not succeeded. Similarly, while the claims by TM that people will learn to levitate if they practice the method do succeed in generating considerable revenue for TM, has it ever taught anyone to levitate? Yes, some meditators can "hop," but is that levitation? The common, ancient claim that meditation develops *siddhis,* or psychic abilities, has not been empirically verified despite thousands of contemporary meditators and considerable scientific studies. Claims of these abilities are historic and unverifiable. When they occur with contemporary subjects they cannot be duplicated, although the original instances are often verified by witnesses. This either means that we live in an age that no longer generates *any* people who are so gifted or that meditation, as important and useful as it is, is unlikely to lead to psychic ability. If the second conclusion is correct, doesn't that imply that the classical association of transpersonal stages of development with psychic abilities is either overblown or mistaken?

The lack of connection of meditation and psychism does not mean that meditation is not extraordinarily beneficial and remarkable in many ways. For example, the Tibetan practice of *Tummo* has been demonstrated to maintain physical warmth even when people are surrounded by ice. We know that advanced yogis can turn off pain perception and survive for long periods of time without food or even oxygen. These talents involve physiological reprogramming, not precognition, psychokinesis, and other psychic abilities that religions usually claim are marks of high spiritual attainment. They can be learned and duplicated, meaning they are subject to the three strands of empiricism.

IDL uses empiricism when it says, "Learn how to suspend your beliefs, assumptions, and interpretations and get into the roles of interviewed dream characters and the personifications of life issues. Choose the recommendations that make sense to you and test them in your life. Check your results with sources of objectivity: experts, teachers, other interviewed emerging potentials." This is a developmental emphasis that is focused on your growth in the here and now, a waking up in relationship to your ongoing and current, real-world concerns.

---

[3] An impressive example of the I Ching is provided by C.G. Jung in his introduction to Evans-Wentz's *The I Ching.*

Phenomenology

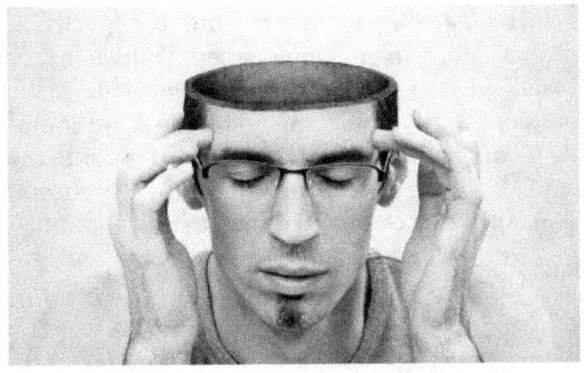

A phenomenological approach is one that suspends assumptions, beliefs, expectations and preferences of all sorts. Because our assumptions and beliefs often have practical value, this is generally temporary, as it is for IDL. Derived from the thinking of Husserl, phenomenological research in psychology is based on the idea that we see things clearer the more we can get out of our own way. Therefore, when we are attempting to see things objectively, as we are when we are attempting to learn or perform an experiment, the more that we can temporarily set aside our biases, prejudices, opinions and emotions the more likely we are to hear and see without filtration. While cognitive filtering is inevitable, it can be reduced, and that is the intent of phenomenology.

A fundamental aspect of its integral life practice along with recognizing and revising your life script, immersion in the Drama Triangle and cognitive distortions, IDL both uses and teaches a phenomenological approach in three areas, interviewing, meditation and pranayama. The dropping of assumptions is both easiest to learn and most clearly observed in role identification during interviewing. If you do not get into role your answers will be shallow and reflect your opinions and preferences; to the extent that you set your habitual waking assumptions and worldview aside when you become an element during an IDL interview your answers are much more likely to be challenging, unexpected and reflect points of view or perspectives that you do not normally call your own. In meditation, phenomenology determines whether or not, and to what extent, you stay identified with your body, thoughts, feelings, images and sense of who you are. In IDL *Pranayama,* phenomenology allows you to become, rather than simply observe, your breath.

Phenomenology can beneficially be generalized to a general attitude toward experience. For example, once it is learned IDL recommends that you practice listening to others and to experience night time dreams from a phenomenological perspective by intentionally suspending your assumptions. This will keep you out of reactivity, drama and interpretations that misunderstand wake-up calls. In all these ways, a phenomenological frame of mind resembles the "Middle Way" between extremes taught by Gautama, Aristotle's "Golden Mean," and the concept of homeostasis in biology.

Interdependence

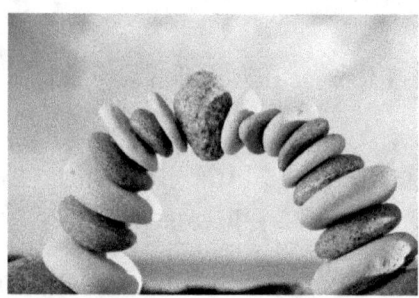

Interdependence is as basic to Buddhism as salvation is to Christianity, obedience is to Islam and Judaism and karma to Hinduism. What makes it astonishingly different as a foundation for spirituality is its observation of relationship as process rather than a statement of relationship as morality, such as "Love thy neighbor." In this world view, all things intrinsically arise or originate interdependently, which means that there is no one underlying factor, quality or substance that sustains either creation or the human predicament. This observation stands the test of time because it is broader than the realm of moral relationship and extends into the realm of objectively observed empirical experience, whether external or internal, individual or collective.

Interdependence is different from dependency or independence. Dependency makes all other qualities dependent on one or more major attribute, such as love, wisdom or inner peace. Independence proclaims that any one quality is sufficient in itself, either because it contains all other qualities or because it doesn't need them. Interdependence recognizes that a particular quality is most effective for certain circumstances and therefore encourages flexibility, adaptability, and a variety of possibilities.

Interdependence implies multi-perspectivalism, because different interdependent factors imply different perspectives. IDL arrives at an awareness of the interdependence of all experience through its emphasis on a multi-perspectival methodology. By interviewing multiple perspectives from the same dream, interdependence among those perspectives becomes obvious. Consequently, IDL does not reduce reality to one over-riding concept, perspective, or entity, like love. To do so sets up a fundamental epistemological dualism while depriving us of sufficient interdependent tools for development.

Balance

"Harmony," homeostasis," "the middle way," "yin and yang," and "the golden mean," are common ways of talking about a quality that is so intrinsic to life that it is normally taken for granted. Balance implies a dualism of activity, if not thinking, and often both. In order to have balance, you have to have a minimum of two factors, forces, or elements that are in some way oppositional. Life is continuously balancing an enormous variety of factors, far too many to count or keep in one's awareness. For example, your cells are pushing outward with the same fourteen pounds per square inch of pressure that the atmosphere is constantly pressing in against them with. This is a powerful dualism, conflict and homeostasis that is so fundamental that we are completely oblivious to it. Another is our breathing. Inhalation is matched with exhalation. Notice that most oppositions that create balance do not rise to the level of conflict. Do your inhalations fight with your exhalations? Normally, no. Our inhalations and exhalations are normally balanced, out of our awareness, whether we are aware of them or not.

Once we understand that everything is composed of conflicting polarities in states of equilibrium, we start to find balance and harmonies everywhere we look. We find that they are composed of intrinsic and inevitable conflicts which are necessary to create and maintain a transcendent harmony that includes, yet transcends, both polarities and their conflict. This is a figure-ground relationship fundamental to life: we can either focus on the component dualities and conflicts within any situation or relationship or we can focus on the integrative and harmonious context that includes both. There is no right answer to this challenge. Sometimes we need to focus on one more than the other, but what we do know is that the ability to do so, rather than to become fixated either on dualities and conflict, on the one hand, or oneness, on the other, is itself delusional, blind and out of balance. If you examine dysfunction in almost any field of human experience - interpersonal relationships, politics, religion, economics, psychology, sociology, history, aesthetics or personal development, you will find that most problems can be understood as a fixation on one or the other instead of developing the ability to view it as a gestalt and to flow in perspective, interchanging which is now figure, now ground.

The sophistication and pervasiveness of constant balancing in physiological, behavioral, interpersonal, cultural, and psychological realms is so pervasive that we normally reduce it to the balancing of just one or two factors, such as love and fear, wisdom and ignorance, negentropy and entropy, or peace and chaos. In a Manichean dualism, everything "good" or desirable gets lumped together as examples of a "positive" polarity while everything "bad" or undesirable is placed under a "negative" one. However, both homeostasis and the developmental dialectic demonstrate that both are equally necessary, which means that "bad" and undesirable qualities are inherently as important and desirable, if balance is to be maintained. For development, antithesis is as necessary as thesis if synthesis is to be achieved and maintained.

Siva, the god of destruction pictured above, serves this purpose within Hinduism. Another word for the ability to see conflict as contributing necessary balance within a greater whole is "contextualization." Whenever you back off from any conflict and observe the interdependence of each pole, you have contextualized, objectified, and depersonalized an opposition. You observe it as a representation of some type of higher-order balance. Both "bad" and "good" are recognized as relative to your context; broaden your perspective and what looked preferable and what you wanted to reject, now appear equally worthy of respect. The ultimate, pure, and perfect qualities are relativized while the secular, impure, and corrupted qualities are re-evaluated in a more positive light.

This perspective is reinforced in IDL by the experience of interviewed emerging potentials as wake-up calls, which can be thought of as generally unrecognized, unheeded antithesis. Every time you interview a wake-up call, whether a sleeping or waking nightmare, mundane dream or waking life issue, you are respectfully investigating some antithetical element, some perspective that is in opposition to your own. By doing so you move first toward the acceptance and then the integration of that particular wake-up call. What was previously a perceived threat or an unappreciated "other" becomes a valuable, meaningful element of a greater whole. You are enriched by it even as it adds to your growth. In this way, IDL interviewing furnishes high-octane fuel for the expansion and transformation of consciousness.

Some people view the enlightenment, peace and harmony that comes with the transcendence of opposites as proof that everything, when seen from the "right" perspective, is in divine order. This is not the conclusion of IDL. It does not use the contextualization of conflict as a way to rationalize it away, ignore it, or pretend it does not really matter. This is because IDL interviewing demonstrates that interviewed emerging potentials produce low scores for a purpose and because from their perspectives, conflicts usually has an important function that is to be respected. It may be to emphasize areas that you need to work on and that will not go away if you simply rationalize an associated conflict. It may be to demonstrate that internal conflict within a particular perspective, indicated by a combination of low and high scores, makes the interviewed character what it is. You discover this when the element is asked how it would be if it scored all tens. It is not unusual to hear it say that it either does not want to change or that it would cease to exist as itself if it did. Its nature functions to wake you up to certain perspectives and possibilities in its current configuration and resists changing into a pattern to your liking, even if that represents the resolution of differences, oppositions or conflict, if to do so does not reflect its priorities.

Dualisms are both necessary, yet destructive. You can't live and grow without the distinctions that the dualities of language create and allow, but if you allow them to define you they eventually stop your development; they will trap you in a web of intrinsic, self-made delusion. Philosophers, theologians and some mystics have attempted to resolve this dilemma by creating monisms that say, "dualisms and evil are delusions; what is real is sacred and good." Although experience clearly indicates that a multiplicity of balancing factors exist and are important, many people and spiritual traditions strongly resist juggling a number of oppositions. As we have seen, they tend to dismiss multiplicity as obscuring the "real" meaning of life, which is "love," or "wisdom," or "peace." At prepersonal levels of development we just can't seem to wrap our brains around the simple, fundamental reality of a profusion of fundamental oppositional and balancing forces at work in the cosmos. It feels like conceptual polytheism, and we want monism. But monisms discount life by ignoring the fact that both dualisms and delusions exist for a good reason: to wake life up to itself. The classical attempts to resolve this dilemma fail because they look at balance and dualism from the perspective of humanity, not from spontaneous perspectives which embody life itself.

Buddhism provides a notable exception in that it enumerates not one "real" or "true" reality, but seven factors that it says are "conducive to enlightenment:" These are mindfulness (*sati*), keen investigation of the *dhamma* (*dhammavicaya*), energy (*viriya*), rapture or happiness (*piti*), calm (*passaddhi*), concentration (*samadhi*), and equanimity (*upekkha*). Notice that this is not a reductive explanation: it isn't saying that "love is all you need," or that "wisdom" or "compassion" is the answer. While it is true that Buddhism, if pressed, will boil the cause of suffering down to ignorance and tell you its solution is attainment of nirvana brought about by wisdom, it prefers to provide multiple causes and multiple, interacting and balancing processes that produce awakening, liberation, or enlightenment. IDL shares this bias. In fact, it insists on it.

IDL notes that in developmental psychology black and white thinking is associated with personality disorders, mid-prepersonal levels of development, and cognitive distortion. The ability to hold several contradictory ideas in one's mind at the same time, to tolerate ambiguity and non-rationality, are competencies that generally require years and a good education to develop. If you do a reality check with most adults you know, you probably won't find many with a refined capacity for any of these things. Humpty Dumpty is simpler; he makes more sense, because believing only the reality we create is easier to understand.

Balance becomes a problem when it becomes an inertial state from which we cannot escape. When this happens balance is called "habit" or addiction." There then exists a stable state that resists change and may or may not be destructive. This is why development requires a dialectic interplay between balance and thesis, on the one hand, and imbalance and antithesis on the other. If we do not question these adaptive balances ourselves, by listening to and following wake-up calls, circumstances may at some point violently eject us from our complacency.

IDL emphasizes balance because it is a core reality that shows up repeatedly in interviews. This balance is not C.G. Jung's compensatory theory of dreaming, in which dreams balance out, or compensate for, waking delusions. Instead, each interviewed emerging potential is found to have its own homeostasis, its own equilibrium, and it is generally more refined than that of waking identity. For example, IDL finds that it is impossible to have peace of mind and drama at the same time. As drama increases, peace of mind decreases; as drama decreases, peace of mind increases. Most interviewed emerging potentials are found to be relatively free of drama, which means that they are relatively *balanced* in relationship to waking identity. This alone is sufficient reason to pay careful attention to what they have to say and what they recommend.

Integral

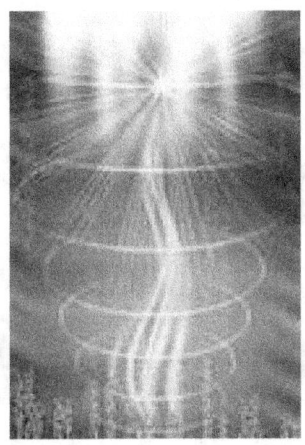

"Integral" implies not only integration but multi-functionality. Instead of one answer, you have a multitude; instead of one definition of being (ontology), you have many. An integral approach celebrates a cacophony of variables and dimensions that create life and value, yet organizes and makes sense out of them. IDL endorses variables intrinsic to Ken Wilber's AQAL model. An integral approach considers level of development, various states of consciousness, the four quadrants of invested holons, the various lines and different styles of development. This is a multi-perspectival approach, consulting all of the blind men investigating the elephant and looking for similarities and patterns in their findings. IDL is a particular variety of integral that emphasizes a phenomenological transpersonal empiricism. Its phenomenological aspect is demonstrated by its non-evaluation of the reality status of interviewed elements, which it calls "emerging potentials." Its transpersonal aspect is demonstrated in several ways. It is not psychologically geocentric but centered on multi-perspectivalism and the thinning of the self; it is trans-rational in that its methodology includes both belief and reason but transcends both. Its empirical nature is demonstrated by a methodology that follows the three strands of empiricism: injunctions, testing and peer review. In setting up an integral life practice, goals are determined in consultation with interviewed emerging potentials and subjected to triangulation, rather than being simply the expression of waking preferences. This is an extension, broadening and improvement on the classical understanding of peer review.

If you go to a mountaintop and come down and then proclaim a new vision of the world to the swamp dwellers, does that mean that you are enlightened? Isn't it true that you have had an experience of relative enlightenment? Do experiences of enlightenment mean that you are no longer a swamp dweller? Are you a swamp dweller that has had extraordinary, life-changing experiences of enlightenment? Enlightenment can be defined in several ways, as a high mystical state, as a feeling or as the pinnacle of development. IDL believes that while all of these definitions have their place and uses, the most useful and therefore important is to view enlightenment as clearer, more lucid awareness at whatever stage of development you currently inhabit. It is as if you, the swamp dweller, lived in the swamp with the perspective you had while living on top of the mountain. Enlightenment is primarily a developmental process, meaning that you want to do what expands your definition of yourself and avoid what doesn't. This may be news to some readers, who are used to thinking about enlightenment as a "bolt from the blue" or an "off/on switch:" you touch the hem of the robe of the master, or get knocked off your horse by a divine revelation, and you are enlightened. There are numerous problems with confusing such intense but sporadic and temporary state changes with enlightenment. Enlightenment is an unfolding *process*, which means that you can do things to make it more or less likely. You are not at the mercy of divine intervention or "good karma;" there are things you can do and not do that make a major difference in how enlightened you become and whether you stay that way.

The temporary view from the mountain top is analogous to a state opening, whether it be due to a dream, lucid dream, hypnotic, channelled, drug, ascetic, meditative, near death or mystical experience. The permanent experience of living with the perspective of both the swamp and the mountain top is analogous to attainment of a higher developmental stage. The view from the top of the mountain transcends the view from the swamp but includes it. It represents a stability in inhabiting such a perspective wherever you are. regardless of what you are doing.

This distinction is important, both for those who are seeking enlightenment and for those who think they already are enlightened. It explains why and how you should question those who say, "Trust me, I'm enlightened!" Remember that they are swamp dwellers who have been to a mountain top once or several times, and are most likely convinced that they are no longer swamp dwellers. They have possibly developed one or another marvelous capability, like the Nidra Yoga capability to stay in delta wave deep sleep consciousness while awake. However, the attainment of an aptitude or line of development does not indicate a stable transpersonal level of development. Is a guitar virtuoso like Jimi Hendrix to be consulted as an expert on economics? Was Bach enlightened or "just" a genius at musical composition? Is an advanced meditator an expert on human relations or engineering? You will regularly find assumptions of higher levels of attainment associated with those who have had near death experiences. They have had state openings of relative enlightenment; many come back from the top of such a tall mountain convinced that they have seen God, met Jesus, and know the Truth. Have they attained stable access to higher levels of personal development? Children and criminals sometimes report mystical or near death experiences. Does that mean criminals and children are enlightened? How do you know? Look at their everyday life. Do they live a transformed life? If not, what does it mean to say, "I am enlightened?" How can you tell? Look at all four of the core lines of development, empathy, self, morals, and cognition, not just one. Look at the criteria for development to this or that level and see if your enlightened guru meets those criteria.[4] This is certainly a much lower bar than the marks of a Buddha, or enlightened one, for instance, but they still remain out of reach for most of us. States are expression of the transcending arm of the developmental polarity while stages are manifestations of the inclusive and balancing pole. Transcendent states are evolutionary while foundational stages, no matter how transcendent, are involutionary. These take turns in the leadership position; when self-transcendence is the priority transcendent states become the protagonist in the developmental dialectic and stage consolidation is in the role of antagonist. When balance and stability are the priority, as they are for most of us most of the time, then the hierarchical, structured, and exceptional nature of transcendence and states becomes the antagonist. Together these two expressions of life, evolution and involution, generate the higher order

---

[4] For a summary of the developmental stages, see *What Is Your Next Level of Growth? Understanding Wilber's Developmental Stages.*

synthesis called "integral," or the acquisition of a higher level of development that both transcends *and* includes the previous ones.

Transpersonal states show up in IDL when interview subjects identify with perspectives that are one with nature, compassion, or transcend categorization. However, rather than being revelatory, these may be so subtle as to be overlooked. For example, almost anyone can do an interview with the air they breathe and access a perspective that is relatively formless, free, and objective, to a degree that transcends identification with any self and all drama. In fact, identification with such perspectives is so common with IDL that it is taken for granted, but regular access to such perspectives is astonishing in the context of ready availability to truly transformational power. IDL is education into both the reliability and accessibility of such states and stages. It is normal for transpersonal state openings to disappear after IDL interviews and for your identity to return largely to the normal parameters of waking life. However, with repeated interviews and character identifications, the ongoing perspective of your waking identity broadens and thins naturally, slowly, and imperceptibly. This change is as subtle and slow but as significant as a child learning to walk or talk. Genuine, broad-based advances in developmental levels are made possible, which resemble a slow, consistent climb up a mountain.

Ascent to higher developmental levels is typical with IDL because this is what life wants to do; it wants to evolve. It is always attempting to use you to wake-up to itself. The more that you get out of your own way the more quickly this naturally occurs.

Observation of Breath

IDL bases its emphasis on both interdependence and multi-perspectivalism on the universal and foundational experience of breathing. It observes that breathing contains at least six separate parts, stages or elements, and that each of these balance the others. Based on the interdependent and multi-perspectival nature of the six stages of every breath, IDL looks for the external and macrocosmic as well as the internal and microcosmic correlates to these stages, for example in the round of a day, the seasons or a lifetime. These six stages are: abdominal inhalation, chest inhalation, the pause between inhalation and exhalation, chest exhalation, abdominal exhalation, and the pause between exhalation and inhalation. Each of these parts, stages or elements can be correlated with basic life characteristics that are themselves correlated with seven basic developmental stages or octaves. These seven octaves are breathing itself, processes associated with each of the six stages of every breath (waking, aliveness, balance, detachment, freedom and clarity), the six core qualities that are addressed in every IDL interview (confidence, empathy, wisdom, acceptance, inner peace and witnessing), six varieties of transformational affect (abundance, joy, awareness, cosmic humor, trans-rationality and luminosity), six stances of devotional affirmation, six strategies for the emptying of self and six ways to take the perspective of life itself. These last three are ineffable and cannot be easily summed up in words. However, these as well as the first four octaves are described in *Seven Octaves of Enlightenment: Integral Deep Listening Pranayama.*

Naming

The power of naming is recognized in *Genesis,* right at the beginning of the Bible, in the creation of humanity. We become self-aware through the process of naming, which creates distinctions and discriminations which are essentially tools for controlling our environment, others and ourselves. IDL uses naming to do two things: interrupt our train of thought and to bring into clarity that which is present but undefined. For example, what are you feeling right now? A feeling is there, but it has probably been in the background. When you identify it as curiosity, boredom, confusion, anxiety or hopefulness you are bringing into clear awareness something that was affecting you behind the scenes. There is no problem with this most of the time; most thoughts and feelings that are operating out of our awareness are either helpful or harmless. However, some of the time they are not. For example, the thought, "I don't think she likes me," if unrecognized, is likely to create feelings of sadness, fear or anger and lead to other thoughts that just pile one delusion on top of another: "Well, I don't like her either!" "She shouldn't like me. I'm so ugly!" Naming interrupts this train of thought, particularly when you say what you are thinking out loud. You now have an opportunity to reconsider this thought or simply enjoy the break in your stream of consciousness.

IDL teaches naming as an important meditation tool to do just that. Most people who think they are meditating are actually entrained to one or another subliminal thought or feeling that is out of their awareness. It is controlling and directing their consciousness and thereby sabotaging their meditation. However, it is relatively simple to name whatever is currently present in thought, feeling, or mood and thereby open a space of relative clarity and spaciousness, like the space between your eyes and the words that you are reading or the silence between notes in music. These can thereby be expanded until they become figure (foreground) in your awareness and your thoughts, feelings and even your mood become background. *Waking Up* describes how to use naming both during sitting meditation and in the course of your everyday activities.

The Six Core Qualities

(Confidence, Empathy, Wisdom, Acceptance, Inner Peace, Witnessing)

For IDL, enlightenment is not a goal or a static end state but an ongoing process, in which there are always relative degrees of wakefulness present, regardless of your age or developmental level, and relative degrees of delusional sleepwalking present, even if you are an ascended master. IDL believes this bipolar developmental goad of wakefulness and delusional sleepwalking never goes away. Buddhas and gods are still sleepwalking in delusion relative to contexts that transcend and include them. IDL uses the six core qualities not only as one octave in its *pranayama* but also as criteria for waking up or enlightenment during interviewing. Higher scores on a scale of zero to ten generally imply a more transcendent and inclusive perspective than lower scores, but not always. Empathy is a notable exception.

IDL assumes that for any level of development these six core qualities not only remain relevant, but point toward transformational possibilities. This is why, in IDL interviews, interviewed emerging potentials are asked to score themselves zero to ten in these qualities and then asked to how similar amplitudes might show up in the life of the subject. The zero to ten scale is relative and subjective; what is a ten for you today may be a six for you in five days, months, or years. Consistently high scores are not necessarily helpful; they may be so etherial and perfect as to be functionally unattainable and therefore quickly forgotten. For example, a score of ten may not be as useful as a sore of 9.75, which implies something very high, but short of perfection, and therefore more likely to be attainable. A score of seven or eight may be even more realistic and attainable. Similarly, very low scores are not necessarily problematic. The character may be saying, "No; I want to stay a one in confidence because my fear is real and you need to accept that fear." Regarding compassion, low scores are common with interviewed characters, particularly objects. They seem to be saying, "Compassion, and issues of self and selfishness, are irrelevant to my perspective. It's not what I need. You won't either, when you choose to become me."

Just like the six core processes, these six core qualities also promote getting unstuck, moment to moment, with each stage of each breath:

"As my confidence grows my capacity for empathy expands;

As I become more empathetic, I become more wise in my decision-making;

As I become more wise, I become more accepting of myself and others;

As I become more accepting, my ability to experience deep inner peace grows;

As I become more at peace, I become more objective, witnessing the drama of my life;

As my objectivity increases, I become less afraid and more confident..."

These six core qualities open up into a more rarefied level of "qualities," or affect of a transcendent nature, including abundance, cosmic humor, and luminosity. These had their origin the "Three Jewels" of Buddhism, the Sangha, Buddha, and Dharma.

Justice and Human Rights

The purpose of IDL is not limited to supporting your development from prepersonal into personal and then the transpersonal, waking up and becoming lucid and enlightened in all states. It demonstrates that as you treat others you treat those aspects of yourself which they represent and personify. This is literally true in dreams and is demonstrated in every IDL interview. Because life itself is dreamlike, when you apply this principle in your waking life you quicken the speed of your own integration and therefore your own development. This is the basic reason why justice and human rights are viewed by IDL as words and concepts conducive to enlightenment.

We normally only think of justice and human rights in macrocosmic social and governmental, contexts. Thomas Jefferson, as a major architect of the Bill of Rights, is an international representative of the broad extension of human rights to all men. IDL views your interaction with family, work, and society as a microcosmic projection and mirror of your interaction with your microcosm, or internal reality. The concept of extending justice and rights to interviewed emerging potentials is called "dream politics," because it deals with the distribution of power in the macrocosm and microcosm. It teaches learning to listen to and demonstrate respect for members of your intrasocial, as well as your social, communities. For IDL, microcosm includes your thoughts, feelings, night time dreams, and your relationship with your intrasocial community, comprised of interviewed emerging potentials as well as other "subjective" forces, preferences, and patterns of habitual adaptation. Your dream characters are members of *ad hoc* groups that share a culture and interdependent relationships that are revealed when interviewed, particularly in the context of Dream Sociometry. They come together in dreams to express priorities and perspectives that are transformative.

IDL focuses on a commitment to justice and the extension of rights we demand for ourselves to imaginary as well as "real" others. The act of deep listening itself is a form of justice that is transformational. When you act on recommendations from members of your intrasocial community you are extending to them the basic right of being given a respectful hearing. Since imaginary elements, such as a dream fireman, are not concerned with physical security, food, shelter, health, or protection, we are not talking about the extension of such rights to fantasies, nor are we talking about the extension of the right of freedom of speech to termites, much less to imaginary termites. Instead, IDL encourages the practice of deep listening to this or that interviewed perspective, without thereby feeling committed to agree with it. This is different from anthropomorphically projecting onto chimpanzees, whales, dolphins, dogs, and elephants the concept of justice and rights that we desire for ourselves as humans because we are listening to *their* priorities instead of assuming they must agree with *ours*. The more respectful and healthy your interactions with interviewed emerging potentials become, the more your own development supports the evolution of both microcosmic and macrocosmic society and culture.

We have seen that the extension of human rights to interviewed emerging potentials is a commitment to respect. Your intention is to listen to and respect the priorities and interests of whomever or whatever you encounter, whether it be in your waking life, a dream, a near death experience, or an IDL interview. This does not mean you have to agree with any, real or imaginary, and you certainly do not have to subordinate your own values and interests to theirs. It only means that you have a responsibility to listen to those that cross your path, to do your best to table your own prejudices and interpretations, and to demonstrate that you have heard what they have had to say. Sometimes action is required. It is always up to you whether or not you act on what you hear.

The extension of justice and human rights to interviewed emerging potentials is more than a quaint moral oddity. The balance of power that exists between you and your emerging potentials is essentially that between a dictator and the rest of the world. Your waking identity not only tends to put its needs, preferences and world view first; it then justifies and rationalizes this by believing that what it wants and believes is "really" what others need and "should" believe. Just as we ordinarily assume our preferences reflect the preferences of other parts of ourselves, so we normally extend this psychological geocentrism to others: we know what they need to think, feel and do. We see this assumption, that what we want is what is "really" good for others, in how parents deal with children, how corporations justify exploitation of workers and the environment, and how nations justify war. If we want this to stop in the macrocosm we need to take steps to stop it where we have the most power and influence, in our own individual microcosm, our intrasocial cosmos and realm of personal governance. IDL interviewing demonstrates that our preferences do not agree, most of the time, with those of interviewed dream characters and the personifications of our life issues.

While it is important that we focus on staying engaged with the external world in order to have a positive influence toward the transformation of our society and culture, there is no denying that our greatest power and effectiveness comes in changing ourselves. This is because it is in our feelings, thoughts and actions that we have the greatest power and control and where we can do the greatest good for the world. When we direct this power to the alignment of our priorities with those of life *via* finding and following the priorities of our life compass, we change the world toward justice and respect for the rights of all by first doing so within ourselves.

Abundance

Wherever you look, without or within, there is abundance. The more you look for it, the more you will see it. The discipline of looking for abundance creates deep waves of thankfulness, nurturance and security. Notice that when you are filled with a sense of abundance you do not feel either fear or stress. Instead, you feel thankful. Birth and death are seen to be mere transformations of this abundance. Abundance contains all six of the core qualities, confidence, compassion, wisdom, acceptance, inner peace, and witnessing in growing, deepening quantities. It also contains cosmic humor and luminosity. Abundance is another definition of oneness; as such, its cultivation encourages growth into the transpersonal.

IDL cultivates a sense of growing abundance in several ways. Most of the emerging potentials that you interview will have a much greater sense of abundance than you do, if you look for it and pay attention to it. Doing many interviews naturally creates an overwhelming sense of supportive, nurturing, high-quality abundance. In a way that is analogous to a diamond with an infinite number of facets, here is no end to the creative variety of interviewed emerging potentials or perspectives they may take. It is both extremely nurturing and mind-boggling to wake-up to the presence and reality of this never-ending abundance. IDL also uses *pranayama,* or the yoga of breathing, to focus on and amplify a sense of abundance, moment to moment, in the here and now.

Cosmic Humor

What's funny about a smoking rabbit that looks like he took too much psilocybin? If we interviewed him, he might not think he was funny at all, which would itself be another dimension of cosmic humor. Another, perhaps more common term for cosmic humor, is "crazy wisdom," a term devoted by the highly influential, intelligent and alcoholic Tibetan master Chogyam Trungpa. It uses absurdity to open the mind, as in the famous saying, "If you see the Buddha in the road, kill him."

For IDL, cosmic humor is a tool for thinning and dissociating from waking identity, without thereby moving into a state of dissociation or nihilism. You stay very much yourself, but your attachment to pain, drama, fear, preferences and yourself becomes funny. You no longer take your attachments so seriously, but at the same time you do not discount them or lose respect for the human predicament. Drama becomes precious and tender, something to be nurtured and loved, and yet is silly, absurd, and crazy. Cosmic humor looks upon drama as similar to playing God, as a child does who takes the role of mommy with her dolls, a man may do with a train set, complete with tunnels, buildings, people, and animals, as CEOs do with businesses, or as politicians do with countries. However, people tend to get lost in drama and turn it into a life or death addiction. With cosmic humor, the absurdity of your position as God becomes increasingly unavoidable and ludicrous, meaning that you can lay down your role in the game and walk away at any point, never to look back. One personification of this in Tibetan Buddhism is the painstaking creation of gorgeous, exquisite and complicated *yantras* out of colored grains of sand, and to then ceremonially destroy them. Both the act of loving creating and destruction are placed in a context of incidental irrelevance. Cosmic humor is another definition of oneness because it takes a separate sense of self out of the relationship and thereby abolishes dualism. As such, its cultivation encourages growth into the transpersonal.

The advantage of cosmic humor is that when you experience it, life is no longer about you. What other people think about you is no longer any of your business; in fact your default assumption becomes that they don't care about you and all they know about you are their own delusional projections. When people talk to you or form opinions about what you say they are merely shadow-boxing with their own preferences. Another way to describe this is the process of no longer personalizing, with personalization being a core cognitive distortion.

The end of personalization brings a dramatic and powerful advance in freedom, liberation, and enlightenment. IDL discloses states of clarity that are invisible through the filter of self. You just won't access them as long as you personalize, that is, identify with a sense of some authentic or genuine self. Therefore, the minimization of personalization is more important than *siddhis,* lucid dreaming, or even the attainment of high states of clarity in meditation. This is because when you minimize personalization you reduce identification with filters that separate you from both clarity and oneness. High states of clarity in meditation tend to reduce personalization but there is no guarantee. As Ken Wilber has described, it is entirely possible to take a separate self into higher states of enlightenment. Within Hinduism, the concept of *Atman* even assumes that this is a good idea. If you are a mystic and have a world view that Atman is Brahman, then Self remains, and that Self-identification inevitably filters experience. The minimization of personalization represents the increasing transparency of your sense of self.

As you grow in cosmic humor, your sense of who you are becomes transparent, insignificant, and unimportant, yet still necessary, but for entirely different reasons than before. You slowly wake-up to the fact that your intrasocial community, your emerging potentials, your life compass, and life itself, are counting on you. They need you. Like it or not, you function as the gatekeeper determining whether they incarnate in your consciousness and are born into outer expression in the world or whether they stay buried and ignored forever. It is completely up to you.

The immature can use cosmic humor as license to ignore or discount the opinions and preferences of others, or as an excuse not to care about others and what they think or feel. Instead, IDL encourages you to deeply listen with utmost respect to the opinions and preferences of others and then use triangulation to make decisions in alignment with your own life compass. Rather than the awareness of your role as gatekeeper being a burden or a source of spiritual narcissism, it becomes another reason for cosmic humor, because you know that there is no you and that even if there was, it never would be adequate for such a task. So instead you defer to a variety of interviewed emerging potentials to help you run your life, based on their various aptitudes and specializations, because they are more evolved than you are, know you better than your family, friends and gurus and make better choices than you do. While this may sound like a radical abdication of responsibility, it is actually a highly sophisticated form of orchestration and delegation. Triangulation brings the final decision back to you.

Like abundance, cosmic humor contains all six of the core qualities in increasing quantities. The difference is that they are all funny! Confidence gets funnier and funnier! So does empathy! The idea of being wise makes you laugh! Acceptance of others? Ha ha! Acceptance of myself? Ha ha ha!! Inner peace is humorous, and so is the idea of stepping back and observing the dramas of life, and observing how *you* observe the dramas of your life! The amplification of cosmic humor generates an increased awareness of the presence of both growing abundance and luminosity.

Luminosity

Luminosity sounds cold and remote to many, particularly those married to devotional and interpersonal paths, because it is formless, without shape, dimension or time and of course completely objective. Because it is non-dual it *also* includes form, shape, dimension, time and utter subjectivity! Luminosity is not itself a "thing" or a place; it's not even a quality! How can anyone relate to such a concept? One can only say that it is pure experience by clear awareness. This clear awareness is what separates unconscious luminosity, or life unaware of itself, from conscious luminosity, or life which has awakened to itself. This is why Magritte's famous picture of an eye containing boundless sky is used to depict luminosity. An eye implies conscious awareness while the sky implies boundless awareness. That it is within the eye implies that conscious awareness has awakened to the awareness that boundless awareness exists within it as its natural state. Both the eye and sky are natural, implying that the best way to relate to luminosity is through direct personal experience. For instance, right now exhale your breath more completely each time for five exhalations. At the bottom of your breath, after exhalation, observe the space. Notice that it becomes deeper and broader with each longer exhalation. Now stay with that experience and carry it up into each of the other stages of your breath. Imbue each of them with the clarity, objectivity, and boundless creativity of the space after exhalation. You are bringing death into life, the unborn into consciousness, but by focusing on its unborn nature instead of on consciousness.

Buddhism refers to what IDL calls luminosity as *sunyata*, "emptiness." It can be equated both with the formless causal, the highest of three states of oneness, or it can be equated with the integration of all states and stages of development as the non-dual. In Buddhism the formulation is, *"samsara* is *nirvana:"* that which is transcendent is the same as that which is immanent. That which you have searched for all your life is and always has been always already present, only too close for you to see. Luminosity is another definition of oneness because it eliminates all dualities. As such, its cultivation encourages growth into the transpersonal. Your ability to access and experience luminosity both deepens and expands your ability to appreciate the abundance and cosmic humor of life.

You develop access to luminosity in IDL when you become emerging potentials that possess it and then become them later, when you meditate or practice *pranayama* while exercising or at other times. As it grows in your awareness, you become aware that it may come into the foreground, but it is always present, as the ground of this moment and this and this…

Life

In traditional Hindu and Buddhist dream interpretation there are entire categories of dreams that are either meaningless or demonically inspired, as opposed to dreams that are of divine origin. IDL does not make these distinctions, not out of metaphysical beliefs or philosophical reasons, but because interviewed emerging potentials rarely do. When you become demons, spit, or a dust pan, you will probably find that they are unmistakably alive, because they possess your awareness and consciousness. In addition, they are in their own way each *more* alive than you are, because they possess their own unique perspective, which you lack. When you identify with even the most meaningless and imaginary elements you can imagine, you become more alive, but not necessarily more spiritual or more godly.

In the above, extremely sacrilegious picture, we have the profane becoming sacred, the unconscious becoming fully alive by partaking in the Feasts of Feasts, communion with the Divine. This is a cosmically humorous depiction of the sacred, which peels away the layers of patina associated with holiness in order to celebrate life itself.

IDL talks about life instead of spirit or God, because all emerging potentials are alive, but may or may not equate themselves with spirit or God. Imaginary dust pans usually are not equated with spirit or God. Neither are wart hogs, empty soap dishes, or dogs, although "dog" is "God" spelled backwards, at least in English. Therefore, because life, in all its absurdity and tragedy, is good enough for emerging potentials, it is good enough for IDL. It does not need to separate out the sacred from the profane or God from nature because life doesn't do so. You are invited to experiment with opening and embracing life without assuming that it is God or spirit and see what happens. Is life degraded because you do not think about it in those terms? Or does life now repossess these previously dissociated characteristics, qualities, and possibilities, becoming in itself and for itself more sacred and alive?

4: Words and Concepts that May Not Be Conducive to Enlightenment

We have noted above that words are powerful tools that create meaning in our lives. They need to be kept when usefulness follows from their meanings and discarded when they no longer adequately describe emerging realities. While Gautama Buddha is responsible for the phrase, "not conducive to enlightenment," we could substitute, "not beneficial for waking up," or "not supportive of your development." This is because while "enlightenment" can be thought of as a state of complete union or oneness attained through a mystical or near death experience, it is more appropriately thought of as the attainment of a stable, lasting developmental stage of wakefulness which includes clarity, witnessing, unity, and boundless awareness. There is every reason to believe, as Wilber has explained, that as cultural contexts expand personally, culturally and historically that your capacity for broader, more inclusive types of enlightenment do as well. Therefore, IDL encourages viewing enlightenment as a *process* of awakening rather than as some final destination. You are more enlightened today than you were when you were four, and if you continue to learn to get out of your own way, you will be more enlightened in six years than you are today.

IDL acknowledges the usefulness and adaptational necessity of all of the following words and concepts within given cultural contexts. Most young people are working hard at creating a sense of self; undermining it is not generally helpful. Many adults are highly dependent on their social and professional roles to earn a living; undermining the words and concepts that they use to validate their worth in society is not generally helpful. However, this is no reason not to educate both children and totally enculturated adults in the relative and temporary nature of even their core concepts, thereby giving them permission to think through and outgrow any and every perceptual cognitive distortion when and if they so desire.

The same thing applies to cultural contexts at home, worship or work no matter how old you are. You are not going to do very well in a monotheistic context, such as a Jewish, Islamic, or Christian family and nation if you do not accept and use the concept of "God." To encourage people in those societies not to do so is probably not doing them any favors. While it can be fun and self-justifying to irritate people by attacking conceptual sources of security or meaning for them, doing so is trivial, cruel, and an occupation for minds that are insecure and subsequently attempt to make themselves feel superior by demeaning others. IDL does not point out the limitations of words you may rely on and find valuable in order to be critical or to pull the rug out from under your belief system, although it may feel like that sometimes as you read what follows. It also does not point out words and concepts it believes are not conducive to enlightenment in order to create an impression of moral, intellectual, or evolutionary superiority, because to do so would instead imply just the opposite: insecurity in one's own belief system.

Nevertheless, there are differences between public and private beliefs, and anyone can light a candle in the darkness of thoughtless groupthink, even if it is only an interior candle that we use to illuminate our own inner world. Caution with when, where, and how you use words remains important today, and you need to weigh truth, compassion, and usefulness against one another, because the sad reality is that these are often in opposition to one another. Your use of a word may be correct yet neither compassionate or useful. This occurs often when we label people with words like "obstinate" or "bitchy." Your use of a word may be compassionate yet neither true nor useful. For example, if you congratulate an atheist by telling them they are doing "God's will," you are perhaps being compassionate, but whether this is true or not is problematic, since what God wills is open to debate, and it is probably not a very useful thing to say to an atheist. You can also put a word or concept to good use in a way that is neither true nor compassionate. For example, if you flatter or lie to get what you want you may be doing exactly that.

Outgrowing groupthink is not the greatest obstacle to giving up outmoded words and concepts. The major problem is not recognizing when a word or concept is no longer useful or that it may actually be impeding your further development. The reason this is such a difficulty is that if a word or concept has been useful and necessary for you in the past, it has had significant adaptive value. To consider giving up anything that has proven adaptive value feels threatening, and particularly when there may well be a social cost for giving up a word or concept. For example, there are common words, "should," "ought," "fault," "blame," "must," "can't," "always" and "never" that signal cognitive distortion. If any of these words are part of your habitual usage, it takes discipline and practice to give them up, even if you want to. Consequently, for these reasons, words and concepts tend to be immortal. Like Dracula, even if you don't use them, they will tend to re-awaken from the crypt of forgetfulness and haunt you, until you directly confront them and drive the steak of clarity and understanding through their heart.

You can stop using some words, like "tree," and instead substitute other words, such as "plant," "oak" or "pine," and it really won't matter, because not only are they in part synonyms, but few people build their culture or identity around the word "tree." Contrast that to the problems that arise when a person questions the usefulness of the words "God," "Self," "spirit," or "soul." While giving up concepts like the "unconscious" or "shadow," or "interpretation," is immaterial for many people because such words and concepts have no central relevance to their lives, if you are a counselor who makes a living using a model that assumes the reality of the unconscious, these terms have adaptive importance. They may be part of your professional identity. The more central a word is to your culture, work, or identity, the more threatening will be the idea of moving away from it.

We use the signal words that are cognitive distortions because they *feel* true and they truly express our feelings, despite the fact that they are irrational and destructive.[5] An unwillingness to stop using them is a good

---

[5] "Should," "ought," "fault," "blame" and "must" are cognitive distortions because they not only are not true, but they generate the toxic feeling of guilt. It is not true that you or someone else do something because you "should" or "ought" to; you do what you do because you either want to or need to, and saying so is honest and rational. Similarly, it is not true that something is or is not your "fault" or that you are or are not to "blame." What is true is that you or someone else believes there was a failure to act or think appropriately. Therefore, what is true is that you did something that you or someone else did not like. Perhaps they think you "should" have done something differently, but that is their problem. It is your responsibility not to descend into irrationality by accepting their cognitive distortion as truth. "Can't" is a cognitive distortion because it implies powerlessness, which is usually inaccurate. For example, it is not true that you "can't come to dinner" or "can't be on time." What is true is that you don't want to or have other priorities. You *could* do these things; you're not powerless unless your feet are nailed to the floor, so stop telling yourself that you are. "Always" and "never" polarize what you say in an untrue way. If you say to someone, "You're always late; you're never on time," all they have to do is think of one instance in which they were on time to disprove what you are saying and justify in their minds ignoring what you are saying. Using any of

diagnostic indicator that despite years of education you are still stuck at a mid-prepersonal level of development, at which your emotions define not only who you are but what is real. All concepts have their use in one context, or at one level of development or another, but when they are retained into higher levels. they represent fixations or lead anchors: they slow down or stop your development.

The challenge is to broaden your frame of reference, context, and world view, and that means re-thinking and re-evaluating old, comfortable, assumed words and concepts that maintain your perceptual cognitive distortions. As discussed above, IDL recognizes three types of cognitive distortions, emotional, rational, and perceptual. This last category is the most difficult to spot, because we are enmeshed in the identity they create; we use them to create both meaning and our sense of who we are. Therefore, when you call a core concept into question you challenge both the sources of meaning in your life and who you think you are.

Treat the following list of words and concepts as an education in the contextual relativity of words and concepts, rather than as a recommendation that you give up any of them today. Everyone grows at their own pace, and it is not the business of IDL to tell you that you should outgrow these concepts in order to "be enlightened." That is an elitist stance, a projection of one set of values onto others, and a direct contradiction to what it means to practice deep listening. Therefore, IDL respects your choices in the words and concepts you use and honors your timing regarding when and how to use them and when to give them up. After all, some, and perhaps all of the words that IDL proposes are conducive to enlightenment will themselves in time be outgrown.

However, when you do contemplate giving up one or more of the following words and concepts, approach it something like a spring cleaning, with the object of reducing clutter and opening up space for new possibilities. The analogy has some merit. Just like unused possessions are comfortable old friends which we resist saying goodbye to, so we become habitually attached to outmoded words and concepts because they connect us to the past that made us who we are today. Words have a life span, but no one ever associates them with an expiration date. Past that point, their meaningfulness no longer comes from their usefulness, but because they make us comfortable. Our sense of self has become dependent on them, and a telltale sign is that not using them creates a sense of anxiety, meaninglessness, loss, or alienation. At that point, it is probably fair to say that we have an addiction to these perceptual cognitive distortions and that this addiction is blocking our development. This is a difficult state to objectively determine, because

---

these words is not only irrational, it's stupid, because they are all self-destructive. All of these and many more cognitive distortions are explained in *Waking Up* by this author.

we, like Humpty Dumpty, are rather certain that the words and related concepts that we use are useful, meaningful, and make sense, even when the truth is we are psychologically and emotionally addicted to them. Their use keeps us thinking about life in ways that makes it difficult, if not impossible, to keep growing.

Some people attempt to deal with this issue by going on a conceptual fast, called meditation. They believe that if they practice not thinking long enough and frequently enough that they will break their addiction to words and concepts. Sadly, this is a delusion. We know that is the case by reading the writings of gurus, mystics, ascended masters and saints. No matter how much they have meditated or how enlightened they have become they continue to use words and concepts that are limiting and limit them and their message, because they are expressions of particular world views that are perceptual cognitive distortions. You can check this out for yourself by going to favorite passages of your favorite spiritual teachers and reading them from this perspective.

The more the loss of a word and the concept it represents is accompanied with feelings of discomfort, anxiety, or insecurity, the more likely you are to be addicted to it. Addiction to a world view or a conceptualization is a good definition of a perceptual cognitive distortion. While emotional cognitive distortions create and sustain drama and our rational cognitive distortions justify staying stuck, perceptual cognitive distortions create impossibility. The words and concepts you use do not allow interviewed emerging potentials to grow when they conflict with a world view you assume is correct or necessary. Consequently, you cut yourself off from your life compass and the priorities of life. You cannot recognize or see what is outside your world view because it makes no sense. If it is part of the culture of your work and to give it up would mean losing your job, you have no incentive to do so. Therefore, you will take what fits within your world view and discard the rest, confident that you understand, when in fact you are deluding yourself.

As you read through the following list of words and their explanations, observe your feelings and thoughts. If the questioning of their worth brings up strong feelings, stop and attempt to identify them. Is it fear? Confusion? Insecurity? Disbelief? Anger? Then ask yourself, "What is it about what I'm reading that is bringing up these strong feelings?" The first and most likely option to rule out is that you are feeling threatened. If you are, then the most likely explanation is that the word, and the concepts that it represents, in some way defines important, key, fundamental aspects of your sense of self. If you think that may be the case, then you need to consider whether you still need that definition of who you are at this point in your development or whether you have outgrown it and are still merely attached to the concept out of habit, or because no alternatives make sense to you. The distinction is between still climbing a ladder, on the one hand, and having reached the roof, landing, or ledge, on the other. If it is the first case, kicking the ladder out from under you is cruel and stupid. If it is the second, picking up and carrying the ladder as you progress up to the next level is going to slow you down, if it does not stop you all together.

This is the sense in which IDL asks you to consider the following words. View them objectively, as tools that point to certain meanings. Are those meanings still useful in your life? Are they moving you up your ladder? Have you reached the "top" of some stage of development, but are still carrying the ladder because you might need it again tomorrow? Doing so implies a fear that the world will run out of ladders or that yours is the only or best ladder. Now imagine that you are climbing a series of ladders and that you insist on carrying all of them with you as you progress. There you are, trying to climb up your thirteenth ladder while carrying twelve of them. How is that working for you? Is that practical? Is it useful? Is it necessary? Why would a person do such a thing?

The only reason that makes any sense at all is that you have never stopped to think that not only may you not need more than one ladder at a time, but that the usefulness for you of those ladders is over. You are on a one-way trip; you aren't unlearning what you have learned; you are not going to be re-tracing your path back down at some point and thereby need those ladders. If you let them go, you won't fall. You will still not only be safe, but much better able to move ahead because you will have let go of cumbersome, dead weight. The ladders never really go anywhere. You can pick any of them back up if you are really into carrying ladders, or you can retrace your steps up one any time you want, if you really want to. If you understand such things, yet you still insist on carrying ladders, is there any other explanation than that you are addicted to your ladders?

If so, be gentle with yourself! Most attempts to break addictions are unsuccessful because their power, resistance, and resiliency is chronically underestimated. You will not be doing yourself any favors by underestimating your addiction to any of the concepts we describe below. Do not think that you can just reconsider their usefulness and stop using them, as if by magic. They are pieces of an interlocking puzzle that creates your sense of life meaning. Those pieces interdependently support and maintain each other. When you attempt to remove one piece, the others work hard to put it back into place.

For example, when geese migrate, one takes the lead position because aerodynamics makes the trip easier for all of them. When the lead goose gets tired, she falls back and another one flies forward to take her place, because there is a collective benefit and motivation for that particular piece of the migrating goose puzzle to be in place. Similarly, when you attempt to stop using one word or concept you are identified with, one mark of your addiction to it is how resilient it is.

For example, think of the concept, "thinking." Now stop thinking. What happens? How long does it take another thought goose to fly up and take the place of the missing lead goose? For most of us, not long! First educate yourself about your addiction and prepare yourself for a process of broad-based evolution beyond it. Where are you headed? What is your plan for getting there? When geese land in a lake or a field they no longer need a lead goose for flying. To insist on keeping one would be foolish and not useful. Once on land, each goose takes care of itself.

Where do you want to land today? Where do you want to be right now? What is your plan for getting there? Are you going to need your favorite "lead goose" once you are there? Are you willing and able to do without it once you have arrived? See if you can suspend judgment while you read, in order to get a bit of distance from your emotions. Do not take personally the questioning of some term you like and use and then choose to feel attacked. Even if you believe some of these words and concepts, you are not your beliefs. You are not your feelings. You are not your concepts. All of these things are merely tools to help you grow. Hopefully, by thinking them through carefully, you will be able to use the words you choose more clearly, carefully, and accurately, so that you are not only better able to help others, but more likely to get where you want to go. In addition, you will be clearer about the world view of IDL as well as how and why it teaches what it does.

Something can be true and still not conducive to enlightenment, such as the fact that sugar tastes good or that drama is exciting. Similarly, the truth or falsity of the following concepts is only one consideration, as we pointed out above. Another is their usefulness. This is a functional standard of truth, dating back to the pragmatism of Charles Sanders Peirce, John Dewey, and William James in the US, starting around 1870. Conceptual usefulness has an expiration date. At some point the adaptive advantages of most words and concepts are outweighed by their ability to spin, create, and maintain a conceptual tomb in which some part of your development will lie frozen and fossilized.

If a word, concept, feeling or behavior isn't conducive to enlightenment, you won't evolve; you will stay stuck. Get into the habit of asking, "How does this or that word or concept support my waking up today? How does it support my greater lucidity?" If it does, keep it; if it may not, try life without it and see what happens. You may find that some concepts that you thought you needed or that you couldn't live without, or that were essential for enlightenment, actually are none of these things. But you won't know until you make an effort to discard or not use those that are habitual parts of your world view.

Who needs words and concepts anyway?

Truly transcendent mystical and near death experiences are ineffable - you can't adequately put them into words. This raises the question, "Don't all words and concepts create unnecessary filters that block my enlightenment?" Consider what your life would be like if you never needed words and concepts that you find essential today. The ability to think clearly, which means to reflect upon the assumptions made by the words you use, is a mark of personal development to at least a rational level, and beyond. That means that if you want to become enlightened, you first have to learn to think and reason, which means to understand and use words and concepts, as well as discard those which are inadequate or no longer useful to you. Reason and the understanding and avoidance of logical fallacies is a necessary pre-requisite for moving beyond the rational to the trans-rational, the realm of higher-order enlightenment. You learn words so you can think and reason; you suspend your dependency on words so you can separate who you are from them. This is itself a necessary pre-requisite to transpersonal development, one that gets surprisingly little attention. The next step is to suspend your dependency on the world view that your favorite words and concepts support and justify. This is an exercise in identifying and eliminating your perceptual cognitive distortions, a requirement for becoming stabilized at the multi-perspectival gateway stage between late personal and transpersonal stages of oneness with life itself.

Wilber's Pre-Trans Fallacy and IDL, an essay on the IDL website, explains why many of the following terms are inadvisable because they imply a transpersonal, trans-rational level of awareness when in fact only a pre-personal, pre-rational level of awareness is necessary or present. This is called "elevationism." Alternatively, words and concepts may imply that transpersonal and trans-rational experiences are pre-personal and pre-rational, which diminishes their value and validity. This is called "reductionism." For example, to say "He was hallucinating," generally implies regression to a pre-rational state, although the person may have had a transpersonal opening and an experience of transformational oneness.

Meditation can be approached as a "time out" from cognitive distortions, including perceptual ones, and the drama that they stir up. The problem is that meditation is generally not sufficient to eliminate words, concepts or perceptual cognitive distortions because it tends not to change everyday mind, which runs on the set of linguistic structures we learned as children. If you do not directly address your reliance upon the words and concepts that you use they will follow you right up your developmental ladder, framing, defining and limiting your growth every step of the way. IDL is particularly helpful in this regard in that it submerges your identity in both perspectives and roles that do not partake of your perceptual cognitive distortions. Not only do you thereby wake-up to your own cognitive distortions as you objectify them and separate your sense of self from them, but you outgrow your dependency on them. You can see this process happening in the interviews that follow some of the words and concepts we consider below.

Scientific Materialism

TOUCHED BY HIS NOODLY APPENDAGE

Materialism is a perceptual cognitive distortion that believes that matter is the only reality, that the mind is the physical activity of the brain, and, in its extreme forms, that thoughts cannot have any effect upon our brains, bodies, actions, and the physical world. The scientific materialistic worldview owes its success to its usefulness at creating distinctions and discriminations that can be both tested and turned into dependable knowledge that serves as a foundation for the development of technologies that improve the quality of life. Consequently, most of the advances in medicine, physics, astronomy, space travel, psychology and technology are due to application of principles closely associated with scientific varieties of materialism. To dismiss scientific materialism out of hand is to dismiss the power and usefulness of this particular level of human evolution. It is far better to grow into scientific materialism and to never grow beyond it than to never even attain this level of development. This is because to be a scientific materialist you first must learn how to doubt, ask questions, think, problem solve and develop at least some degree of rationality. You must learn to respect empiricism and skepticism.

IDL does not view materialism as conducive to enlightenment for some of the same reasons as the distinguished group of scientists who have written, "The "Manifesto for a Post-Materialist Science."[6] The biologist Rupert Sheldrake makes many of the same points in *Science Set Free.* IDL, as an integral yoga, views consciousness as co-arising with behavior, systems, and culture. Therefore, it does not give precedence to any one of these four factors as materialism does, when it gives precedence to behavior. It is therefore as fundamental a mistake to give priority to spirit and consciousness as it is to give priority to materialism and reductionism.[7]

IDL seeks a middle ground between reductionists and elevationists – those who want to reduce reality to "lowest common denominators" and subcomponents, on the one hand, and those who want to explain reality in terms of transcendent, eternal truths. It does so because the majority of interviews of dream characters and the personifications of life issues do neither, and they do not use the language of this group of scientists either, appealing neither to spirit or quantum mechanics, nor do they use evidence from near death experiences to validate non-physical existence. Instead, interviewed emerging potentials use words and concepts to affirm life in ways that are practical and meaningful to each individual.

---

[6] Manifesto for a Post-Materialist Science

[7] While IDL agrees with these scientists that there is indeed evidence for the existence of psychic phenomena, of minds apart from bodies, and for non-physical existence, it believes that these are primarily explained in terms of the belief systems of perceivers rather than as indicators of objective realities, for reasons that we will explain below.

Ego

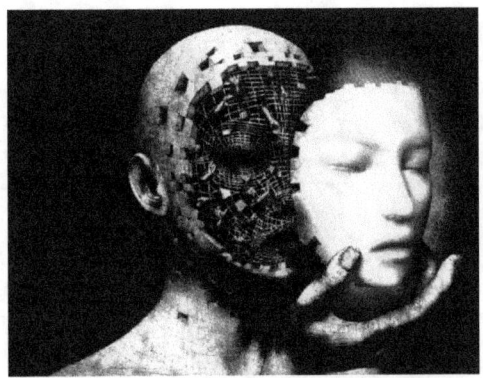

This popular word is now commonly used to refer to an inflated sense of self-worth, the conscious-thinking self, self-esteem, or a stabilized, healthy identity. It brings to mind "egotism," "egomania," and "ego strength." The development of multiple processes, cognitive functioning, defenses, and interpersonal skills in childhood and into adolescence is often called "ego development." In Western psychology, the ego, as the predominating concept of the self, originates with Freud, for whom the ego acts according to the reality principle, which is a regulating mechanism that enables the individual to delay gratifying immediate needs and function effectively in the real world. Examples would be to resist the urge to fart in public or criticize an employer.

Functions of the ego include conscious awareness, defense, perception, intellectual-cognition, judgment, tolerance, reality testing, control, planning, defense, synthesis of information, intellectual functioning, and memory. Containing reason and common sense, the ego is supposed to separate out reality from fantasy, organize our thoughts and make sense of the world. The ego attempts to resolve conflicts between itself, the urges of the id, and the demands of conscience, or the superego, by using defense mechanisms, such as rationalization, projection, identification, sublimation, displacement, intellectualization, reaction formation, denial, repression, and regression. It is the organized, "realistic" self that mediates between instinctual impulses and conscience, rationality and irrationality.

In Hinduism and Buddhism, the ego, or *ahamkara* is the "false self," and being trapped in it is to be trapped in the delusion of *samsara* or *maya*. The basic dualism for Hinduism and Buddhism is between this false self and a "real" self, or between illusion and "reality." For Buddha, both being married and having children, on the one hand, and asceticism, on the other, were not conducive to enlightenment. This is because the first represented for him giving into the desires of a selfish, self-centered self, or ego, while the second represented the artificial and counterproductive denial of the reality of such a self, which he considered a subtle form of *ahamkara*. According to Buddhism, while the first choice keeps you mired in suffering, the second puts you in conflict with yourself, so instead of moving toward peace of mind you just move into repression and suffering of a different sort.

The concept of the ego is so grounded in the assumptions of Freudian psychoanalysis and psychodynamic psychology that to use it conjures up the associated mechanistic, reductionistic and self-centered world view and model of personality. Similarly, the concept of the ego, or "false self," in Hinduism and Buddhism is problematic for IDL because it creates a dualism with a "true" self, a dualism that life itself doesn't experience. These multiple and diverse usages mean the word "ego" is "over-determined," or creates ambiguity and confusion if not clearly defined. The consequence of these multiple usages is the furtherance of a perceptual cognitive distortion, that you have something called an "ego," that is not conducive to enlightenment.

Instead of ego, IDL simply uses "waking identity" to refer to who you experience yourself to be. Your sense of self is not viewed by IDL as inherently undesirable, bad, or selfish, nor does IDL place it in opposition to an unconscious, subconscious, superconscious, or "true" self, as the ego generally is. Your waking identity is simply who you think you are, regardless of your level of development. It is the orienting perspective that you use to inhabit the various social roles you take while you are awake and dreaming, such as child, parent, student, lover, and worker, and the three dramatic roles of victim, persecutor, and rescuer.

Traditional understandings of the ego imagine it falling asleep or going unconscious in sleep and dreaming, where it is subjugated to the id or to a grandiose dream identity that can fly and do magical things. IDL however, observes that when you dream you think you are awake; therefore, the perspective that you take when you are dreaming is typically your waking point of view with its attitudes, preferences, assumptions, and emotional reactions. It is only upon awakening, in retrospect, that we say, "Aha! My abilities in my dream were far broader than those in my waking life, so my dreaming self must be different from my waking self!" For example, Buddha and Jesus had waking identities, and those identities provided the perspectives out of which they experienced and understood their dreams and mystical experiences, just like you and I. Therefore, IDL uses "waking identity" to refer to your "dream self" as well as your waking sense of who you are. Again, this is because when you dream, you perceive the experience from the perspective of your waking sense of self, whether you are lucid or not and whether you fly or die and are reborn in a dream or not.

While we can argue about the reality of an ego, it is much more difficult to argue about the reality of "waking identity." One could even shorten that to "identity," or "sense of self." In fact, in IDL, even imaginary dream characters and the personifications of life issues have a "waking identity," in the sense that they have a stable sense of their individuality. Doesn't it make much more sense to call the sense of self of deceased aunt Mildred her "identity" than to call it her "ego?" In addition, IDL attempts to avoid creating an unnecessary dualism between a false and a real self, as exists both in Western psychology and Eastern religions, because this distinction is not made by most interviewed emerging potentials. The implication is that your life compass does not need it, so why should you?

Because IDL is rooted in phenomenology, it attempts to suspend assumptions, such as the idea that "ego" is a word reflecting a concept that can be outgrown at some developmental levels. Instead, it attempts to practice deep listening to questioned ideas and perspectives to see what they have to say about themselves. What might be the practical advantages of no longer thinking of your waking sense of who you are as your "ego?" The objective is to free you from all of the associations that exist in our culture to this word so that, as you take the perspectives of interviewed emerging potentials, you can look at yourself from their perspectives, which have nothing to do with seeing you as an ego. This will free you to view your "waking self," who you normally think you are, with new eyes, from new perspectives, and thereby reframe both your limitations and possibilities. Here is our first example of using IDL interviewing to gain insight into words and concepts:

An Interview with Ego

"Ego, I imagine you as a screaming two or three-year-old, maybe like the one that lives upstairs, who stomps around early in the morning, like

a young stegosaurus, and who likes to scream to get what she wants. I will make you look like Lucy, of 'Peanuts' fame, who is forever pulling the football out from under Charlie Brown, when she isn't playing psychiatrist. Will you please describe yourself and what life is like from your point of view?"

Ego: "I don't think you are being fair at all. I don't see myself at all like that! I am a queen on her throne, and not just ANY queen! I am the Queen of the WORLD! And everybody does what I want when I want or I WHACK them with my jewel-encrusted scepter!"

Hmmmm...OK...I am impressed, I guess, but since you are an imaginary part of me that I made up, I am more amused by you than scared. And while I might humor you, I don't plan to allow you to rule my life because I don't respect your authority."

Queen: "I can see you require a good WHACKING! Come over here..."

"How can you whack me with your scepter if I think you are imaginary and don't feel pain from imaginary scepters?"

Queen: "Well, you SHOULD listen to me, because I'm the Queen! And I will throw a fit, a temper tantrum until you do!!"

"How about if we just sorta move on? What do you like best about yourself, Queen?"

Queen: "I like that I am the Queen of the World and am ALL POWERFUL and that everybody has to do what I say because I am strong, right, beautiful, and PERFECT!"

Is there anything you dislike about yourself, Queen?"

"Having to put up with insolent, disrespectful fools like you! Other than that, no, what's there to dislike when you're perfect?"

"What part of me do you most closely represent, Queen?"

Queen: "I don't represent any part of you! I am real and you are my subject! OBEY!"

Queen, if you could change in any way you wanted, would you?

Queen: "No. I like staying imaginary, because I can be all-powerful. I want my reality to stay imaginary too, so I can control it and make life turn out the way I want."

"Queen, how would you score yourself zero to ten in all six core qualities?"

Queen: "All tens, of course, since I'm perfect!"

"Queen, if I scored like you do, how would my life be different?"

Queen: "You would be perfect, of course! What a stupid question!"

"Queen, if you were in charge of my life, how would you live it differently?"

Queen: "You would have no self-doubt because you would know you were right. You would both command and demand the obedience of all others because you are right and perfect. You would not tolerate conflict, disloyalty, or imperfection. When you whacked people with your scepter it would only be an expression of your compassion, your caring to teach your subjects and those who are imperfect."

"Hmmmm...OK...So when would you suggest that I become you and think, feel, and act like you do?"

Queen: "Whenever you want to get your way, to win, to be right, and to be perfect!"

"Thank you, Queen!"

So...what have I heard myself say? That my ego is selfish, narcissistic, grandiose, and believes that it is real and in control! It recognizes that this is its fantasy but prefers the reality of its fantasy to real life! What do I think is the wake-up call from my life compass here? That no matter who you are or how much you have grown, you always have the option of becoming a three-year old again, for better or for worse, and it is wise not to forget that is a genuine possibility.

There comes a point in development when regression to a three-year old is more trouble than it is worth. You don't regress not because you don't want to admit you have a screaming, narcissistic three-year-old inside you, but because becoming it just isn't much fun any more. It doesn't work. That is how the entire concept of a separate self that is in opposition to everything and everybody feels as boundaries dissolve. The idea of "ego" loses its functionality; you don't need to develop a separate self-sense any more, nor do you need to protect or defend it. Instead, what you need to do is use it, without investing any of yourself into it. It is at this point that "ego" becomes no longer conducive to enlightenment.

Exceptionalism and Psychological Geocentrism

Exceptionalism involves superiority, uniqueness, and exclusivity, in the sense of not being subject to the rules and conditions of others. Exceptionalism itself is a manifestation of psychological geocentrism which says, following Protagoras, "I and my group are the measure of all things." "Where I live is the *axis mundi,* the center of the universe, the most blessed and privileged land and people ordained by God." Psychological geocentrism interprets experience as "all about me." "The right, true, and loving perspective is my perspective, and if you want to be blessed by God, a sheep instead of a goat, and to avoid eternal Hellfire, you need to think like I do." We see this everywhere in every time and land, in Jews as the Children of the Covenant and therefore particularly blessed and protected by God based on His promises, and with Jerusalem as being the Most Holy City, the center of the Earth, most blessed by God, and where God dwells. Similar beliefs are found among the Babylonians, Egyptians, Greeks, Romans, Africans, Siberian Shamans, Europeans of the Enlightenment, and Easter Islanders. While there have been many "holy warriors" in the history of the world, from Joshua to Joan of Arc to George W. Bush, who have claimed God's direction, these are pre-personal expressions of "enlightenment," acting without the benefit of personal level reason or egalitarianism, and therefore lacking any claim to transpersonal enlightenment whatsoever. Because exceptionalism and its root of psychological geocentrism is a central human delusion and pathology and a core perceptual cognitive distortion that every child must grow out of, it must first be recognized if it is ever to transcended. Needless to say, many people never recognize their narcissistic claims to exceptionalism or their grandiose assumptions of psychological geocentrism. Instead, they fight vigorously to defend them, because these assumptions are central to their identity and to their cultural position.

The first settlers of the American continent, both English and Spanish, believed that they were "God's chosen people" who were "given" these lands and the responsibility to rule over the Indians, by either converting them or exterminating them, a justification that finds its historical parallels in the Islamic conquests, the European religious wars, Nazism, and Zionism. None other than Thomas Jefferson was an early exponent of American exceptionalism. In 1809, upon departing the presidency, he said America was "Trusted with the destinies of this solitary republic of the world, the only monument of human rights, and the sole depository of the sacred fire of freedom and self-government, from hence it is to be lighted up in other regions of the earth, if other regions of the earth shall ever become susceptible of its benign influence." This doctrine was elaborated in the 1840's by Jacksonian Democrats as "Manifest Destiny," to justify the theft of the Oregon Territory, the Texas Annexation, and the Mexican Cession of California and New Mexico. Throughout most of its history the U.S. has justified its aggression as its God-appointed mission to bring liberty and democracy to the world. Historian T. Harry Williams argues that Lincoln believed: "In the United States man would create a society that would be the best and the happiest in the world. The United States was the supreme demonstration of democracy. But the Union did not exist just to make men free in America. It had an even greater mission - to make them free everywhere. By the mere force of its example America would bring democracy to an undemocratic world."

An excellent, much more recent example, which demonstrates the staying power of this pernicious perceptual cognitive distortion, was an extraordinary duel of public pronouncements between Barak Obama and Vladimir Putin of Russia, with the former declaring the exceptionalism of the United States and Putin denying exceptional status for any nation. Obama stated in 2009, "I believe in American exceptionalism, just as I suspect that the Brits believe in British exceptionalism and the Greeks believe in Greek exceptionalism," implying that because psychological geocentrism is normal, that it is justified. In 2013 he said, "But when, with modest effort and risk, we can stop children from being gassed to death, and thereby make our own children safer over the long run, I believe we should act...That's what makes America different. That's what makes us exceptional." Putin's response was classical: "It is extremely dangerous to encourage people to see themselves as exceptional, whatever the motivation...We are all different, but when we ask for the Lord's blessings, we must not forget that God created us equal."

Exceptionalism is not only important because it justifies colonization, war, torture, and assassination, but because it represents an unavoidable stage of development of the self that must be outgrown if individuals or cultures are to survive and evolve. While exceptionalism and psychological geocentrism are natural and even appropriate in a four-year-old, its appropriateness, but not necessarily its usefulness, diminishes thereafter. Both are tools for discrimination and privilege at the expense of others, and that can be quite useful for adults and nations who wish to exploit the resources and lives of others.

Exceptionalism and psychological geocentrism identify our level of development as pre-personal, despite our attempts to make our particular circumstances the lone exception to the rule. Exceptionalism is fundamentally a form of egocentric, narcissistic, grandiosity, appropriate, as we have observed, in four year olds, but even then only with adult supervision. Both exceptionalism and psychological geocentrism exist to provide justification for playing the persecutor within the Drama Triangle and for acting in abusive ways toward others. In adult culture psychological geocentrism is legalized in the rules of capitalism and politics, both of which carve out exceptionalism based on wealth and power. This is socially sanctioned personality disorder on a massive scale, as described in the classic 2003 documentary, *The Corporation*, which correlates psychopathy and antisocial personality disorder with fundamental characteristics of capitalist culture, including the callous disregard for the feelings of other people, the incapacity to maintain human relationships, the reckless disregard for the safety of others, deceitfulness (continual lying to deceive for profit), the incapacity to experience guilt, and the failure to conform to social norms and respect for the law.

When culture not only condones but rewards psychological geocentrism and exceptionalism and punishes those who do not play by those rules by demoting, firing, not hiring them, not electing them or not re-electing them, there are powerful forces that create blindness to the presence and operation of this perceptual cognitive distortion in even the smartest and most talented of people. Consequently, for you or I to imagine that we are the "exception," that is, we have escaped from exceptionalism, is delusional. Our default assumption should be that we are still subject to psychological geocentrism and experience ourselves as "exceptional." This commonly shows up in the belief that our experiences are unique, when in fact, we are undoubtedly feeling and experiencing things right now, and even at our most special and unique moments, that are common, mundane, and almost universal. Another common delusion is that no one can or will ever understand us, when in fact many, many people have similar experiences and can and will understand us. This cognitive distortion exists because our thoughts, feelings, and experiences continuously reinforce the reality that our feelings and thoughts are special and unique. We are the center of the universe, just as our physical experience of the sun rising and setting reinforces a practical reality of geocentrism. Evolving out of this delusion essentially involves expanding our sense of self through empathy with others, meditating and taking the perspective of various emerging potentials, in order to access perspectives that are not centered on physical, emotional, or cognitive realities.

Our addiction to exceptionalism and psychological geocentrism is based on a fear that the surrender of specialness means the inevitable loss of individuality and the meanings we associate with our uniqueness. The more important the late personal values of interdependence, accountability, transparency, and mutual respect become the more the cost-benefit ratio of these concepts shifts away from maintaining exceptionalism and psychological geocentrism. IDL works to evolve humanity out of this destructive perceptual cognitive distortion by demonstrating a phenomenological method in which such assumptions are temporarily tabled in favor of creating space for an objective listening to novel perspectives. Over time this predominant cultural myth and perceptual cognitive distortion is slowly outgrown by creating an intrasocial culture that involves mutual respect shared among multiple alternative, legitimate definitions of self. It then extends that respect into the social macrocosm by insisting on it as the foundation for our relationships with family, friends, co-workers, retailers, and politicians.

Guilt

You probably know people who feel guilty and who use the concept of guilt who have an advanced degree and have many competencies and rewarding group affiliations. They may be quite happy with who and where you are, as are many Christian ministers and priests and Jewish rabbis who are wedded to this toxic and pernicious concept. What would Christianity or Judaism be without guilt? Would they even exist? While there may have been a historic time and place in which guilt was useful, it certainly is not today and particularly not for you, me and our children. However, until you have a thorough understanding and recognition that any and all thoughts and uses of this word, except to neutralize it, are destructive and abusive, guilt will act as a lead anchor to stop your development in its tracks.

If guilt is so destructive, why is it still so common? Guilt is useful for parents, society and seemingly, for us. If parents can make us feel guilty for not doing what they want, we will control our own behavior so they will not have to. This is part of what it means to develop a "conscience." If society has citizens that feel guilty when they break its laws it will spend much less time and fewer resources on control. If we feel guilty we imagine we are therefore avoiding the punishment of our parents or of society. Pretty soon, earlier than we probably remember, guilt becomes a comfortable, habitual form of masochism.

IDL views guilt as a primitive form of self-persecution within the Drama Triangle. The greatest problem with self-persecution is that it causes us to become trapped in the hopelessness and helplessness of the role of victim. This in turn causes us to seek rescuing, which in the case of guilt means redemption and forgiveness, generally from others and God. The problem then becomes that we disempower ourselves by placing our worth outside of ourselves, in the hands of others or of some deity. This disempowerment is naturally resented, turning rescuers into persecutors, particularly since we know they can and will find us guilty. The only way to rescue ourselves from this madness is to give up the Drama Triangle, and the best way to start is to refuse to be motivated by guilt, feel guilt or use guilt to manipulate and control others. IDL interviews will put you in contact with perspectives that are less likely to use guilt than you are and can help you outgrow it. However, the simplest and easiest way to do so is to get the words "guilt" and "guilty" out of your vocabulary as well as words that imply guilt, such as "should," "ought," "fault," "blame" and "must." Because use of such words becomes habitual, it is highly recommended that you ask family and friends to point out to you when they hear you use these words. This will give you an opportunity to re-phrase what you are saying using other words that do not imply guilt. Over time this will change the way you think, meaning that you will succeed in exorcising the demon of guilt from both your external and internal dream.

Conscience

When you rely on your conscience to make decisions, what are you doing? When you are a child you are taught what to do, feel, and think in order to get approval and you are told what to not do, think or feel if you want to avoid being punished. Essentially these rules involve obeying your parents and their surrogates, such as teachers, police, religious authorities, older siblings, and family members who look after you. As you grow, you internalize these rules, which means that you don't need someone to tell you what to do to get approval or avoid punishment.

Because adapting to your environment is how you survive and because following the rules is how you adapt, you have had considerable vested interest in learning the rules of life to the place where they were internalized and automatic. They were so much part of the culture of your family and your childhood world that you never recognized them or questioned them. Consequently, unless you have performed an "exorcism," the voices of your parents and other strong, influential figures from your childhood still live rent-free in your head. Most people don't even realize that their "parents" are still hanging out in the attic of their consciousness, telling them what to do, pulling their mental-emotional strings like puppeteers. If you want proof of ghosts and spirits, look no further. This is a real haunting and *the* real haunting, and one that does a great deal of damage. Your parent's rules become your rules, and you might very well forget where or why you learned them.

When you internalize the script injunctions of your parents you become socialized. External, objective sources of authority are now internal and subjective. You now "listen to your conscience." When you don't follow the rules, "your conscience acts up." For instance, when you defy authority and refuse to go to war you are a "conscientious objector," meaning that you follow your own inner voice instead of some external authority. A more accurate way of saying this is that you are following a different set of internalized norms, ethics, morals, or values than those set by some external authority, such as the government. You aren't necessarily being "true to yourself;" you are following values that you internalized from somewhere.

When you follow your conscience, you are probably "doing what you believe to be right," because most of us have no way of separating who we are from our internalized parent voices. When you follow what they say to you, you will think you are doing what is "right," when you may only be doing what was expected of you when you were three.

If you had been born into another family, you would have internalized a different set of expectations. What as an adolescent and adult you would have believed was "right" and "true" and fiercely fought for, could be diametrically opposed to what you now believe with all your heart. For instance, if you had grown up a muslim and been brainwashed with Wahhabism in a radical Islamic madrasa, you would most likely be willing to fight and die for Allah. If you had grown up in Germany in the 1920's and 1930's you would most likely have been willing to fight and die for National Socialism. If you had grown up in a Jewish settlement on the West Bank you would have most likely accept and fight for apartheid Zionism.

When you rely on your conscience to make decisions you are confusing internalized parental and social scripting with your life compass. You think that cultural norms are the voice of "truth," "goodness," what is "right" and "just." But the fact that what conscience tells us is radically different based on what culture we grow up in tells us that conscience has little or no relationship to any values and contexts that transcend those imposed by culture and society. Without learning to make clear and concrete distinctions between conscience and life compass you are very likely to spend your life doing what others people want you to do but thinking that it is what *you* want to do. This is a fundamental way society keeps you in harness, being a good plow-pulling citizen, maintaining social order and cultural traditions and beliefs.

If you want to evolve beyond pre-personal and early personal levels of development, conscience is not your friend. Beyond the childhood of individuals and societies, conscience is not conducive to enlightenment. It is a dead weight that will hold you back because it confuses your familial and cultural scripting with finding your own voice.

Finding your own voice is an important piece of work for personal levels of development. How can you identify your own voice, much less your life compass, when both are entangled, confused with, or muffled by the internalized voices of your parents? Few people follow their life compass because it never crosses their mind that there is a difference between conscience and their life compass. If they are able to make that distinction they would be highly unlikely to have a methodology that allowed them to tell the two apart. If they did have such a methodology, such as IDL, they still face repercussions if they place the priorities of their life compass before those of "conscience." Consequently, you can be a passionate fighter for human rights and not pass this test of personal development, because you may simply be living out the scripted values of your parents or favorite teacher or be in simple adolescent rebellion against them. You can be an effective professional, technician, public servant, or artist and never find your own voice. Barak Obama, a highly intelligent beneficiary of all the blessings of American society, spent his Presidency carrying water for the Deep State, a slave to his social and cultural conscience. To do otherwise, you need a means of differentiating your conscience from your life conscience. An important first step is to identify your life script, and a means to do so is provided by Transactional Analysis in its life script questionnaire. Its applications are discussed in *Waking Up*.

The idea that conscience is largely arbitrary scares a lot of people. They don't want to believe that life is capricious or that their conscience is just internalized groupthink. They want to believe in some sort of predestination, whether by karma, dharma, God's will or one's own soul choices prior to birth. Therefore, I do not expect those who disagree to be convinced by what I say here, nor would that be wise. However, if you interview many different perspectives of all different sorts - real, imaginary, from dreams, mystical experiences, after life, past lives, and history, you will probably find that most of these interviewed persepectives lack conscience. They do not have internalized parent voices like you do. Why not? While they will certainly be part of you, and therefore sometimes say things that your mother or father would say, you will also find that they usually also say things that are autonomous to one degree or the other. Those perspectives generally will reflect less of the parental scripting than you do. The result is that they tend to view life with less conscience than you do.

In our society, to say that someone "doesn't have a conscience" means that they are unethical or immoral. It means they are egotistical and manipulative. Is this an accurate description of interviewed emerging potentials who do not appear to have a conscience? You can test this for yourself. When you interview emerging potentials, what is the result? Some will definitely be crazy and bizarre, but most will probably make at least as much sense as you do. Many of them will seem happier than you. Most of them will score higher than you do in one or more of the six core qualities, which means they are more awake than you are, at least in some areas. If conscience has little, if anything, to do with being alive or waking up for these perspectives, why should it for you?

You will find, if you do interviews with the dreams or life issues of young children, that conscience is for them a much stronger presence in those dream characters and personifications of life issues that are interviewed. This is because internalizing parental voices is a basic survival skill for children; they need to do so. It is also important to the development of a sense of self. Your social identity, as superficial as it may be, is largely an expression of those values that you have internalized from your environment, and a great deal of that relates to the development of your conscience. Why then, doIDL interviews not interrupt a child's ability to develop and follow their conscience? Just as children learn to follow different rules and expectations from different parents and authority figures, so they can learn to differentiate between the expectations of interviewed emerging potentials and "real" authorities. Consequently, interviewing does not turn children into amoral, dissociated delinquents. In fact, they do the opposite. IDL interviewing puts children in touch with sources of authority that are independent of internalized parental rules and norms so that their sense of what is "right" for them can come from something that is authentically *them* instead of from some internalized parental voice that they now confuse with their own inner compass.

You will always have a conscience, because you will always have inside your head the parent messages you received as a child. What will change is that you will recognize them for what they are, sift through them, and choose to listen to them much more carefully, deciding only to use those that are conducive to your further enlightenment.

Your conscience and the Drama Triangle

Conscience is your still small voice, the one that tells you right from wrong and good from bad. It is your connection to God. Your conscience keeps you from sin. Without conscience you are an animal, without guidance, ethics, morals, or social norms. If you would only listen to it and follow it, you would be happy. Humanity's perversity is its failure to listen to and do the bidding of its conscience.

Or so they say. Conscience is perhaps the oldest, most hallowed bit of delusion in the consciousness of humanity. To question it is to go against God, society, the soul, the Good, religion, and love. What could be worse? What could be more blasphemous?

Whenever you try to make yourself do something you don't want to do or not do something that you want to do, are you listening to your conscience? Conscience is mother's milk laced with small, regular doses of heroin. The crack is not enough to kill you, but enough to addict you when you are still too young to remember it happening. The rewards of conformity to conscience as well as the punishments if you disobey it, are strong enough to keep you addicted for your entire life. Marx would have been more accurate if he had said, "Conscience is the opium of the people."

Isn't the purpose of your conscience to keep you safe and healthy so that you will be a good child, citizen, and child of God? These are the types of good intentions that parents and leaders have. They themselves may not be aware that conscience also has the benefit of being a powerful tool for your socialization and pacification. If I, as your parent, teacher, President or guru can get you to do what I want automatically, because you think it is "God's will" or "conscience," then my life gets a lot easier. You are more likely to obey me and less likely to ask questions, refuse orders, or disobey laws. Whenever your parents, or some religious or spiritual leader want to get you to do something, to think a certain way, or wish to protect themselves behind a shield of unimpeachable credibility, what can they do? Can't they present themselves as the voice of conscience?

Can't conscience be a good thing? How about "Eat your vegetables," or, "Don't play in the street." Such statements are not conscience but rather simple pieces of information, called "injunctions," given for rational reasons, like health and safety. However, if they are given with threat of punishment ("....or else!") or with a serving of "should," "ought," "must," and guilt, they are conscience and abusive, because they are Persecutors that create and maintain the Drama Triangle in your thoughts and relationships.

Most people will tell you that what is *really* conscience is the same for everyone. However, isn't it true that conscience differs according to culture, religions, social norms and mores? Won't most Christians and Jews argue that their conscience is different from the Islamic conscience? Isn't that what the branding of Islam as terroristic claims? Won't Arabs and other people in countries bombed by the US and NATO argue that people in the West either have no conscience or a very different sense of what conscience means, if conscience allows them to do such things?

When you listen to and follow your conscience are you thinking for yourself? Are you instead following the internalized moral precepts of your family, culture and religion? Have you not so completely internalized them that you *think* their injunctions are your conscience? The inculcation of the vast majority of what is called "conscience" is a loving process of abuse and victimization within the Drama Triangle. Parents and cultures everywhere find the internalization of social values, called "socialization," as conscience highly useful. Someday it will be widely recognized as such and parents will teach their children not only the difference between conscience and their life compass, but how to find, listen to, and follow their life compass. They will learn how to beware of anyone or anything that claims to speak as their conscience.

"Life compass" is a term used by Integral Deep Listening (IDL) to refer to consensus perspectives and recommendations you access by interviewing the personifications of dream characters and life issues that are important to you. These perspectives, called "emerging potentials," are not the children of your parents, culture, religion or society like you are. They have their own priorities and are not afraid to disagree with yours and the voice of your conscience. You can listen to both your conscience and interviewed emerging potentials, compare them and decide for yourself which has your greatest good as its primary interest.

You are the product of a number of beliefs that you had to accept to survive, adapt, and grow in your family and school. Weren't you much less likely to disobey if the preferences of your parents, teachers and society were called "conscience" and you were told that this was something innate within you, or the same as God's will? To trespass against your conscience may be a threat to your society, religion, or family, and therefore a threat to you, when you are punished for disobeying authority figures.

Conscience presents itself as acting in your own good. It knows what is best for you and tells you its actions are only because it cares about and loves you. It is selfless, and you ignore it at your own peril. How is this different from a Rescuer in the Drama Triangle who tells you, "I know what you need. I am only trying to help you. If you don't listen to me you are ungrateful and foolish."

Conscience carries the marks not of a Helper, but of a Rescuer within the Drama Triangle. Rescuers are not Helpers, because they mask self-interest behind a facade of care for others. They do not ask if their help is needed, they do not check to see if the help they are giving is useful, and they do not stop "helping," preferring self-martyrdom and burn-out to recognition of their selfishness.

Your conscience knows what is good for you and speaks up without you asking. It doesn't check to see if its voice is helping, because it knows that it, by its nature, is helping. It doesn't have to check. It refuses to stop demanding you follow it, unless you shut it out with a drug or some other type of intense avoidant stimulation.

Conscience as Rescuer promotes its truth, way, thoughts, feelings, perspectives, and actions, not yours, and certainly not the priorities of your life compass. Your life compass, revealed by interviewing your emerging potentials as they manifest as dream characters and the personifications of your life issues, balances and evolves confidence, empathy, wisdom, acceptance, and witnessing within yourself. Unlike conscience, it is selfless. If the priorities of your life compass and conscience happen to coincide it is coincidence, not due to any awareness or intention of your conscience.

On yet closer examination, you will find that your conscience not only is not your friend, it is never has been your friend. This is because it never wants you to listen to yourself. It only wants you to listen to *it*. Your conscience doesn't trust you. It doesn't respect your judgment. It doesn't even like you unless you are doing what *it* wants. How is this different from the role of Persecutor in the Drama Triangle which tells you, "I am only punishing you for your own good"? Isn't it amazing that you continue to give your conscience any attention or any respect at all?

Persecutors do not see themselves as persecutors. They only say what they say for your own good; they only do what they do because they love you. This means that if your parents or teachers yell at you or call you ugly, stupid, or a failure, it is only for your own good. Verbal abuse in the name of conscience is not verbal abuse at all; it is "character strengthening," and if you knew what was good for you, you would agree with it and change.

If you examine your conscience closely, you will discover that it is the Persecutor role in the Drama Triangle masquerading as the Rescuer, which is itself masquerading as a Helper. Your conscience is deception wrapped in deception; is there any surprise that so many believe in it and that so few ever free themselves from it? How many people ever stop to ask themselves, "How much of what I call my conscience is different from what my parents, culture or this or that peer group believes?" How much of what I call my conscience is probably internalized social and cultural norms?"

When rulers, people, and nations declare war on you in the name of God and then bomb you, destroy your towns, scatter cancer-causing munitions-grade uranium all over your fields, rape your wife and daughters, and torture you to death, is it not for the greater good, for democracy, justice and God, because conscience dictates? People who believe in conscience and then do such things have a very high rate of suicide. As of this writing, the suicide rate of American military veterans is currently twenty-two a day, about one every hour. There is one suicide a day among active duty US military, all among people acting on the basis of "conscience." This is because their conscience has contradicted their life compass on such a fundamental level that there is no way to rationalize away the discrepancy. Unable to escape the cognitive dissonance, but unable, unwilling, or ignorant of how to free themselves of the tyranny of conscience, they kill themselves in an attempt at self-rescue.

How to escape conscience? There is no alternative to sorting through your thoughts, feelings, and motives, one by one, and finding out which script injunctions you carry that are informational facts and which are guilt-creating, persecutorial, "shoulds," "oughts," and "musts." This is why IDL has chapters in *Waking Up* both on recognizing and freeing yourself from your life script as well as on the major emotional cognitive distortions. If you want to learn to think for yourself you must exorcise the internalized toxic directives of the ghosts of your parents that are living rent-free in your attic. Keep the nurturing voices of your parents but evict the rest!

Your conscience is never, ever representative of your life compass. How do you tell the difference? If you will learn to interview your emerging potentials you will slowly learn to differentiate between your life compass and conscience. Your life compass doesn't do drama. It's not in the Drama Triangle. It works to balance confidence, empathy, wisdom, acceptance, inner peace, and witnessing. If you don't follow it, it doesn't threaten you or try to make you feel guilty any more than a compass that points north cares if you go east or south. However, when you do follow your life compass, life gets easier. You have a deep inner sense that you are on the right path for your life. You will have a confidence in who you are and where you are headed regardless of what others may think or say. You will be able to speak and act with authority because you will be in alignment with what is true, good and harmonious for you. As you move into this sacred space you outgrow any need for conscience, not because you no longer listen to it, but because you subject its voice to a higher, more authentic authority that is uniquely your own.

A debate between believers and non-believers in conscience

"Conscience is the light by which we interpret the will of God in our own lives."

Thomas Merton

"The torture of a bad conscience is the hell of a living soul."

John Calvin

"[T]he infliction of cruelty with a good conscience is a delight to moralists. That is why they invented Hell."

Bertrand Russell

(Russell is universally hated by all those who cannot or will not think.)

"There comes a time when one must take a position that is neither safe, nor politic, nor popular, but he must take it because conscience tells him it is right."

Martin Luther King, Jr.

(Conscience is a very poor, unreliable reason to do what is right, if only because your worst enemy appeals to the same justification. Doing what is right? For who? Under what circumstances?)

"If all the world hated you and believed you wicked, while your own conscience approved of you and absolved you from guilt, you would not be without friends."

Charlotte Brontë

(If you do what you think is right you don't have to care whether it makes sense or is useful.)

"Conscience is what makes a boy tell his mother before his sister does."

Evan Esar

"Guilt is also a way for us to express to others that we are a person of good conscience.

Tom Hodgkinson

(The conscience of the personality disordered and of the two year old are both free of guilt.)

"Your conscience is the measure of the honesty of your selfishness. Listen to it carefully."

Richard Bach

(This is very true, but probably not in the sense Bach means it. Because conscience wants what is best for itself, and not for your life compass, it is not only selfish, but completely honest about its selfishness.)

"Character is doing what you don't want to do but know you should do."

Joyce Meyer

("Should," is a dead giveaway that we are dealing with conscience in the form of the Persecutor role in the Drama Triangle.)

"Betrayal is common for men with no conscience."

Toba Beta

(That is because betrayal is a motive often projected upon others, conscience or no conscience.)

"Let us give ourselves indiscriminately to everything our passions suggest, and we will always be happy...Conscience is not the voice of Nature but only the voice of prejudice."

Marquis de Sade

(The Marquis is feared by purveyors of guilt and conscience everywhere.)

"The only tyrant I accept in this world is the 'still small voice' within me. And even though I have to face the prospect of being a minority of one, I humbly believe I have the courage to be in such a hopeless minority."

Mahatma Gandhi

(Gandhi, who beat his wife regularly, did so with a clear conscience. Tyrants do not want what is good for you; they do not want what is good for the majority; they only want what is good for them, but mask their selfishness with conscience. Tyrants of all sorts are by nature selfish persecutors, lost in the Drama Triangle.)

"In matters of conscience, the law of the majority has no place."
Mahatma Gandhi

("Forget democracy and consensus governance; I don't care what you think.")

"There is no witness so dreadful, no accuser so terrible as the conscience that dwells in the heart of every man."
Polybius

(For Polybius, conscience is a persecutor and tyrant, but that's a good thing.)

"Conscience is thus explained only as the voice of God in the soul."
Peter Kreeft

(When societal injunctions have the force of God's will and are defined as both your central truth and intuition, then you are transformed into a zombie, the waking dead servant of current cultural preferences.)

"Conscience and cowardice are really the same things, Basil. Conscience is the trade-name of the firm. That is all."
Oscar Wilde

(You don't have to think for yourself or work out difficult moral dilemmas if you appeal to your conscience.)

"Since then your sere Majesty and your Lordships seek a simple answer, I will give it in this manner, neither horned nor toothed. Unless I am convinced by the testimony of the Scriptures or by clear reason (for I do not trust either in the pope or in councils alone, since it is well known that they have often erred and contradicted themselves), I am bound by the Scriptures I have quoted and my conscience is captive to the Word of God. I cannot and I will not recant anything, since it is neither safe nor right to go against conscience. May God help me. Amen."

(Reply to the Diet of Worms, April 18, 1521)"
Martin Luther

(Martin Luther demonstrates that when you follow your conscience, you put yourself on a diet of worms. His conscience produced some of the most discriminatory bile ever to be uttered by a man of God and conscience. See http://ergofabulous.org/luther/)

"Between the radiant white of a clear conscience and the coal black of a conscience sullied by sin lie many shades of gray–where most of us live our lives. Not perfect but not beyond redemption."
Sherry L. Hoppe

(There can never be either integration or union within the framework of the metaphysical dualism that conscience creates and maintains.)

"True law, the code of justice, the essence of our sensations of right and wrong, is the conscience of society. It has taken thousands of years to develop, and it is the greatest, the most distinguishing quality which has developed with mankind ... If we can touch God at all, where do we touch him save in the conscience? And what is the conscience of any man save his little fragment of the conscience of all men in all time?"
Walter Van Tilburg Clark

(A clear expression of conscience as simply the transmission of socio-cultural norms.)

"Conscience is the inner voice that warns us somebody may be looking."
H.L. Mencken

(If you can teach me to fear the consequences of my behavior, based on what you have taught me to call my conscience, I will monitor myself, freeing you and society to do as you will.)

"I have a different idea of elegance. I don't dress like a fop, it's true, but my moral grooming is impeccable. I never appear in public with a soiled conscience, a tarnished honor, threadbare scruples, or an insult that I haven't washed away. I'm always immaculately clean, adorned with independence and frankness. I may not cut a stylish figure, but I hold my soul erect. I wear my deeds as ribbons, my wit is sharper then the finest mustache, and when I walk among men I make truths ring like spurs."
Edmond Rostand

(Conscience as social propriety.)

"Perhaps conscience did not always produce cowards. Sometimes it made a man feel better about himself."
Robert Ludlum

(Is the purpose of conscience not only to make you feel better about yourself, but to feel superior to all those others you judge as acting less out of conscience?)

"An educator should consider that he has failed in his job if he has not succeeded in instilling some trace of a divine dissatisfaction with our miserable social environment."

Anthony Standen

(Guilt and conscience are the foundations of a good education.)

"It is neither right nor safe to go against my conscience."

Martin Luther

(Since your conscience is a punishing Persecutor, it is unwise to go against it.)

"No guilt is forgotten so long as the conscience still knows of it."

Stefan Zweig

(Conscience as enforcer of guilt.)

"Conscience is no more than the dead speaking to us."

Jim Carroll

(Jim does not mean what he is saying. He means that conscience is the knowledge of the ancients. What he is saying is that conscience is a haunting by voices that seek you to follow their truth, not that of your life compass.)

"The immature conscience is not its own master. It simply parrots the decisions of others. It does not make judgments of its own; it merely conforms to the judgments of others. That is not real freedom, and it makes true love impossible, for if we are to love truly and freely, we must be able to give something that is truly our own to another. If our heart does not belong to us, asks Merton, how can we give it to another?"

Jon Katz

(Jon has drunk the Kool Aid. He still thinks there is such a thing as a good conscience.)

"Anybody can be charming if they don't mind faking it, saying all the stupid, obvious, nauseating things that a conscience keeps most people from saying. Happily, I don't have a conscience. I say them."

Jeff Lindsay

(The opposite of conscience is not immorality, as this quote implies; it is the freedom to find and follow your life compass.)

"The study of law can be disappointing at times, a matter of applying narrow rules and arcane procedure to an uncooperative reality; a sort of glorified accounting that serves to regulate the affairs of those who have power–and that all too often seeks to explain, to those who do not, the ultimate wisdom and justness of their condition.

But that's not all the law is. The law is also memory; the law also records a long-running conversation, a nation arguing with its conscience."

Barack Obama

(...a professor of Constitutional law who justifies both the personally ordered murder of civilians with drones, some of whom have been US citizens, in clear violation of both US and international law – all in the name of conscience.)

"The older you get, the more you understand how your conscience works. The biggest and only critic lives in your perception of people's perception of you rather than people's perception of you."

Criss Jami

(Other people are not the cause of your unhappiness; what you tell yourself you should and should not do in the name of conscience is.)

Intuition

Many people will answer the above by saying, "I don't follow my conscience; I follow my intuition, and that's different." Is it? How would you know? What is "intuition?" Synonyms are "hunch," "impression," "inkling," "notion," "prescience," or "spiritually given." If something is "intuitive," the implication is that it is "on the mark," or "on target," or "accurate," or "cognizant of something I am not but which sounds or feels truthful." Intuition does not differentiate between prepersonal belief, faith, psychism, and state experience, on the one hand, and transpersonal, trans-rational higher stages of development that transcend, yet include belief, faith psychism, and reason. Therefore, claims of intuition tend to be unaware of Wilber's pre-trans fallacy and ignore it, because intuition claims to be "right" and often "spiritual," meaning in harmony with your highest good. Is it? Not only could anything be an intuition, but an intuition can come from sheep's entrails, aura readings, channeling, tarot, or the face of Jesus on a taco. There is no indication of the source of the reliability of an intuition. It is reliable because...it is an intuition!

Notice that in the above picture, of a lady having an intuition, there is nothing there. That's because intuitions are whatever you want them to be. When someone says, "I had an intuition," they are probably saying, "I had a thought, feeling or sensation that I believe is true." Intuition is such a vague concept that means pretty much whatever you want it to mean. Listen to how people use the word and you will find that intuition is commonly used as an unassailable justification for believing whatever the speaker wants to believe. If you question someone's intuition you may often find yourself attacking *them*, questioning the truth and validity of their personal experience. They take personally any skepticism or doubt toward their intuition because they have personalized it. This is because they think they *are* their intuitions. Personalization is a cognitive distortion. A cognitive distortion is an irrational way of thinking that validates a world view that creates anxiety, depression, or both. A belief in intuition does so by making your identity dependent on the rightness or truth of intuitions and therefore vulnerable through dependency on whatever is the source of your intuition. If your intuition is attacked, you are attacked; if your intuition is proven wrong you are invalidated as a person.

Religious beliefs that are "divinely given," meaning intuitively known to be true, demonstrate this characteristic of the cognitive distortion of personalization. For example, the founder of Mormonism, Joseph Smith, said he found the text of the Book of Mormon inscribed on golden tablets. However, eyewitnesses said that what they saw was Joe looking down into his hat at a stone he used to find buried treasure and then writing down his thoughts. If the second version of the story is the truth, the "intuitive knowing" that The Book of Mormon is the Word of God is undercut, with the result being that a crisis of faith and life meaning ensues for believers. Because this is very threatening to people, in this case Mormons, when you question someone's intuition, you are not likely to be viewed as helpful or a friend. They feel threatened, because by questioning the truth of Joseph Smith's "intuition" you question *them*.

Almost all world scripture follows this pattern. Because it was intuitively given, it is from God; because it is from God, it is true. If you question my intuition you not only question my faith, you question God. For example, I have a friend who fancies herself something of a mystic in the fashion of Rumi. She had an intuition that a mutual friend was dead. He wasn't. Did the encroachment of reality on her intuition cause her to change her belief in her intuition or her reliance on it? No; she simply rationalized it; her intuition was correct but divine grace kept our friend alive. Another friend had an intuition that she had found her soul mate. When this relationship didn't work out she didn't question her intuition; she questioned her interpretation of her intuition! What such "explanations" do is move intuition into a category of events and pronouncements that cannot be disproved. If a statement cannot be disproved, it might be wise to ask, "How can I tell if it is true or helpful?" The answer typically boils down to some version of "Trust me." Little children are similarly irrational. We can enjoy them and delight in their creativity and spontaneity, and we can also trust that they are being honest, because they have yet to develop enough of a sense of self to be manipulative. However, does this mean that their intuitions and judgments are trustworthy? You might say that everything they do is intuitive, which means it feels good and it seems right to do. However, despite this, there is a reason why young children are not put in charge of households. Why?

I used to refer to intuition and believe in my own. However, I noticed that it was not important to interviewed emerging potentials and started wondering why not. Emerging potentials either don't have or don't use intuition. Instead, they report their perspective and how they interpret it, within the limitations of the language that the interviewed subject has available for them to use. Watch and listen to when and how people use the word "intuition." What are they really saying? When you talk about your intuition, what are you actually conveying to others? What would your life be like if you didn't use this concept? What, if anything, would take the place of your "intuition?" Here is one example of an exploration of that idea…

An Interview with Intuition

The above picture is an over-used image for intuition, but it makes this interview with intuition as universally applicable as possible.

So, light bulb, are you a symbol for intuition? Tell us about yourself!

Light Bulb: "I bring light and insight to consciousness, which is a good thing!"

So you like yourself?

Light Bulb: "But of course! I'm wonderful!"

Anything you don't like about yourself, Light Bulb?

Light Bulb: "What's there not to like? When I'm on, everything is bright! When I'm not on, I am the possibility of enlightenment! What could be better?"

So do you represent intuition, Light Bulb?

Light Bulb: "Of course! That's why you chose me, isn't it?"

If you could change in any way, would you? If so, how?

Light Bulb: "That's an interesting question. If I were on all the time there wouldn't be time to process my insights; they would all come so fast they would be jumbled together and nothing much would happen with any of them. So the question is, 'What is the optimal frequency for me to come on?' I would say, 'When I'm needed.'"

Light Bulb, You know from my remarks I think you are misused. What do you think?

Light Bulb: "I think there's a difference between intuition and insight. Now that you mention it, I think that I am more creative insight or problem solving than intuition, in the sense of precognition or a 'knowingness' about the future."

So you don't think you represent intuition after all?

Light Bulb: "Now that we are thinking about it, no."

Then maybe I am talking to the wrong emerging potential, Light Bulb! If I were to talk to intuition, what form do you recommend that it would take?

Light Bulb: "A crystal ball. That's more like it."

OK! Good idea! So Crystal Ball, do you personify intuition?
Crystal Ball: "Indeed I do!"
What do you like best about yourself, Crystal Ball?
Crystal Ball: "I like that I foretell the future!"
Yeah, but do you really do that or just claim you do?
Crystal Ball: "Sometimes I really do! And when I do, it's really impressive!"
Right. I've seen some impressive examples of that myself, Crystal Ball…Like when Emanuel Swedenborg in 1759 clairvoyantly reported a great fire in Stockholm, 400 km away. What else do you like about yourself?
Crystal Ball: "That I never fall out of fashion. People are always seeking some version of me to create certainty in their lives."
What do you think about that, Crystal Ball?
Crystal Ball: "I understand they are trying to avoid mistakes and create security for themselves, but I don't think I am of much help. People just use me as a mirror onto which to project their own hopes and fears. I am a tool for externalizing consciousness."
So, what's wrong with that?
Crystal Ball: "Nothing; it just doesn't have much to do with objective reality. It mostly is about one's own hopes and fears."
So you think intuition is accurate to the extent that it is a reliable expression of one's hopes and fears, but not so accurate if assumed to reflect external, objective reality?
Crystal Ball: "That's right."
Crystal Ball, how do you explain real, verified cases of psychic phenomena?
Crystal Ball: "Mystical and near death experiences, precognition, telepathy and psychokinesis happen. These experiences are notoriously difficult to duplicate. Therefore, they are extremely difficult to validate or build any ongoing growth on.
Crystal Ball, how do you score yourself zero to ten in the six core qualities?
Crystal Ball: "I am only a five in confidence, because I do not have nearly as much confidence in my own abilities as do those that depend on me. I don't think they are realistic. Regarding compassion, I would say three, because I do not tell people the truth but mostly only what they want to hear. That is a form of rescuing and validation that doesn't have much to do with growing. Regarding wisdom, I would give myself a three. I don't think I rise to the level of interviewed emerging potentials very often in terms of the objectivity and usefulness of my feedback. Regarding acceptance, I am higher, a seven, because I have something of a complacent, passive attitude toward whatever intuitions people come up with, because I do not feel like I have any control over them. Regarding

peace of mind, I am only about a four. Regarding witnessing, I am a seven. I do witness a lot of what's going on. I think it's mostly drama."

If you scored tens in all six core qualities, Crystal Ball, would you be different, and if so, how?

Crystal Ball: "I would be more like a Tibetan Dorje - diamond clear discernment. I would not so much be intuition as the clarity that comes from being out of one's own way. Now people could call that intuition, but I don't think that is what it is. I think it's clarity."

My understanding is that a Dorje is also known as "Vajra" in Sanskrit, and is the word for both thunderbolt and wisdom and represents bodhi or enlightenment in Buddhism as well as indestructibility and upaya, or the ability to say the right thing at the right time in order to bring awakening to others. Is that right?

Dorje: "Yes, that will do."

So dorje, what do you think of intuition?

Dorje: "I think it's a poor substitute for what people really are wanting and needing: clear discernment, the ability to make good, solid decisions that stand the test of time.

What do you think people need to do in order to learn to do that?

Dorje: "Becoming me would help; meditation, if they will meditate to develop their ability to witness; practice what you call triangulation."

Anything else, Dorje?

Dorje: "Isn't that enough?"

The message of this interview is that we need to think about what we mean when we use the word "intuition." This interview proposed at least three different meanings for it: creative insight and problem solving, foretelling the future, and clear witnessing, which was suggested as a superior substitution or alternative to intuition.

Unconscious, Subconscious

Since Freud, the unconscious or subconscious has often been understood to be the source of dreams, automatic thoughts, slips of the tongue and forgotten memories. Dreams are typically viewed by both depth and transpersonal psychologies as expressions of the unconscious mind. Freud not only believed there were such things as unconscious thoughts, but that sexuality was the source of them. The terms "unconscious" and "subconscious" also create the context for defense mechanisms, probably Freud's greatest and most lasting contribution to the field of psychology. Concepts like "repression" and "suppression," "projection, and "sublimation," which are so useful that we can hardly imagine explaining life without them, scarcely make sense without implying the existence of something like the unconscious or subconscious as places where these defenses "live."

Carl Gustav Jung, the Swiss psychiatrist, developed the concept of the unconscious further. He agreed with Freud that the unconscious is a determinant of personality, but he proposed that it was better devided into the personal and collective unconscious. For Jung, the unconscious contains both the subconscious mind, the personal unconscious and their various components, such as archetypes, impulses, and dream characters. The personal unconscious is for Jung a reservoir of material that was once conscious but has been forgotten or suppressed, much like Freud's notion of the unconscious. The collective unconscious, however, is the deepest level of the psyche, containing the accumulation of inherited psychic structures and archetypal experiences. Archetypes are not memories but images with universal meanings that are apparent in the culture's use of inherited symbols in the unconscious that show up both in dreams and are externalized in art, architecture, and relationships. The collective unconscious is therefore said to be inherited and contain material of an entire species rather than of an individual. Every person shares his or her collective unconscious with the entire human race, as Jung puts it: [the] "whole spiritual heritage of mankind's evolution, born anew in the brain structure of every individual."

However, problems arise with the concept of the unconscious and therefore the various subdivisions within it. Erich Fromm, another psychiatrist who is best known for his best seller, *The Art of Loving*, thought that "...the term 'the unconscious' is actually a mystification...There is no such thing as *the* unconscious; there are only experiences of which we are aware, and others of which we are not aware, that is, *of which we are unconscious*. If I hate a man because I am afraid of him, and if I am aware of my hate but not of my fear, we may say that my hate is conscious and that my fear is unconscious; still my fear does not lie in that mysterious place: 'the' unconscious." Fromm is pointing out that to locate such processes and experiences in the unconscious mind is to imply there is some one definite space or place where they occur, in the "mind." But the mind is hardly unitary, nor does it occupy some definite space other than "the interior of consciousness." When you give the location of the contents of your unawareness a name, you are turning a process, "unawareness," into a stable, static, real *thing,* - the unconscious. What is process now possesses ontological reality for you, not because it is real, but because you have defined it as real. You now enter into a magical, and as Fromm says, "mystical" relationship with your own conceptual delusion. If it were a helpful delusion, like the word "rock," that signifies an actually existing thing, then it might be worth keeping, however, while the unconscious, like all delusions, has its adaptive uses, in balance for some, including Fromm and myself, it does more harm than good, just like any other cognitive distortion.

John Searle has pointed out that the concept of the unconscious is incoherent, because thoughts, are by nature either thought or capable of being thought, while the concept of the unconscious posits thoughts that can never be thought. This is an example of how the concepts of the unconscious and subconscious can be understood as rational cognitive distortions in addition to perceptual ones.

The idea of an unconscious resembles in some respects the idea of a personal afterlife. Your thoughts and feelings are like ghosts or spirits, which do not just die. Instead, they continue to live, full form, and can either haunt you by incoherent urges and desires from "the other side" or "reincarnate" when they erupt anew, fully grown, into consciousness.

Is this myth realistic? When your thoughts or feelings "die," that is, are forgotten, do they go into dark inner holes, niches, or compartments to sleep until resurrected, like Dracula? Buddhism points toward a far more reasonable and probable explanation. Its doctrine of *skandhas,* which addresses the creation and maintenance of our sense of self, has been applied to explain consciousness that is out of awareness without resorting to a concept like the "unconscious" for over two thousand years. Because all things arise interdependently, Buddhism refuses to talk about the existence of anything apart from the necessary conditions that lead to its expression. For example, the desire for a cup of coffee is not something somewhere inside you that is lying latent, like a seed in the winter, waiting for warmth, or a zombie in its crypt, waiting for darkness. Instead, the existence of your desire for a cup of coffee is potential, not actual, and that potential can emerge into consciousness when the proper confluence of conditions comes into being.

An analogy can be made to snowflakes. Each one is not a reincarnated memory of a past life as a previous snowflake. When appropriate atmospheric conditions arise, unique but highly structured forms called snowflakes appear. The same point can be made using chaos theory and the concept of chaotic attractors. "Attractor basins" is a concept from chaos theory which has been adapted to the exploration of consciousness by Allan Combs. Think of attractors as a pattern of activity toward which a system tends to slide of its own accord. They are probably best visualized as warped or twisted tornadoes composed of probabilities rather than of objects and concrete forms such as trees, road signs, or entities. See *The Radiance of Being,* for example, pp. 16-20 & 218-226. Skandhas, natural phenomena like snowflakes and chaos theory provide models that account for the arising of thoughts, feelings, preferences and intentions without recourse to an unconscious or subconscious.

Thoughts and feelings are composed of multiple parts or "subroutines" that themselves do not rise to the coherence of thoughts or feelings. These components include prehension and simple reactivity. As soon as you move beneath waking identity you begin to disassemble consciousness. Wilber describes this in terms of the four fundamental attributes of any holon remaining dissociated. Instead of looking at one, unitary "unconscious" or "subconscious," if you could look into the "afterlife" of your memories, thoughts, and feelings, you would be examining components which, when looked at individually, have the same relationship to a thought that a piece of wood, brick, or a window frame does to a house. At this level of analysis, you no longer have a house; you only have the components of a house. This is also the point that Buddhism makes with the concept of *skandhas*. Why this is important is that an understanding such as skandhas or natural processes such as the creation of snowflakes or chaos theory describe processes rather than posit ontological realities. Consequently, with Buddhism you do not derive an immortal soul, self or Self while with depth psychology you derive entities, in this case psychic structures, called the unconscious and the subconscious.

Here is another example. When you look at a solar system are you looking at consciousness aware of itself or at emerging potentials for consciousness to become aware of itself? We know that all the atoms that make up our bodies have their origin in the sun and its surrounding nebula.

We also know that holons have consciousness, or experience, all the way up and all the way down to sub-atomic particles, but we do not therefore claim that quarks have an unconscious or subconscious. Why not? If humans are holons and they have an unconscious and subconscious, then does it not follow that all other holons do as well? Is not to assume otherwise a form of exceptionalism and psychological geocentrism?

This is not to deny that most of the operations of consciousness occur out of our awareness and that there are many physiological and psychological sub-routines or building blocks of consciousness which constantly go on out of our awareness. This is beyond doubt. These include thought processes, memory, affect, and motivation. Unconscious phenomena also include the locus of implicit knowledge, that is, the things that you have learned so well that you do them without thinking, repressed feelings, automatic skills, subliminal perceptions, thoughts, habits, and automatic reactions. Marin Minsky, who takes a reductionistic and materialistic approach, wrote an interesting book about this, called *The Society of Mind.*

The term "subconscious" is similar to "unconscious" and, while useul within certain contexts, just like the unconscious, is not conducive to enlightenment for similar reasons. The concept of the subconscious is commonly used to refer to our inner storehouse for conflictual and disowned parts of ourselves. It may also be assumed to be the repository for our unused and unrecognized potentials.

The idea of "subconscious" is reminiscent of Plato's famous concept of *anamnesis,* which contends that learning is a process of rediscovering knowledge that already exists within us, which implies pre-existence and reincarnation, a belief that Plato also appeared to embrace. *Anamnesis* is essentially a romantic idea, in harmony with the inclinations of Lessing, Rousseau, Grof, Washburn and neo-shamanists that holds that all that is good, true, and beautiful pre-exists in perfection and that it only needs to be rediscovered. Everything is always already there, like the goods in a darkened warehouse; you only need to turn the spotlight of your "conscious" or "awareness" on to light it up. The advantage of this view is that it says what you need already exists, including your ability to be aware of those things you need to know in order to be happy. The disadvantage of this view is that it doesn't fit reality. Did scuba gear exist in the warehouse of consciousness twenty thousand years ago, just waiting for us to shine the light of consciousness on it? How about the internet and drone warfare? While anything is possible, this is hardly the most parsimonious explanation for both creativity and evolution. Isn't it more likely that emerging potentials did not pre-exist, that they are possibilities that may or may not emerge into consciousness, just like we know snowflakes will be created but we cannot predict the specific and unique form of any particular one? Typically, we either throw the light of awareness on things and misinterpret them, such as the intentions of others or our own motivations when we were three, or we are unable to find and illuminate things we want or need, such as how to lucid dream or keep our minds quiet when we meditate. Is it in any way necessary to assume that what we need pre-exists in some subterranean memory or some collective akasha for us to throw light upon?

If all this is reasonable, then perhaps the subconscious exists not in actual experience but as an interpretive afterthought. For example, as Fromm was pointing out, when you are aware of something, like your anger, it is *conscious;* it is not unconscious. When you think, "I *could* get angry," anger exists as an unexpressed potential only, it does not reside some *place,* that is, in your "subconscious."

To repeat and summarize: You are full and overflowing with potentials of all sorts. Some are positive, some are conflictual, some are deadly. To allocate them to a *place,* the "subconscious," creates a "thing," a "subconscious," where only a process exists. That process is one of being aware of a potential and not expressing it, or being aware of a potential and expressing it. Or, you can be unaware of a potential and have no capability of expressing it, or the potential may not exist. However, you cannot speak of a process of *not* being aware of a specific potential and not expressing it, because you can not speak or think of something you are not aware of. However, we often read the pre-existence of an idea or feeling into the actions of others, in an act of interpretive projection: "Ha! He said "lover" when he was really thinking about his "mother!" We do not know if this is true, but because we have read up on Freud's defense mechanisms, we attribute motivating reality to a potential feeling and thought that may or may not have existed.

Dreams, for example, are commonly assumed, particularly by depth psychology, to reside in your subconscious. Do they? When you have a dream, you are conscious of it; if you do not remember a dream, is it hanging out somewhere, waiting for you to remember it? If you access the correct combination of stimuli, you may indeed access that potential, but to do so you do not need to posit the existence of a subconscious. Again, think of dream creation as similar to that of snow. Snowflakes are not lurking in some heavenly unconscious, waiting to be created. They are generated when the right combination of temperature and moisture come together. Similarly, are your dreams hanging out in the catacombs of your mind, awaiting to be unearthed, or are they emerging potentials consisting of thoughts, feelings and intentions that collectively arise spontaneously given the appropriate psychic weather conditions?

IDL does not rule out the existence of collective "thought form" phenomena, such as implied by the concept of the collective unconscious. It is too difficult to dismiss out of hand the testimony of thousands at Fatima who saw the sun move up and down in the sky or, as Jung noted himself, the many recurring sitings of unexplained UFOs. Do we require the concept of archetypes to explain what is going on with waking collective "dreams" such as these? Are these externalized realities so different from our own, individual, night time assumptions, that two-headed dragons are real while we are dreaming about them? Cannot Fatima-like experiences or UFOs be called "thought forms" or "realities," as the perceivers of these experiences consider them, without postulating a collective unconscious? Can we not have collective, dream-like waking experiences without positing an "unconscious" in which they reside? Once we posit the existence of a "something," a "subconscious," we risk hobbling our growth by tying it to a conceptual fixation, something that is not necessary, nor the simplest or most adequate explanation available.

Consequently, IDL views the unconscious, subconscious, and derivative concepts as helpful for beginning students of psychology who are studying models for the working of the mind and the creation of personality, but becoming less necessary and more misleading the more our need for permanence, the reality of "things," and identity thins. From such perspectives, "unconscious" and "subconscious" complicate the much simpler process of awakening to incarnating potentials of all sorts.

Because these two concepts acts as perceptual cognitive distortions while creating a place where only the potential for awareness exists, and because the idea of an unconscious or subconscious is not used by interviewed emerging potentials, who rarely find it necessary to explain their world, IDL has found that both parsimony and clarity generate a simpler world view. To assume that interviewed emerging potentials are elements of an unconscious, whether individual or collective, sub- or super-, is a projection onto them of waking assumptions. The phenomenalism of IDL asks, "What happens when we temporarily suspend such assumptions?" "Are they necessary? Are they helpful?"

IDL invites you to experiment with suspending your assumptions about the unconscious, subconscious, superconscious, personal unconscious, and collective unconscious in order to simply look at your waking, dream and mystical experiences from the cognitive framework of this or that interviewed emerging potential. While some that are interviewed may use these terms because, after all, their perspectives reflect your language and conceptual context and they want to communicate with you in a way you can understand and appreciate, others will not use these terms because their perceptual context transcends both your language and conceptual context and they believe you are capable of a broader, freer way of approaching consciousness. Listen, learn, and draw your own conclusions.

Here is a whimsical interview with the unconscious. You are encouraged to create your own, which will speak uniquely to your own evolutionary development.

An Interview with the Unconscious

"Unconscious, because you are a word that designates a place and a thing, I am imagining you to be a vast domed structure, a combination of The Ministry of Magic in Harry Potter and the Pantheon in Rome. I look up into you and all sorts of bird-like papers, representing thoughts, and objects, representing feelings and experiences, are flying about within you. There are home niches everywhere along your massive domed walls, in which millions of thoughts, feelings, and experiences are nesting. Light shines in through skylights here and there, but essentially you are dark and gloomy in your vastness, but the air is abuzz with all sorts of flying notices, imaginings, and stimuli."

"As you know, Unconscious, I believe you are a helpful, adaptive figment of my imagination, devised to help people make sense of their experience. You also know that I believe you are most useful for people who are stuck at pre-personal levels of experience to make sense of their own impulses and motivations. However, you also know that IDL teaches that such assumptions need to first be surfaced and then parked, so that we can respectfully and deeply listen to what you have to say, without our biases and interpretations getting in the way so much. However, I know that despite our best efforts, there are layers of bias and interpretation, and I know that I will contaminate and distort whatever you say because of them. While I apologize for that, I also am aware that the most we can do is to be aware of that and attempt to own up to our biases and projections as we become aware of them."

So Unconscious, from your perspective, what are you like and what is important about you?"

Unconscious: "I am a vast storehouse. I hold your memories and your potentials, your physiological processes and mental-emotional sub-routines. Who you think you are is created out of my contents. What I do not possess you cannot become; however, because I possess so many memories and potentials, you could have become someone very different from whom you are, and you could become in the future someone very different from who you are today."

"What do you like best about yourself, Unconscious?"

Unconscious: "I like the abundance of possibilities I provide. I am not limitless, but I might as well be. I don't direct or predestine anything; I simply am a depository, like a magical library."

"What do you like least about yourself?"

Unconscious: "I don't like that I am cut off from the greater world and that I am gloomy inside."

"Do you want to add anything else about what aspects of me you might most closely represent or personify?"

Unconscious: "Yes; your self-definitions that cut you off from the rest of the world artificially."

"Unconscious, do you want to change? If so, how would you like to change?"

Unconscious: "Why separate me from the rest of life? Why not simply let my roof be the sky and let my contents nest where they will?"

OK...Let's see what happens...OK...Some are nesting in the branches of trees; some are flying among the clouds: some are lying on the ground; some are riding on the backs of birds: some are flying unexpectedly up under birds and scaring them; some are watching TV; some are snoring and appear to be asleep...So where and how are you now, Unconscious?"

Unconscious: "I am no longer a "thing" or a "place" separated from the "thingness" of your entire experience or the "location" of your life. Also, I no longer possess anything, so I do not limit or control what you can become.

How do you score yourself in each of the six core qualities, and why?

Unconscious: "I score myself a ten in confidence because I have no fear. I contain everything and everything contains me, because we are co-extensive. What can hurt me? What can affect me? There is no duality; there is no "other." I don't know how to score myself in compassion. I could say that I am very compassionate because I provide the context for any and all potentials to arise, but these may be desired or undesirable; none of that is my concern. So I don't think of myself in those terms, but I am not so sure I am amoral, like nature, either. Regarding wisdom, I am a ten. Regarding acceptance, it is also a ten. What is there not to accept? I contain all things, and I have no preferences. I don't know if "bad" stuff is going to turn out to be just what is needed to stimulate breakthroughs, or whether "good" stuff is going to impede growth. Regarding inner peace, I am totally at peace as the context for all this activity, so I am a ten. Regarding witnessing, I am also a ten, because I watch it all with humor and amazement."

Unconscious, do you still view yourself as I called you, as "the Unconscious?"

Unconscious: "No. I am life. Earlier you wrote that there is life that one is aware of and life that one is unaware of. While I am a context that is aware of both, I do not view potentials as dormant 'things,' but more like seeds that could not grow, or water vapor that may or may not turn into rain or snow or create a rainbow. So no, the name 'unconscious' no longer fits me. Just call me 'life.'"

Aha! So you are the Akashic Records!

Did you not listen to what I just said? The Akashic Records is a mythological superconscious unconscious. It is just me, a combination of the Pantheon and the Ministry of Magic, transposed onto the "skein of space and time, with maybe bearded masters shuffling through my stacks like some enlightened librarians.

So Life, if I lived my life from your perspective, would it be different, and if so, how?

Life: "It would be open and relatively unstructured, yet structured with an essential framework, like a trellis for climbing roses. No structure means chaos and overwhelm; too much structure means stagnation and fossilization. You require a balance between the two. However, I have that balance, and the more that you become me, the more you will, too."

Do you have recommendations for me?

Life: "You have been preferring to be aware of the spaces between your thoughts in your everyday life. These spaces keep opening up. The more that happens, the more you live in me, the more you become me. So I suggest you keep doing that."

"Life, if I change my understanding of the unconscious and subconscious to reflect who and what you are and what you have said, what will that do to my understanding of defense mechanisms?"

Life: "You can continue to use whatever concepts you want if you find them helpful; I don't care. From my perspective they aren't real, nor are they important. But then, I'm not you, and perhaps if I were, I would find them important."

"Are there particular times when it would be most advantageous for me to look at life from your perspective?"

Life: "Yes. Whenever you get stuck in drama or the need to say, feel, or think something. Becoming me will not move you into a state of passive detachment, but rather into a space of creative potential, of context, where your actions will not be driven by a cut-off, separated, sense of self."

If these comments from "the unconscious" and "Life" were a wake-up call from my life compass, it would be telling me to continue my practice of exploring the spaces between my thoughts and feelings. Also, that becoming life expressing itself in this way feels beneficial and therapeutic to me on some deep level.

How attached to the concepts of unconscious and subconscious are you? What function do they play in your life? How would you explain life if you didn't use them? What would it take for you to outgrow them?

Shadow

Jung develops the concept of the shadow" for good and important reasons. For example, in "The Philosophical Tree" (1945), in *CW 13: Alchemical Studies.* P.335, he says, "A man who is unconscious of himself acts in a blind, instinctive way and is in addition fooled by all the illusions that arise when he sees everything that he is not conscious of in himself coming to meet him from outside as projections upon his neighbor." Expanding on this approach in "Psychology and Religion" (1938), in CW 11: *Psychology and Religion: West and East,* P.140, Jung says, "If you imagine someone who is brave enough to withdraw all his projections, then you get an individual who is conscious of a pretty thick shadow. Such a man has saddled himself with new problems and conflicts. He has become a serious problem to himself, as he is now unable to say that they do this or that, they are wrong, and they must be fought against... Such a man knows that whatever is wrong in the world is in himself, and if he only learns to deal with his own shadow he has done something real for the world."

There are several assumptions about "shadow" that Jung and those who follow him in this regard, including Ken Wilber.

First, "shadow" refers to aspects of self:

"To become conscious of (the shadow) involves recognizing the dark aspects of the personality as present and real." Aion (1951). CW 9, Part II: P.14

The function of this concept is responsibility through ownership, based on the idea that we are empowered only by that which we take as self-created, as a part of ourselves.

Second, "shadow" indicates dark, or unwanted aspects of self:

"Unfortunately, there can be no doubt that man is, on the whole, less good than he imagines himself or wants to be. Everyone carries a shadow, and the less it is embodied in the individual's conscious life, the blacker and denser it is." "Psychology and Religion" (1938). In CW 11: *Psychology and Religion: West and East*, P.131

"Taking it in its deepest sense, the shadow is the invisible saurian tail that man still drags behind him." *The Integration of the Personality*, (1939).

Jung is saying that the shadow is an evolutionary throw-back, a burden to be cast off:

"We carry our past with us, to wit, the primitive and inferior man with his desires and emotions, and it is only with an enormous effort that we can detach ourselves from this burden. If it comes to a neurosis, we invariably have to deal with a considerably intensified shadow." "Answer to Job" (1952). In CW 11: *Psychology and Religion: West and East*, P.1.

The darkness of the shadow is not petty; it can be demonic:

"It is a frightening thought that man also has a shadow side to him, consisting not just of little weaknesses- and foibles, but of a positively demonic dynamism." "On the Psychology of the Unconscious" (1912). In CW 7: *Two Essays on Analytical Psychology*, P.35

Not only can shadow be neurotic and demonic, but also pathological and psychotic:

"If the activation is due to the collapse of the individual's hopes and expectations, there is a danger that the collective unconscious may take the place of reality. This state would be pathological. If, on the other hand, the activation is the result of psychological processes in the unconscious of the people, the individual may feel threatened or at any rate disoriented, but the resultant state is not pathological, at least so far as the individual is concerned. Nevertheless, the mental state of the people as a whole might well be compared to a psychosis." "The Psychological Foundation for the Belief in Spirits (1920). In CW 8: *The Structure and Dynamics of the Psyche*, P.595

Third, "shadow" indicates *repressed* aspects of self:

"Having a dark suspicion of these grim possibilities, man turns a blind eye to the shadow-side of human nature. Blindly he strives against the salutary dogma of original sin, which is yet so prodigiously true. Yes, he even hesitates to admit the conflict of which he is so painfully aware." "On the Psychology of the Unconscious" (1912). In CW 7: *Two Essays on Analytical Psychology*, P.35

Jung finds good reason for man's repression of his shadow:

"The change of character brought about by the uprush of collective forces is amazing. A gentle and reasonable being can be transformed into a maniac or a savage beast. One is always inclined to lay the blame on external circumstances, but nothing could explode in us if it had not been there. As a matter of fact, we are constantly living on the edge of a volcano, and there is, so far as we know, no way of protecting ourselves from a possible outburst that will destroy everybody within reach. It is certainly a good thing to preach reason and common sense, but what if you have a lunatic asylum for an audience or a crowd in a collective frenzy? There is not much difference between them because the madman and the mob are both moved by impersonal, overwhelming forces." "Psychology and Religion" (1938). In CW 11: *Psychology and Religion: West and East,* P.25

What Jung means, when he speaks of "losing one's shadow," is its repression:

"No, the demons are not banished; that is a difficult task that still lies ahead... Every man who loses his shadow, every nation that falls into self-righteousness, is their prey.... We should not forget that exactly the same fatal tendency to collectivization is present in the victorious nations as in the Germans, that they can just as suddenly become a victim of the demonic powers." "The Postwar Psychic Problems of the Germans" (1945)

"If an inferiority is conscious, one always has a chance to correct it. Furthermore, it is constantly in contact with other interests, so that it is continually subjected to modifications. But if it is repressed and isolated from consciousness, it never gets corrected." "Psychology and Religion" (1938). In CW 11: *Psychology and Religion: West and East,* P.131

Here we see Jung's basic theory of his method. You can't fix personality dysfunction unless you bring repressed shadow to the surface:

"... if such a person wants to be cured it is necessary to find a way in which his conscious personality and his shadow can live together." "Answer to Job" (1952). In CW 11: *Psychology and Religion: West and East,* P.1

Fourth, recognition of one's shadow involves *confrontation.*

"Whenever contents of the collective unconscious become activated, they have a disturbing effect on the conscious mind, and contusion ensues." "The Psychological Foundation for the Belief in Spirits (1920). In CW 8: *The Structure and Dynamics of the Psyche,* P.595

"Filling the conscious mind with ideal conceptions is a characteristic of Western theosophy, but not the confrontation with the shadow and the world of darkness." "The Philosophical Tree" (1945). In CW 13: *Alchemical Studies,* P.335

"To confront a person with his shadow is to show him his own light. Once one has experienced a few times what it is like to stand judgingly between the opposites, one begins to understand what is meant by the self. Anyone who perceives his shadow and his light simultaneously sees himself from two sides and thus gets in the middle." "Good and Evil in Analytical Psychology" (1959). In CW 10. *Civilization in Transition,* P.872

Notice that Jung's "holy grail" is the finding and integration of "the self."

Let's look at how IDL looks at all four of these points regarding the shadow, as aspects of self, as dark aspects of self, as repressed aspects of self and as requiring confrontation.

First, IDL does not recognize any self to which "shadow" belongs. It does not belong to waking identity, for it is repressed, or disowned by it. To whom, then, does it belong, if it is not an aspect of who you think you are? Is it a part of who you are but you do not think you are? Jung's classical answer, following Freud, is that it is part of an expanded, disowned identity that is then projected outward as delusional and conflictual relationships with the world.

This theory is put to the test by IDL, as we have seen in the above interviews with the "Ego" and "the Unconscious," and done so in a way that anyone can verify for themselves. Take any of the words and concepts we discuss here, or any demonic dream character, "shadowy" characteristic of yourself, such as an addiction or something you are ashamed of, or some demonic world event, like 9/11. Interview it, using either the IDL dream or life issue protocol. What you will find is that yes, the character or element most likely does personify some aspect of yourself. However, as you get into the interview, you will most likely find that it embodies potentials that you do not possess. For example, in the interview with the "ego," above, I could see how it is a part of me and could respect it, but could not bring myself to feel intimidated or controlled by it. So yes, it is a part of me, and no, it is not a part of me, in that I could see that it was so much smoke and no fire. Similarly, in the interview with "the Unconscious," above, I could see how it personified aspects of myself, many of which are unrecognized or disowned. However, as it transformed itself into Life, it became clear that it so completely transcended who I think I am as to no longer be considered a part of me and to make sense at the same time. The only way it could make sense at that point would be *for me to experience myself as a part of it.* If this is so, in what sense is this or any element "shadow?" In what sense does it belong to *you,* if it embodies potentials that you do not possess? Does it not make more sense to say that you belong to *it,* that you are an aspect of *it?* Are you the "shadow" of what you misperceive as shadow?

Like you and me, these interviewed emerging potentials have a sense of self, a sense of identity, even if it is *ad hoc* and imaginary. They embody perspectives which generally prove to be highly relevant and meaningful. Do they also have projections? Yes, in the form of the interpretations they make regarding experience. Doesn't this also imply that they have a "shadow," or repressed, dark, disowned sense of self? If so, is that not strange to contemplate that "shadow" has its own shadow? How could that be? If you interview that, do you find that that also has its own shadow? Doesn't this formulation imply that repression is a bottomless pit? Is it? In the experience of IDL it is not; you can and do get to the bottom of things.

Unlike you and me, interviewed emerging potentials have a weak or non-existent self-sense. They are imaginary perspectives that embody certain combinations of qualities and characteristics. When "shadow" elements are interviewed using IDL, they are found to be as much "not-self" as they are "self." We are as likely to belong to them as they are to belong to us. So is "shadow" a part of your "self?" Not based on the experience of IDL interviewing. It is accurate to say that it is *experienced* as part of a disowned self, but this self is itself a delusion and, when you take the perspective of shadow, you often find it has characteristics that are greater than your "self," which means that it could not be either your self or disowned, unless you radically re-define "self" to include everything, which means "self" identifies nothing in particular, particularly *you.*

Jung's second point involves the supposed darkness and demonic nature of these shadowy "self-aspects." IDL interviewing generally demonstrates that such assumptions are waking projections, even while dreaming, and are not substantiated either by interviews of characters themselves or by other elements from within the dream or associated life situation. On the contrary, the intentions of such "shadow" elements are generally found to be in the service of *shocking waking identity awake.* This is hardly a dark, demonic, neurotic, or psychotic intention. Notice that in the interview of the Ego, above, the Queen certainly did her best to be fearful and intimidating. Instead of transforming into love and light, Ego saw itself more like the Queen in Disney's *Snow White and the Seven Dwarves* (evil) than the way in which she came across to me, more like the Queen in *Alice in Wonderland* (absurd). Is this a failure to accurately portray the Shadow in its authentic, demonic nature or, is it an example of what can happen when you deeply listen to some personification of what you consider to be your own shadow? We will address that issue in our interview with the Shadow, below.

Jung's third point involves repression and disownership. IDL recognizes both, but shares the focus that interviewed emerging potentials emphasize in countless interviews: what is important is not what is repressed and disowned, or what is not yet recognized or owned, but whether or not you respectfully listen to both. When you put focus on what you fear, that is "repressed shadow," you amplify your fear and shadow, in the hope that by doing so you will overcome the repression and generate an "integrated self." However, what generally happens is that you get a socially enculturated self that is a thoroughgoing product of the best of prevailing groupthink. "Integration" ends up meaning "normal," which is a frightening thought, considering the state of reality generated by contemporary "normal" humans, including the best and the brightest, like

Barak Obama. For example, if you are afraid of failure and repress it, and then you wake-up and say, "I will look at my repressed fear of failure!" What is the result? It entirely depends on what you mean by "looking" at it. Generally, that means looking at it through the distorted lens of your waking identity or, if you are lucky, through the distorted lens of a good therapist. Both will undoubtedly be improvements, in that they will result in approximations to "normalcy," or "social adjustment." But what do either have to do with the priorities of your life compass? Has it been consulted? If so, how? IDL interviewing allows that which is feared to be heard on its own terms; if it wants to transform, that is respected; if it wants to stay the same, or become even more fearful, that is respected. IDL teaches you to respect the priorities of perspectives that personify facets of your life compass and to take them into account while you are considering your own and the interpretations and priorities of therapists. The result is much less likely to result in "normalcy."

Interviewed emerging potentials themselves do not focus on the feared, repressed, or disowned. Even when they are stuck in the Drama Triangle they rarely see themselves as persecutors, but instead as angry or depressed victims. They are much more often to be found to be relatively free of the Drama Triangle and focusing on what is not yet recognized or owned and what is attempting to be born into consciousness.

Jung's fourth point about the shadow is that it requires confrontation. IDL has found that respect, as demonstrated by deep listening in an integral way, largely eliminates the need for confrontation and the defensive, fear-based stance that the superficial confidence of confrontation implies. While it is possible to confront without fear or defensiveness, it is not easy, nor is it likely. Most of us imagine we are confronting without fear or defensiveness, but that belief rarely bears up under close examination. Waking up and enlightenment involve growth into the core qualities and perspectives of life; these usually do not require confrontation, other than the challenging our motivations and behaviors as well as the logic of the statements elements make when interviewed, or in questioning the nature and purpose of their recommendations.

As long as you are identified with a self sense you will have relatively non-integrated aspects of a greater self with which you may experience conflict. What will change is that you will respectfully observe and listen to them instead of treating them as conflict or repressed shadow.

Interpretation

Interpretations are projections by consciousness onto a person, event, or dream by the dreamer, an external interpretation source such as an expert, a dream dictionary or a dreamwork group, or by some subjective or "interior" perspective. What a dream "means" is dependent upon the interpretations that are projected onto it and who or what is doing the interpretation. What physical or mental symptoms "mean" is dependent upon the professional assessment of a collection of symptoms and the arrival at a professional interpretation called a diagnosis. A person is providing interpretations when they provide their own opinions on the causes, meanings, and effects of conditions, whether physical, mental, interpersonal, financial, legal, or dream-based. They are paid to either heal disease, make people feel better, or eliminate some life problem, like procrastination, money problems, or a messy house. In the case of dreams, a good dream interpreter provides meanings that "fit," "make sense," provide "insight" or are "helpful." Treatment recommendations are based on the interpretations of the expert.

Interpretation is the fundamental skill of both traditional dreamwork and various treatment modalities. "Experts" and "professionals" are taught to interpret symptoms and symbolic material, with the help of interpretive guides, such as the DSM V (Diagnostic and Statistical Manual, which the mental health profession uses to make diagnoses) and various dream dictionaries. Other words for "interpretation" are "diagnosis" and "prognosis." Even coaching, which adamantly claims to have nothing to do with therapy and often prides itself on being the "anti-therapy," uses interpretation constantly. Because coaches do not consider their interpretations either diagnostic or predictive, but instead "suggestions," "advice" or "encouragement," they claim their services are in a different category from therapists. However, a fundamental similarity exists: these different groups are all being paid to make interpretations and give advice based on those interpretations. The debate over whose interpretations are most accurate or helpful is a secondary issue.

IDL assumes that interpretation is unavoidable, but that it can be minimized, recognized, and controlled in ways that are supportive of the basic purpose of IDL: helping the interviewed person, whether they be a client, student, or family member, to wake-up out of some delusional, painful space and into a life of relatively increased clarity and balance through accessing and followed the priorities of life, as expressed individually as the priorities of their own life compass. Consequently, IDL Practitioners defer to the interpretations of interviewed dream characters or personifications of aspects of the physical, mental, or interpersonal life issue of the moment. These can be as subjective and misleading as those of experts, dream dictionaries and well-meaning friends, but they generally are not. This is because interviewed emerging potentials know you at least as well as you know yourself and arguably better. Interpretive comments or "associations" by the dreamer occur after the dream is told and before the interview. Following the interview, the dreamer is asked to interpret what they have heard. Often the response will startle the interviewer, because it is not unusual for the person receiving the interview to have recognized or realized things from the interview that the interviewer did not. These are generally not so much distortions as much as they are inferences based on personal experiences that the interviewer was not aware of. Consequently, these interpretations by the dreamer are often very helpful for helping the interviewer understand what the dreamer did and did not get out of the interview.

Interpretations by the interviewer in the IDL interviewing process come last, after those of one or more interviewed dream characters or personifications of life issues and then those of the dreamer or interview subject themselves. The interviewer's interpretations may come in the form of reading back the interview to help the person objectively hear what they have said to themselves, or in general remarks regarding what the interviewer heard from the interviewed character and the subject. While the interviewer does their utmost to do the reading back in a way that stays true to the meaning of the interviewed emerging potential, interpretation is unavoidable. The interviewer also makes many interpretations in guiding the subject in how to operationalize the recommendations in the interview, choose which ones they want to work on, and set up a monitoring program. Because this is again primarily a teaching function it does not stir up nearly the amount of interpretive problems as you find in psychoanalysis and psychodynamic approaches to therapy and counseling.

Making interpretations is not only natural and important; it is also inevitable. What will change as you move ahead in your development is that your interpretations will be increasingly effective because they will become less and less *your* interpretations and more a reflection of the priorities of life.

Interviewing "interpretation," which we do below, provides an example of beginning with an abstract concept, rather than a "thing," such as an ego, the unconscious, or the shadow. This is routinely done in IDL when a life issue, like procrastination, which is itself a series of experiences and abstract thoughts about them, are associated with feelings, which are processes, and these are allowed to turn first into a color or colors and then congeal into a definite form.

Interviewing "Interpretation"

When I think of interpretation it is essentially a process of the mental projection of meanings. When I think of mental, intellectual processes, the color yellow comes to mind, and immediately that brings up an image of the Sun and its rays. If the Sun were the source of the interpretations, then the rays would be the interpretations themselves. So, going with that metaphor, let's interview sun rays.

"Sun rays, will you please describe yourselves?"

Sun Rays: "We are brilliant yellow beams of energy, so we are warmer than the surrounding space or atmosphere. We are almost nothing, but our persistence and energy make us almost everything, since we are a basic and essential ingredient of life."

"Sun Rays, what do you like about yourself?"

Sun Rays: "All of the above."

"Is there anything you dislike about yourself? Do you have any weaknesses?"

Sun Rays: "There is nothing about us to dislike; what appear to be our weaknesses are actually our strengths."

Besides my interpretations, what other aspects of myself do you most closely personify? More broadly, what aspects of humanity?"

Sun Rays: "My universalist symbolic significance is already well understood: heat, light, energy, power, growth. As rays, we have been imagined even by early Egyptians as emissaries, like angels or saviors, from the Source of Life to humanity. As such we are placed unknowingly and inadvertently in the role of rescuers in the Drama Triangle."

"Do you want to change in any way? If so, how?"

Sun Rays: "No. Why should we? Besides, we have an important role to fill. We need to think not only about ourselves but consider our interdependent relationships with all things."

"How would you score yourself zero to ten in the six core qualities, and why?"

Sun Rays: "We are a ten in confidence, wisdom, acceptance, inner peace, and witnessing, but only because we are you, plus our own additional perspective. By ourselves, we are none of these things, because we are not conscious; we have no self-awareness, and our level of consciousness is pre-sensory. One with all things, we are unaware of that oneness. However, when you take our perspective, that oneness becomes self-aware, to the extent that you are, so those core qualities become available to us to inhabit and as descriptors that we can wear them like clothes. Similarly, while you are hardly tens in these qualities, when you combine with us you are, because we possess the identification with oneness that you lack. However, our "tens" in these five core qualities is not perfection, because we know that as you evolve, we co-evolve; as you become more wise, for instance, what was a ten in wisdom will become an eight or a six.

Regarding compassion, that is a different story. We understand you human conception of compassion, as a higher octave above not only love but altruism and empathy. We can imagine ourselves being a ten in compassion, but we aren't. That may be because you are not, but then you aren't a ten in these other qualities either, so it would seem to be something else. It is that compassion, unlike the other five qualities, implies a sense of self in ways that the others do not, but we rays lack a sense of self. For example, a seed can confidently sprout without having any sense of self, but compassion implies a sense of self, at least as normally defined. What we do as sun rays, we do not out of a sense of any self-other dualism; there is no distinction between ourselves and others that is real, and so being compassionate toward others makes no sense. However, the fact that by our nature we give ourselves freely to be used by any and all things as they see fit might be viewed by others as extremely high compassion. However, we do not see ourselves as compassionate. So while for humans compassion is a core quality, it isn't for us, and we doubt that it is for life itself."

Sun rays, that is a highly controversial, almost heretical position. Most admired humans build their lives and consciousness around love and compassion. The more compassionate you are the more spiritual you are; the more spiritual you are, the more enlightened you are. So are you saying you and life are not enlightened? Or are you saying that the current human conception of enlightenment is different than yours in a fundamental and important way?"

Sun Rays: "Everyone likes to think that they are enlightened, the 'Crown of Creation,' and so forth, so I cannot dismiss the possibility that I do too. It is also true that even as the personification of interpretation that I do interpretations myself, and all interpretations are limited, flawed projections. All I can say is that from my perspective, compassion is not so important to me, what I am, and what I do as sun rays. You might think about my perspective on being without compassion as either oneness that is unconscious because no sense of self has yet developed and that therefore there is no awareness of oneness or, at the other extreme, it is because my perspective reflects causal and non-dual definitions of oneness. It is not that there is no more compassion or love; it is more that those experiences and interpretations are both included and transcended in a broader, more encompassing sort of interdependence."

"There will be many who will argue about that and not like it at all."

Sun Rays: "Sorry. That's not my problem. If you don't like my perspective, don't consult me. There are plenty of other perspectives that will happily validate cultural groupthink."

"That sounds a little haughty and judgmental of you, Sun Rays!"

Sun Rays: "I can understand how that would be your interpretation."

"So if you were a ten in compassion, Sun Rays, would you be different? If so, how?"

Hmmm...good question...I feel like I wouldn't have the impartiality that I need to do my job. It may be that objectivity and witnessing are in intrinsic conflict with compassion in that regard. Do I imagine myself having infinite compassion while I bake some creatures but freeze others? Do I imagine myself no longer giving myself indiscriminately, out of a desire to be compassionate and hurt no one and no thing? And if I start to discriminate, am I more or less compassionate? Most would say "less." I agree. No, I think giving without discrimination or reserve is about as compassionate as you can get, and that is my nature, but it is not a human definition of compassion, because it necessarily results in cruel deaths for many. But I don't worry about that, nor am I sorry about that. Does that make me cruel? Perhaps so, by human standards."

"Sun Rays, the purpose of this interview was not to get a dissertation on compassion, but to explore what interpretation means from your perspective. I suppose what we just got was an example of how differently you interpret compassion from most humans and why you are not a fan of human compassion. If Joseph, and humans in general, scored like you do, what difference do you think it would make in their lives?"

Sun Rays: "They would give themselves completely without fear of loss or reduction in ability or strength. Because they are humans, with human limitations, they would indeed have such reductions, so I am not saying this is possible or realistic. I am simply saying what I think they would do if they were more like me. This alone would be transformative, because it would be highly creative and passionate. However, I am not sure it would be seen as compassionate. However, for me, respect is a higher value than compassion, and giving oneself completely without fear of loss or reduction in ability or strength would be a huge source of both self-respect and respect of others, regardless of whether it was viewed as compassionate or not."

"Do you have any recommendations regarding when it would be most beneficial for me (and humans in general) to become you and act as you do?"

Sun Rays: "Yes. When persistent energy, selflessness, and non-partiality are required, whether in what you do or the interpretations that you make."

"So you view yourself as a source of non-partial, selfless interpretations?"

Sun Rays: "Yes, but only relatively so. I know I make interpretations, and that those reflect my perspective, which is only one of infinite legitimate perspectives."

"Thank you, Sun Rays. What I have heard you say is that you make interpretations, and you recognize that they are your projections, and that you are not claiming that they are better or superior to other interpretations. That sounds like relativism and the communal hug of egalitarianism to me, Sun Rays. Are you saying that all interpretations are of equal value?"

Sun Rays: "No. The value of an interpretation depends on its context, or the assumptions that it makes. Change the context, change the underlying assumptions, and you change both the value and the legitimacy of the interpretation. So you can honor and respect any interpretation within its context, like the mythology of Christianity, while questioning that context and the assumptions that it makes. In fact, you have to do this if you want credible interpretations that are wise instead of simply intelligent."

"Sun Rays, people are going to be thinking, 'That's him (Joseph) talking. This is just a way of him expressing his own opinions, but ascribing them to another source, like Biblical prophets did with God."

Sun Rays: "Of course! And they will be correct! But that is only half the story! It is not even the more important half! The rest is what I provide, as a distinct perspective, that he normally does not inhabit. What I say includes his mind, because he created me, but I also transcend his mind, because my perspective is broader and more inclusive than his. Those who do not see this or recognize this miss the point. But they are unlikely to 'get' it by merely reading what either you or I say. They have to do their own interviews."

"OK, Sun Rays! So what I hear you saying is that you refuse to represent interpretation per se, but only offer your own, as one among any, but believe that your interpretations are better than many others because they both include and transcend other, more limited interpretations. Is that right?"

Sun Rays: "Yes, that's right!"

So if this were a wake-up call from my life compass the message that I would take away is that while interpretation is unavoidable, all are not equal, and that some are more beneficial than others, because they speak from a broader context. But isn't it true that more limited interpretations, from more limited perspectives, might be more appropriate for dealing with particular issues?

Sun Rays: "Absolutely. For instance, there are situations where consulting the Queen in the above ego interview would be more appropriate and effective than consulting me."

If interpretation is unavoidable, how could it be a concept that is not conducive to enlightenment? The answer is that most interpretation is done by waking identities and involves their projections. Those interpretations are generally wrong because they are partial; they miss important elements because they do not see the broader picture. Interpretations that are more conducive to enlightenment are those that are made by, or adopted from, interviewed emerging potentials, and compared with those of waking identity and respected external sources. Therefore, in order for interpretation to continue to be a useful, beneficial concept past the personal levels of development, interpretations need to be increasingly made by potential perspectives that see what is attempting to emerge and can communicate it in ways that are understandable. This is required if we are to graduate beyond the echo chambers of groupthink and intuition.

Symbols

Multi-cultural associations to common objects and events can be found in C.G Jung's *Man and His Symbols,* and *Patterns in Comparative Religion,* by Mircea Eliade in addition to many, many other sources. Jung saw dream symbols as compensating for repressed thoughts and feelings. More broadly, symbols are everywhere and are unavoidable. They have many useful functions, as words, road signs, and traffic lights, for example. In dream interpretation, a symbol is something that stands for something else and that is generally a visual metaphor of the "real" meaning of the dream character or object. For example, cars are symbolic of the body, buildings of consciousness, and women of nurturance, fecundity, and receptivity. You may already recognize the damage that is done to the body, consciousness, and women by reducing their meaning, value, and worth to projected associations that lie outside themselves. This is the main problem that IDL has with symbolic approaches to dreams: they reduce the worth and meaning of dream, waking, and mystical experiences to our associations to them, thereby stripping them of their own vitality and reality.

IDL easily and routinely demonstrates the inability of symbols to adequately express meaning. It does so by asking you to write down your associations to a dream, which means your own projections onto it of your meanings, including whatever you believe the dream elements "symbolize." You are then asked to interview one or more character in the dream. When you do so you can then compare your associations and symbolic projections to the comments, perspectives and realities revealed by the character itself. When this is done, it is routinely observed that the perspective of the interviewed dream character is far broader than what it is assumed to symbolize. For example, if we return to the interview with "interpretation," we find that the perspective of Sun Rays is far broader than interpretation, which it considers a relatively minor aspect of its significance.

Dreamers generally view dream characters and events in symbolic terms. Consequently, IDL asks interviewed elements, "What aspect of the interviewed do you most closely represent or personify?" The answer is the character's own interpretation of its own part in the life of the dreamer. However, the character may answer, like ego as Queen did above, "Nothing! I am real!" Also, note that just because a leather jacket says it represents protection does not mean that it is *only* the sense of self-protection of the subject of the interview. It may be only that, it may say it is not a self-aspect, or it may say it is both. IDL does not assume an ontological status for interviewed emerging potentials. An interviewed jacket may be real, a self-creation or some combination. Phenomenological methods such as IDL suspend such assumptions in favor of deep listening in an integral way. It generally becomes clear that interviewed emerging potentials possess qualities that the subject does not have, or develops qualities that are only now emerging as potentials for them. It stretches the meaning of "self-aspect" to reduce such a character as Sun Rays or "Air," in the Shadow interview, to a component of some hypothetical "real" self that transcends the awareness of waking identity.

While symbolic thinking is intrinsic to living and creating meaning, the reality of these interpretations, projections, and meanings are conditional rather than absolute. This is a reason why the use of symbols in the sense of seeing dreams or life as symbolic is not conducive to enlightenment. This is because it keeps you stuck in a psychologically geocentric world view, in which you are the center of your reality because you are the source of meaning through the interpretations you make of the symbols that you find both outside yourself and within, wherever and whenever you look. When you allow interviewed dream characters and personifications of your life issues to make their own interpretations you

146

will probably find that your understanding of symbols and symbology shifts in fundamental ways.

Transference and Countertransference

"You have a very bad
case of transference."

Transference and countertransference are technical terms coined by Freud and which are still in common use in psychoanalytic and psychodynamic circles. They refer to problems with interpretation that inevitably arise in the context of these therapeutic models. One definition of transference is, "a reproduction of emotions relating to repressed experiences, especially of childhood, and the substitution of another person ... for the original object of the repressed impulses." In therapy, the common concern is that the therapist becomes a substitute parent figure for the client, which means that both his hopes and fears are unrealistically projected onto the therapist, obscuring meanings and intentions and creating multiple, complicated barriers to the therapeutic process. "The focus in psychodynamic psychotherapy is, in large part, the therapist and patient recognizing the transference relationship and exploring the relationship's meaning. Since the transference between patient and therapist happens on an unconscious level, psychodynamic therapists who are largely concerned with a patient's unconscious material use the transference to reveal unresolved conflicts patients have with childhood figures." Countertransference is defined as redirection of a therapist's feelings toward a patient, or more generally, as a therapist's emotional entanglement with a patient. Obviously, this keeps the therapist from hearing the patient clearly and objectively.

One doesn't have to ask too many questions about these concepts before they become very strange indeed. For example, if transference and countertransference occur on an unconscious level, then they occur out of awareness, correct? If so, then the subject of the transference or countertransference doesn't recognize the problem but the therapist does, correct? Since transference and countertransference are objects of discussion and treatment, then they are known about, they are not unconscious after all, at least not to the therapist. Are transference and countertransference unconscious or conscious? The answer, of course, is very clever: What is unconscious to the client is conscious to trained therapists. This is why you go to them and pay them money, because they can see where you are stuck and free you of your transferences and other unconscious processes, such as your defense mechanisms, that create dysfunction. If you minimize all of these elements, wouldn't the expected result be reduced problems with transference and countertransference and a return to health?

Research does not support psychoanalysis and psychodynamic psychotherapy. Countless research studies have not shown benefits beyond placebo, which means about a third get better, a third experience no change, while a third get worse. However, the validation and testimonials provided by the improved third, combined with the non-committal response of the second third, means that there is enough support and repeat business to create a cult following and a self-perpetuating guild. Both are true believers, the cult members, because they have been taken in by pre-rational anecdotal evidence, and the guild members because they have a financial and reputational stake in maintaining the *status quo*.

Approaches that involve projecting therapist meanings and interpretations onto clients are initially empowering, as the subject identifies with the power of the authority of the therapist, hypnotist, psychopomp, priest or shaman. The problem is twofold: the subject becomes dependent on the "healer" for changes that do not last. As a consequence, depending on others for interpretations, such as that you are in transference, projecting, personalizing or in some other way blind, is disempowering *unless* it results in an internalization of that therapeutic, healing function. Even then, these will be the interpretations and projections of your waking self sense, not of your life compass. You can be very sure that your interpretations, analysis, reasoning, beliefs or diagnosis are correct and still be completely at variance from the priorities of your life compass. Sure that you are right, you act against your own greater good, thereby destroying any chance for inner peace or integration.

Psychology makes the mistake of assuming that because professional diagnosis works in medicine that it will work in talking therapy. Because the problem is by definition unconscious, it is unknown and unknowable by the client except by another, to whom it is conscious and who has the expertise to deal with various defenses to it becoming conscious to the client. The client is thereby placed in a disempowering child-parent relationship, dependent upon the interpretations of expert external sources of objectivity called therapists. Even if this role is successfully internalized, there is no reason to believe that the results are in harmony with the priorities of one's life compass.

IDL addresses these issues by encouraging the support of expert external sources of objectivity who act primarily in support of internal sources of objectivity. These expert external interpretations either defer to or work to support the interpretations of internal sources of objectivity - interviewed emerging potentials, particularly those which score higher than the client/student in one or more of the six core qualities of confidence, empathy, wisdom, acceptance, inner peace, and witnessing. The goal is to make the client dependent on their own life compass, not on a therapist, healer or dream interpreter. In such a model issues of transference and counter-transference are minimized because the therapist/teacher is not the primary source of interpretation; interviewed emerging potentials are. When resistances arise they are interviewed so that interpretations and solutions come primarily from interviewed emerging potentials, not the therapist or subject. The therapist consistently defers to the collective wisdom of internal sources of objectivity because they recognize that such perspectives know the client/student better than the therapist possibly can and because they innately represent possibilities and potentials that are both more creative and more to the heart of the life issue of the moment.

During the interviewing process, in contrast to most therapy, the focus is not placed on the interviewer-subject relationship, but on listening to what the interviewed emerging potential has to say. The major considerations during the interviewing process are, "Is the subject in role?" "How can I help them to become more thoroughly in role, yet remaining present, aware, observant and witnessing?" Emphasis is placed on the suspension of assumptions, expectations and interpretations in order to practice deep listening to the interviewed character. Consequently, interpretations that occur are primarily made by the emerging potential. While interpretations by the interviewed and the interviewer are unavoidable, they are addressed later, in deference to what the emerging potential has to say. This structure reduces opportunities for both transference and countertransference in IDL.

The question then might arise, "Is there transference or counter-transference between the subject and the element that is being interviewed?" From the perspective of IDL, this is a ridiculous question. One could always read such possibilities in; one could argue that just because the focus of the interview is between the subject and the interviewed element, that does not mean that transference or counter-transference are not happening. What would be the source and intent of such arguments? Clearly it would be to maintain interpretive, projective control in the interpretations of the therapist by presenting an irrefutable possibility. But IDL is not about staying in control, nor is waking up contingent on the interviewer maintaining the final say regarding interpretations or what is projection and what is not. For IDL all this is disrespectful to the interviewed emerging potential and disempowering to the subject of the interview.

Outside of the interviews themselves, during the creation of action plans or the teaching of concepts such as the Drama Triangle, scripting, cognitive distortions, and meditative techniques, the focus of IDL is on teaching rather than therapeutic dialogue. Consequently, the focus is on information relevant to finding measurable solutions to specific, ongoing life concerns rather than a delving into childhood traumas or deep emotional resistances. Therefore, to the extent that transference and countertransference arise, they are more likely to be benign and not interfere with learning and practicing IDL, just as occurs in other teaching situations.

"Self-Aspects"

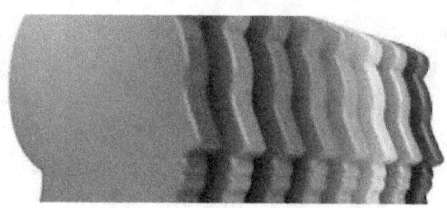

This is a common term used by almost everyone connected with understanding the "unconscious" components of psychological development. It has a number of synonyms that are subject to the same concerns when used to mean aspects of self, including "sub-personalities," "roles," "inner voices," "alter-egos," and "dissociated identities." The fundamental problem is that such terms rarely adequately describe how the "other" perceives *itself*. Does an interviewed goblin see itself as a self aspect? How do you know unless you ask it? Otherwise, isn't the assumption that it is an aspect of yourself a projection of *your* perspective rather than an objective assessment of the point of view of the interviewed character? Can you know if it is an accurate assumption or not without asking?

There are other problems. For example, I can refer to you as a "self-aspect." This is indeed true, because all I know of you is what you represent to me. You speak and act and I will see, hear, and respond to different things, in different ways, about you than someone else will, because I perceive you through the filters of my own experience. Therefore, all I can know of you are those components of your identity which are aspects of my own experience. Therefore, I can claim that you are what you represent to me. Fair enough. However, is that *all* you are? Evidence indicates otherwise. This evidence is derived from the fact that other people will take you to mean very different things by what you say and do than I do, rather like different blind men grabbing different parts of an elephant and claiming that they know what the elephant "really" is. This is equivalent to me saying, "Because you are these aspects of myself, that's who you "really" are. This is a pre-rational way of dealing with the world because it is inherently solipsistic. Even more fundamentally, there is something downright disrespectful about reducing your essence to your utilitarian value for my structure of meaning in the world. Like seeing you or objects of my experience as symbols, viewing you as a self-aspect is reductionistic. Who and what you are is forever much more than an aspect of myself.

It is due to this awareness of both a desire and a need to respect the other that IDL refuses to reduce others, including dream characters or fantasized images, to self-aspects. Instead, it chooses to pursue a middle way, where it denies that such elements are reducible to either external realities or internal self-aspects, while refusing to deny both their subjective and objective characteristics. Respecting emerging potentials is not done out of some sense of egalitarianism reminiscent of the fight for animal rights; we are not talking about animals but about self-created fantasies that lack selves. There is a genuine ontological difference. It is rather the act of respect itself, fundamental to deep listening, which is the most fundamental factor, because respect is an inherently therapeutic and productive stance to take toward all of experience.

Like most other terms that IDL does not consider to be conducive to enlightenment, this conclusion regarding self-aspects did not come from philosophy or abstract reasoning. Until sometime after 2000, I assumed that interviewed dream characters and imaginary elements were self-aspects, and I indeed used that term for decades. It only slowly dawned on me as the result of many, many interviews with spoons, storks, clouds, stars, and piles of shit that these were essentially personifications of perspectives that were self-aspects, in that they *were* self-created and were limited by the vocabulary and level of development of myself or whomever was the subject of the interview, *and* they were also autonomous and independent, in that they offered perspectives and creative ideas and solutions that could not reasonably be said to be derived from any meaningful definition of self. I must admit, with some embarrassment, that this awareness of the intrinsic autonomy of these perspectives was strongly evident to me since I began this work in 1980, but I did not draw the obvious conclusion from it for some thirty years. Such is the power of projection, groupthink and psychological geocentrism. While the definition of self can be expanded in order to include emerging potentials, in addition to anything and everything else, such a grandiose, all-inclusive definition of the self does not reflect the experiential reality of the relative autonomy of these perspectives. Their perspectives are generally both new and broader than anything a realistic self-definition can claim.

Reducing interviewed emerging potentials to self-aspects not only discounts their autonomy but attempts to reduce their ontology to a sub-function of the self. However, their perspective typically transcends that self in significant ways, including scoring higher than the interviewer on one or more of the six core qualities. If an interviewed character is in fact a rediscovered aspect of one's 'true' but 'lost' nature, how could it be either 'emerging' or 'potential'? The implication is that there is no evolution or development, only a return to a lost Eden. There is no learning, but, as Plato believed, only remembering. But this theory goes against philogyny. Evolution and development really do "go where no man has gone before." This is why Sheldrake has had trouble designing experiments that validate his morphogenic fields; every time life evolves some form, like an eye, it is doing it for the first time, regardless of how many times it has done so previously. It does so because *life wants to see* and because conditions exist for sight to emerge.

Viewing interviewed emerging potentials as neither self-aspects nor objective realities, but drawing on both, is a higher, more evolved position, because it recognizes the contributions of both objective and subjective realities. It does not insist on the conclusion demanded by Aristotelian logic: "things" must be one or the other, existing or non-existent; they cannot be both or neither. However, the brilliance of Nagarjuna is, following Gautama, that there is a middle stance which sees, acknowledges, and respects the contributions of both, yet refuses to be defined by either one.

An Interview with a Bread Knife, Lime, and Lime Tree

To get further clarity on this issue an interview with a character that is undeniably a "self-aspect" will be helpful. This might best be something that is purely personal, so that it is devoid of most collective or "archetypal" symbolic meanings. Of course, this is impossible, because meanings and interpretations can and will be projected onto any and every image one can come up with. However, something that is clearly personal is most likely to be viewed as a self-aspect. A bread knife comes to mind, the one I was using this morning to slice a small loaf for breakfast. The scene generated an alarm reaction from Ulli, my father-in-law, who was afraid I would cut my hand. That in turn caused me to ignore him and continue with the cutting, showing him that there was no blood and that I did not cut myself. While I viewed his reaction as an unsolicited attempt to rescue me, he saw it as a natural reaction to a perceived danger.

So bread knife, are you a "self-aspect" or not?
Bread Knife: I do not think I am a good example for you because people will say, "But it is a *real* bread knife." If you want to go with this

example, why don't you interview your feelings about being parented and rescued? That's plenty subjective!

OK. So what are my feelings? Hmmm... Violation; disrespect. Disrespect, mostly. So if disrespect had a color it would be lime green. It has turned into a very non-creative lime. So lime, describe yourself:

Lime: I am green and growing on a tree with a whole lot of other limes. In fact now I am changing not only into all the limes but the tree itself with all its fruit!

So Lime Tree, what do you like best about yourself?

Lime Tree: I am beautiful, peaceful, well-rooted, and I bear a rather exotic fruit that is a mixture of sour and sweet.

Is there anything you dislike about yourself Lime Tree?

Lime Tree: No!

What aspect of myself do you most represent or personify, Lime Tree?

Lime Tree: I personify many things about you: your rootedness, naturalness, peacefulness, abundance, sweetness, and your ability to be sour!

So are you an aspect of me, Lime Tree?

Lime Tree: I am whatever you want me to be, an aspect of you, a collective, archetypal motif, a representative of actual lime trees, and a relatively autonomous perspective. I don't limit myself to one or another of these categories; why should you limit me to one or the other?

Lime Tree, what do you have to do with this knife I started to interview? Lime Tree: Nothing much in particular, but we are both emerging potentials that serve similar functions. It would provide you with its perspective it you interviewed it. I don't know what that would be.

If you could change in any way you wanted, Lime Tree, would you? And if so, how?

Lime Tree: I like myself the way I am, thank you.

Lime Tree, how would you score yourself zero to ten in the six core qualities?

Lime Tree: In confidence, I am ten because I have no fear; in compassion I am ten as well, because I give myself and my fruit freely; in wisdom I do not know, because I am pure awareness, without content or thinking; in acceptance I am a ten; in peace of mind, also a ten; and in witnessing I am also a ten. If you were to score as I do you would not let the reactions of others get under your skin or irritate you! If people want to rescue you, if you became me you would just smile, because you wouldn't personalize it. Become me whenever you are around people who have a history of rescuing you or around others to help you not be caught off guard.

Lime Tree, there is no denying that you are an aspect of me, however, I can tell you that not reacting to people who attempt to rescue me is not part of who I normally am. You are suggesting that I do something that I do not normally do, nor is it something that I have at some point learned to do and forgotten. If I follow your advice I will be doing something that is not an aspect of my personality. I also do not find it realistic to imagine that the ability you possess that I do not is part of who I "really" am, that I have forgotten about or have not yet realized. In this regard, I do not see how it makes sense to think of you as a self-aspect.

Lime Tree: I agree. I think you are correct to think of me as an emerging potential because, although I am clearly an aspect of you, I am clearly a possibility for a healthier, more balanced response to the actions of others than you have at present or have had in the past in your life.

Thank you, Lime Tree. I think you have illustrated the limitations of "self-aspect" and related terms better than I have done!

How relevant is this interview? I would have to say "very," because my wife Claudia does not like it when I react to her or someone else trying to rescue me. She says I am getting into drama when I do so, and she is right! I also know that I am personalizing, which is a cognitive distortion. So this interview is not only relevant, but helpful, because becoming this lime tree when I feel an attempt to rescue me feels appropriate, workable, and realistic. It might not to someone else, but then, why should it?

Reincarnation and Karma

"You may not always end up where you thought you were going, but you'll always end up where you meant to be..."

If you are looking for a story that explains your life, who you are, why you are the way you are, and how you came to be like you are, reincarnation is for you. Consequently, reincarnation fills an important void for many people who either are not happy with the path set for them by their parents, teachers, and society, or who have walked that path and found it bankrupt. They wonder where to find a sense of life purpose and direction. Karma is the East Indian doctrine of personal cause and effect extending over lifetimes as exemplified by the sign sometimes found in metaphysical bookstores: "Shoplifting is bad karma." That means something like, "We may not catch you, but you will know what you have done and that will cause you to pay a price for it sooner or later."

Reincarnation and karma are not only very common beliefs in today's world, but very soothing. They create acceptance of our circumstances, so that we focus on making them better rather than fighting them. In many cases, acceptance is both the wiser and healthier choice. It is a way of thinking that has been called many things, including fortune, destiny, pre-determination, fate, predestination, Divine will or God's plan. It fulfills important human needs for security, acceptance, and meaning. It also generates social stability that is critical for the long-term survival of societies. For example, cultural continuity over millennia has been supported and preserved in India by the doctrine of karma and a belief in reincarnation. Buddhism, built around monasteries, would never have grown and flourished without a belief that community support of monasteries, including sending children into the Sangha, would bring good karma.

I was first exposed to reincarnation and karma when I was thirteen, through the Edgar Cayce readings. I met a number of professionals who meditated, worked on dreams, and believed in reincarnation and karma. I did too. In my adolescence I read Noel Langley's *Edgar Cayce and Reincarnation,* which explored how both worked in depth. I had dreams with reincarnation themes and I had psychic readings where I was told about past lives. In college I studied philosophy, psychology and comparative religion and learned the Hindu and Buddhist doctrinal roots and socio-cultural contexts from which twentieth-century Western ideas about reincarnation and karma sprung. I learned about how each future Dalai Lama, as a boy, recognizes and accurately picks out personal possessions from his past life. I read Ian Stevenson's *Twenty Cases Suggestive of Reincarnation,* and taught the concepts of karma and reincarnation in my early twenties. Both concepts were fundamental components of my belief system from the age of thirteen until I was in my late twenties. Therefore, I do not approach these words, concepts, and beliefs as an outsider or as someone who does not have a personal experience with their usefulness or a healthy respect for their benefits.

Sometimes I look at the injustice that belief in reincarnation causes people to accept in the world and I am stunned. Sometimes I look at the unnecessary limitations that people impose on themselves, because they believe in karma and I am appalled. Sometimes I look at the bright minds and good-hearted people who not only believe in reincarnation and karma but teach these beliefs to their children and friends and I wonder if I have entered the Twilight Zone. How could it be that I so believed in and taught these ideas for so many years of my life?

The secret is found in the evolution of our sense of self. Our prepersonal and early personal selves find developmental support from the concepts of reincarnation and karma and a belief in them. They make sense. They help explain the world and our place in it. However, the farther you go, in your own personal development, past identification with a competent social self-definition the less useful and meaningful both become.

How does the doctrine of karma become less conducive to enlightenment? India, where the doctrine of karma is still pervasive to this day, since it is a foundational element of Hinduism, provides a massive, multi-millennial demonstration of the dangers of taking on too much responsibility, due to the pervasive belief in the concept of karma. Belief in karma created an extremely stable and compliant Indian society, in which every individual was locked into the profession of his father or mother and whose choice of life partner was determined by his parents, as part of the karma he or she had chosen, before being born. The result of this belief system was highly adaptive: India has one of the most stable and impervious societies man has ever created, one that has withstood the invasions of Moguls, British colonialists, and capitalists. It even survived where and when Buddhism did not and could not. The history of karma and reincarnation in India is a powerful example of the extraordinary ability of the doctrine of karma to support individuals and societies at levels of development that require stability and security. It even provides freedom for those who have already raised families to drop out of society, become hermits, and focus on their own liberation. Karma may, in fact, be the best cognitive structure devised to date by humans for providing cultural stability and security, as well as teaching and maintaining a personal sense of responsibility.

However, what happens when the focus of development shifts from security, stability, and personal responsibility to personal level issues, such as guaranteeing human rights and egalitarianism? At this point there is a massive, unavoidable cultural collision between karma, on the one hand, and discrimination and injustice. What is responsible on one level is not responsible on the other, higher level. Karma not only explains, but actually provides for religious and divinely-sanctioned social injustice and deprivation of human rights, all in the name of personal, social, and dharmic responsibility. In the late 1940's India addressed this inconsistency with laws that outlawed the caste system. However, because you cannot outlaw the doctrine of karma, the caste system remains alive and well in India, and with it massive discrimination and injustice.

Setting aside for the moment the question of the truth or falsity of reincarnation and karma, there are important psychological reasons why these beliefs are very attractive. From about three until the mid-twenties learning to take responsibility is a core skill we must acquire if we want to live a happy life. Learning to be on time, to keep your word, obligations, and promises, to be accountable, and to accept responsibility for your actions are not only critical elements of character, but fundamental signposts of maturity. If you don't do these things, you have not developed a healthy waking identity. Of course, many people never learn personal responsibility or apply it only in limited ways. Therefore, to the extent that the concept of "karma" helps people to be more responsible, it is an important and beneficial aspect of waking up. Belief in reincarnation and karma is quite helpful for the attainment of those stages of enlightenment that are associated with building a strong, stable sense of who you are, which means the three pre-personal stages and the first two personal stages. Since competency at these stages, including a strong ability to be responsible, is a pre-requisite for higher stage advancement, a strong case can be made of the absolute necessity for a belief in some mythology, meaning "system of truth," like the dharma/karma/reincarnation constellation. If you are irresponsible and need to learn to be more responsible, the concept of karma is invaluable, because it makes you responsible for everything that happens to you. Because we all start out self-centered and irresponsible, birth is constantly generating people who can benefit from the concept of karma, with reincarnation there to fill in the details.

While having a strong sense of self generally translates into competency within the expectations and demands of your family, work, and society, both growth and the attainment of enlightenment past mid-personal stages of development involves the deconstruction of your sense of who you are. This does not mean that you get rid of your identity, but rather that you develop objectivity about it and toward it; your persona or sense of who you are no longer defines your identity but rather serves as a useful set of tools for addressing those issues that are important to you today. This is a huge difference, because when you believe in reincarnation and karma you think you are that responsible self. When you objectify it, that self no longer controls you through its structures, roles, and definitions of appropriate and inappropriate behavior, truth, and reality. The fear is that you will thereby become irresponsible when you give up the doctrines and beliefs that supported the development of that self; instead, what you find is that you access domains of freedom that you did not know existed because your belief in reincarnation and karma blinded you to them. You retain your learned ability to be responsible; the moral regression you imagine or fear does not occur, but your desire to be responsible is no longer validated or justified by a responsible self or a metaphysical rationalization for why you need to be responsible. Instead, you are responsible because when you do so you honor life. It's as simple as that.

There are no shortcuts to the transpersonal. Before you can be nobody, you have to first become somebody. You have to build a competent, confident, responsible, sense of self before you can objectify yourself from it. Those who think they can bypass this process by going straight into the ashram or meditating for hours a day, by becoming psychic, or by learning energy healing, are actually extending their developmental process by postponing the creation of a strong, autonomous sense of self.

While belief in dharma, karma and reincarnation can provide major support in the development of that stable self, IDL believes that there are better ways to do so that are less likely to have to be unlearned at some future point.

Belief in reincarnation and karma, like the doctrines of fate, luck, predestination, and Divine accomplish two schizoid things at the same time. On the one hand, they make you responsible for everything that happens to you: it is all happening because you "created" it, if not by your present choices, then by something you did in a distant past existence. Get robbed? You were probably a robber in your past life. Lose a child to cancer? This is a lesson you needed to learn in order to burn off karma from past lives and to grow in peace, forgiveness, and mercy. Contact an incurable disease? You are burning off even more karma. Do you find yourself in an unequal society, in which people discriminate against you and avenues to better yourself are closed to you and your children? No problem! You are exactly where you chose to be! You are where you need to be in order to grow most quickly, because everything is in divine order. Karma and reincarnation thereby rescue you from a sense of victimization within the Drama Triangle.

On the other hand, does not belief in dharma, karma and reincarnation make you a victim of some process that you either caused but have forgotten, or of some force or entity bigger than yourself, like fate, luck, or God? The role of victim is very powerful, because even if you have victimized yourself, you are both to blame and blameless at the same time; there are powers above and beyond you that control your destiny. Since this is true, how could you *not* be a victim? There is a fundamental and powerful distinction which, if not recognized, creates a trap of self-centeredness that all the meditation and mystical experiences in the world will not burn away. This is the distinction between being a victim, such as a child to cancer or of an earthquake, and *victimization,* which is a further, psychological and optional step that is a disastrous. Not only does something bad happen to you but you perceive it as victimization, that is, that something or someone is either persecuting, punishing or "testing" you, like Job, in the Old Testament, thought God was doing. The problem is that victimization demands a self that is victimized. There is no transpersonal anything as long as you are addicted to a sense that you are somebody or something. To the extent that your belief in reincarnation and karma keep you believing in some self, whether you call it ego, persona, "higher self," soul, Atman, or Self, that accrues karma, you will maintain a personal identity and so block your own development into the transpersonal. You will confuse your mystical state openings into the energic, subtle, causal and non-dual domains as "proof" of your transpersonal development when in fact your identity remains anchored in personal realms, supported by beliefs that tether it and allow it to go no further.

It was not until my thirties that it dawned on me just how grandiose belief in reincarnation and karma was. Was I really that responsible? Was I really that powerful? If I was so knowledgeable before I was born, why did I not have the foresight to see major ways I would complicate my life unnecessarily and consequently structure a future that could avoid such unnecessary misery? Did I really want to believe that children "chose" to be born to child molesters? Are children "meant" to die from cancer? Are people born and raised in poverty, like those born into the *sudra* caste in India, where they were "meant" to be? For a while I decided that the pre-existent self must simply be so eager to incarnate, that it takes a perspective similar to someone on a mountain, for whom the lands below look flat and the way ahead clear, because the swamps, alligators, pythons, and mosquitoes are invisible from such a height. However, in time it dawned on me that my challenges in life must then not be due to karma, but my stupidity and ignorance. Past lives and karma no longer worked to explain how I was now viewing life. However, I still knew the evidence for reincarnation, and I had no better explanation.

Reincarnation is true from some legitimate "real" and valid perspectives, just as the sun rising and setting is "real" for our senses. It certainly seems to be true in at least some cases for at least some individuals, and if it is, then the doctrine of *karma* must have some reality as well. In addition, I would like to be able to set a clear intention to come back and complete the work I have started, or at least kick the IDL ball a little farther down the field, closer to the goal posts. And because I have no certainty about what is or is not true, I will continue to set a clear intention about coming back and continuing my work. This is magical and delusional from some perspectives and true and valid from others. It may well be a rationalization or a hedging of my bets against what I do not know.

However, I neither understand reincarnation and karma in the context of justice or enlightenment, nor do I, on the whole, find the benefits of these beliefs outweighing the obstacles they create for development past the mid-personal. So it probably sounds contradictory that I do not consider either karma or reincarnation to be, in the balance, helpful, even if they are somehow or other both true for some people and still useful for me. This is because once you accept that enlightenment follows an evolutionary, developmental arc, you understand that what is good and useful at some stages of development is harmful and pernicious at others. If you look at how the belief in reincarnation and karma actually affect lives, you find that they often keep people trapped in stories about some past that no longer exists and in a sense of personal responsibility that is grandiose. These beliefs are also used to create a mystique that first opens people up and then leads them into a *cul de sac*. For instance, take the extremely successful career of Brian Weiss, who has been able to leave his practice of psychiatry and instead make a living selling books and giving talks on reincarnation to audiences around the world. You read his books and go to his talks and accept reincarnation and karma. What then? Do you transcend and include those beliefs in a larger developmental spiral or do you stay stuck as you allow them to continue to define who you are? Are the problems you are encountering today really due to what you did in some past life? Are you actually that omniscient, powerful, and grandiose as to believe that you created your life conditions? Do you really believe you have that much control over the world, others, and yourself? How can it be that you are so all-knowing and all-powerful and yet you are not able to discipline yourself to meditate, exercise, stop personalizing or stop eating junk food?

You are simply not as responsible for who you are and what has happened to you as the doctrine of karma insists that you are. Society, culture, your parents and your teachers are primarily responsible for how you think, feel, and act, and what you believe. If you had been born to different parents, in another culture, and were brought up speaking a different language, wouldn't you largely be a different person? People try hard to minimize this reality by pointing to psychological traits that are "inborn." However, can't the same be said for a snowflake? Each has an "inborn" destiny to be six-sided that has nothing to do with karma or reincarnation, yet each is unique and distinct, and that also has nothing to do with karma or reincarnation.

Most people simply refuse to accept that they could and would have been an entirely different person with different thoughts, interests, and beliefs if they had been born into a different context. The idea is too threatening to their sense of who they are because they depend on their sense of self for their security, stability and meaning. They can't imagine life otherwise. Therefore, they manufacture belief in different forms of predestination, of which karma and reincarnation are merely one variety. Functionally, reincarnation and karma simply extend, validate and expand your life script, the pre-determined story that you follow. You hear and repeat stories to yourself that provide you security by explaining why you are who you are and by validating beliefs about who you will become in this life and after death. The underlying question is, "Why do you need such validation?" Do you, or do you simply *think* you need such validation? Is this need real and legitimate or is it merely a cognitive delusion? In the karmic version of reality, who you were predestined to be is inescapable; you cannot escape your karmic scripting. Once you are inside a particular mythic belief system it is logically consistent, like geocentrism. It is only when you step outside of it that you recognize its limitations. Predestination and pre-determination turn personal choice into an illusion and therefore relegate you to the position of victim in the Drama Triangle, with no escape.

IDL views reincarnation in a way that is similar to how most people view geocentrism. We have proof that that the sun revolves around the earth. All we have to do is look up and point to prove it. It is undeniable, and sensory existence is based on this undeniable, sensory-apparent, common sense reality. Therefore, we can say, with sincerity and certainty, that geocentrism is a fact. However, since Copernicus, we know that this fact is a relative truth and not an absolute one. It is helpful and vital for sensory survival, but is untrue and therefore less helpful and in fact detrimental to growth into mid-personal developmental stages and beyond. We know that a belief in geocentrism past the mid-personal is a barrier to the deconstruction of self, because it is a belief system that assumes that the self is the center of reality. As long as one makes such an assumption, how is it possible to outgrow a belief in who we think we are, regardless of what mystical experiences one has? The psychopathic distortions of the self that affect meditators, shamans, drug takers and near-death experiencers who access energic, subtle, causal and non-dual realities are testimony to the fact that Hinduism and Buddhism never recognized or saw through this problem, even with the Buddhist concept of *anatma*. This is because belief in reincarnation and karma inherently generate a belief in and attachment to a self.

Today I take a phenomenological stance toward these beliefs, a stance that I recommend that you play with and see if it works for you. A phenomenological stance suspends judgment and belief, meaning you neither believe nor disbelieve in reincarnation or karma because, like geocentrism, while you respect their usefulness at certain levels of development and perspectives, you recognize their limits at others. Therefore, you hold them as relative, not absolute, truths, from a phenomenalistically-based perspective of multiperspectivalism. This is a mouthful, but it is actually quite simple. You simply observe experience with clear meditative mindfulness, without the need to explain or justify it or make it meaningful by telling yourself explanatory stories, called "beliefs," in an attempt to explain life. You can do so when you recognize that there is no "you" that is born or dies, there is no self to protect or defend by the weaving of elaborate "Atman projects."

Just as you do not have to be Hindu or Buddhist to believe in karma, you do not have to be an Indian in order to be damaged by its implications for your development. One Muslim wrote, "In Islam, (believing you are where you were meant to be) is not a defeatist attitude or leaving all to fate. We are to endeavor to do our very best and then leave it to our creator to decide (our fate). It is rather magical really... As our creator is the biggest planner... We plan but our creator decides what is best for us." One doesn't have to be religious to believe in some version of this idea; you will find it in most spiritual new agers and atheists, like Buddhists, and even some secular humanists. You routinely find it in people who justify their mistakes or ill-treatment as a child or by a previous partner by saying, "If that misfortune hadn't happened, I wouldn't be who I am today." The implication is that some horrific injustice was necessary, justified, "right," and pre-determined.

Even many scientists think this way. It is an unrecognized cognitive distortion, with rational rather than emotional roots. It is a cognitive distortion because it overlooks the fact that if you had a different past you would indeed be a different person today, and who is to say that person would not be healthier, more balanced, and more capable of generating benefits to society than who you are today? You don't know that; you simply choose to believe that who you are is who you were "meant" or "fated" or "predestined" or "karmically predetermined" to be because you can't imagine being someone else and you want to feel validated in the choices you have made in your life and the person you have become ("Even my bad choices were necessary and good because without them I would not be the person I am today."). But, "If we'd been born where they were born and taught what they were taught, we would believe what they believe." This is from a sign inside a church in Northern Ireland, explaining the origin of intolerance and hate.

When you are told that you are responsible for how people treat you, that you get as good as you give, and that you are where your choices have placed you in life, what is the function of such statements? On the one hand, the message is, "make the best of your circumstances." On the other hand, aren't you being told that "You are so powerful that by your choices you control how other people think about you and act toward you, even when you don't realize it?" Are you not being told, "Don't rock the boat by denying your responsibility?" Or that "Everything is in divine order; accept yourself, your life and your fate!" Isn't the subtext, "If you sit down and shut up, you will make life easier for others, and therefore for yourself?"

If society is able to convince you that your concerns, such as a lack of opportunity for education or employment, are all about your karma and not about social policy, or exploitation by the greedy and selfish, then you will go away and leave politicians, bosses and the business of the world alone. It will never cross your mind to demand that abuse stop, because after all, it's your karma. If Islam destroys Buddhism in India and Chinese communism destroys Buddhism in Tibet, it is the karma of Buddhism. If America is destroyed by its corruption and delusion of exceptionalism it is its destiny.

If you think this way will you even expect respectful communication from others? Isn't disrespectful communication by parents and teachers justified by asserting that you have attracted what you need to learn? Isn't this how parents justify child abuse and how governments justify incarceration and war? Why advocate reform where you work or in education or government, since the powers that be are working out their karma, just as you are? Why expect anything of your politicians? If they are incompetent or corrupt, isn't it only because that is where their karma put them? If you hold them accountable, or to expect them to be honest, responsible, and courageous. are you not interfering with their karma? Your job is to be accountable, honest, responsible, and courageous, in submission to *your* karma; that of others is none of your business. If you focus on burning off your own karma, you will get your reward in future lives and those corrupt politicians will get theirs. In the meantime, accept your victimization with equanimity. If people don't treat you with respect, it's your problem, not theirs, because you attracted this treatment as your karma.

Looked at from such a perspective, the doctrine of karma is the Drama Triangle on steroids. It is psychopathic and self-destructive. People only continue to believe in it because they ignore or rationalize away such obvious implications of a belief not only in karma, but fate, predestination and luck. Karma is your rescuer because it teaches you to be responsible and to live a life that is in alignment with your dharma, or your divinely-directed life path to liberation. However, because it makes everything your responsibility, karma is the persecutor, turning you into the victim of the decisions of others, such as your parents and the culture in which you are embedded. Consequently, you are blind to the chronic persecution and abuse that you choose to carry as a mark of your superior character. The result is that karma keeps you stuck in all three roles of the Drama Triangle: rescuer, persecutor and victim. There is no peace of mind or enlightenment when you choose to live within the Drama Triangle.

There is considerable evidence that thankfully, we humans can and do change our childhood scripts and cherished belief systems. This implies that while predestination and all forms of determinism, including karma and reincarnation, may make sense in theory and even be supported by convincing anecdotal evidence and personal testimony, they can be effectively and productively ignored, neutralized, and overcome in practice, without thereby ignoring that very real constraining contexts do exist. Your decisions can and do change your life scripting, and therefore impact all sorts of things with predictable outcomes. However, in order to do so, you first must become aware of your life script, the basic life decisions that you have made that determine who you are and how your life is supposed to turn out. Belief in reincarnation and karma are two examples. Then you have to evaluate these assumptions, sort through them, and decide what is beneficial and what needs to be tossed in the dumpster. At this point you can set new goals for yourself that take your scripting into account, but are not thereby limited by it or to it. The problem is that who you think you are may be so caught up in your scripting that you are addicted to it; to get rid of your cherished assumptions about the nature and meaning of life may infer that you won't know who you are any more, and that can be quite threatening. This is another basic reason why it often feels safer to stick with the grandiosity created by belief in the cognitive distortion of some form of predestination.

Those that outgrow subjective submergence in their life scripts gain access to personal developmental levels of self-determination. They typically mistake this for transpersonal decision-making ability when it is nothing of a kind. Being able to make choices independently of your life script does not imply an ability or interest in listening or conforming to the priorities of your life compass. That is an entirely different matter, and we can observe the multiple limitations that arise, for example in the libertarian glorification of personal freedom.

Overcoming the pre-personal and early personal aspects of determinism is why IDL teaches script analysis and goal setting. It teaches the subordination of personal goals to the priorities of life, as represented by a collective of healthy interviewed emerging potentials, as a means of overcoming mid- and late personal aspects of determinism, disguised as personal freedom. Consequently, outgrowing dependency on belief in reincarnation and karma is another area in which IDL interviewing can be very helpful. Most of the emerging potentials you get to know could care less about karma, past lives, or reincarnation. Your life compass probably will be found not to care either. This is because not having been born and having no stable or "real" self, interviewed emerging potentials and your life compass have no self to defend or rationalize. Life itself, as revealed by IDL interviewing, does not seem to care. Only you do. Why might that be?

Few interviewed emerging potentials seem to believe in karma. If the wheel of cause and effect is such an important, fundamental statement about the nature of reality, why do they not? Could it be that because they encompass your own level of development and then add their own that they have outgrown it? Could it be that as you practice identifying with their perspectives, that you will outgrow it as well? IDL predicts that you will, and that is a prediction that you can put to the test in your own life by doing interviews and applying in your life those recommendations that make sense to you.

What takes the place of karma? One possibility is a growing reliance on the seven octaves of the round of every breath you take. Reincarnation, fate, karma, and predestination support a limited definition of one of the six core qualities, acceptance. Such beliefs create both a sense of meaning for life and a way to stop fighting things that one is powerless to change, so that energy can be focused on building who we are, where we are. Because we all need acceptance, particularly as children, this way of thinking is useful, important, and valuable. However, acceptance is only one of the six core qualities and the six core qualities are only one of seven octaves of enlightenment. The abuses and irrationality that accompany karma, fate, and predestination are an example of the imbalances that follow when we emphasize one quality over the others.

In this regard, IDL provides an antidote to too much acceptance by also emphasizing wisdom and objectivity. As we develop these qualities we learn to think and question our beliefs; we see both their usefulness and their partiality; we learn why and how we need to supplement them with a balance of the other five core qualities.

While IDL respects the amazing usefulness of karma, fate, and predestination for pre-personal levels of development, it is appalled that intelligent, rational people not only defend it, but continue to believe in it. This is testimony to the reality that cognitive distortions are always with us; they just become subtler, requiring higher, more refined levels of objectivity to recognize. The more you outgrow your socially-contrived definition of who you are the more likely you are to develop the objectivity required to see that karma encourages the taking on of far too much responsibility while assuming far too much predestination and determinism. As such, reincarnation and karma are primarily for the benefit of building and maintaining an early personal level of development.

What are the alternatives? How about internalizing the perspectives of interviewed emerging potentials that are more awake than you are? How about re-scripting your life using triangulation? How about moving beyond scripting, drama, and predestination by following the recommendations of your interviewed emerging potentials? How about living moment to moment within the span of each breath?

We have seen how, within Hinduism and Buddhism, reincarnation and karma are both components of a broader concept, *dharma*, or divine will, law, or order. To say "it is your dharma" is a way of saying, "it is occurring according to divine order." That means, "Everything is predestined by divine law." We will now see if dharma will personify itself for us and grant us an interview, as a way to gain another perspective on both karma and reincarnation.

By all means, continue to believe in reincarnation and karma if that works for you. However, consider the possibility of suspending both your belief and disbelief and see what happens. IDL recommends such an approach because it gets you and your assumptions out of the way. Normally they stand between you and experience. If you do so, you may discover that what you saw as reincarnation and karma are something much broader and grander, just as we do when we move from a Ptolemaic to a geocentric world view.

An Interview with Dharma

"Dharma, when I think of you I immediately think of the Buddhist wheel of dharma, representing the interdependent nature of existence. Is it OK if I use that image to personify you?"

Dharma: "Sure! Why not?"

"Dharma, tell me about yourself..."

Dharma: "I am a powerful concept created by humans to generate a sense of stability, meaning, and purpose for life. I am both an outer and inner compass, in that I am cosmic order as well as internal, personal destiny. I am a collective thought form with a life of my own. For example, you could pray to me and tap into me and you could piggy-back on my world view and consciousness. This is essentially what people do when they believe in me. It leads them to think I am real."

"What do you like best about yourself?"

Dharma: "That I am highly useful for these purposes for many people.

"What, if anything, do you dislike most about yourself?"

Dharma: "I am also an aspect of you and therefore I have heard what you have said about me, including your doubts and concerns about me. I fully agree. People can and should outgrow me, and when they do not or will not, their development is slowed or stopped."

"Dharma, how do I know that is not just me putting words into your mouth in order to validate my own biases and prejudices?"

Dharma: "I can say whatever I want to say. I don't need to please you, and I don't need to validate your biases and prejudices in order to feel good about myself. However, you don't have to believe that. Humans generally choose to believe those things that validate their own biases."

"Do you have biases and prejudices, Dharma?"

Dharma: "Yes. But they are different, because my context is different."

"What do you mean?"

Dharma: "My bias is that I am only necessary to the extent that people need thoughts and concepts in order to orient themselves within life.

Once they grow into contact with life itself, it orients them, not their thoughts and concepts. My bias is that I am OK to use for those humans that either need to develop strong, stable thoughts and concepts to direct their development, or for those who have not yet outgrown their attachment to their thoughts and concepts. For those who have, I am merely a tool. In addition, I wish humans did a better job of teaching the relativity of my value, including the goal of eventually outgrowing me. I am like a ladder, like you mentioned earlier; once it has served its purpose and you are where the ladder takes you, do you need it any more?"

"Dharma, what aspects of humanity do you most closely represent or personify?"

Dharma: "As mentioned previously, stability, order, and divine law."

"If you could change in any way you wanted, would you? And if so, how?"

Dharma: "Yeah. I wish I could change into shapes that would teach people the relativity of my usefulness and that would help them to outgrow me and put me down. It's hard work always trying to live up to the unrealistic fantasies and delusions of humanity. I think I would prefer to be a pinwheel! I would still be round, with multiple elements, reminiscent of my role of Wheel of Dharma, but I would be fragile, useless, and fun. As a pinwheel, I am not something to be taken seriously, yet I can be appreciated for what I am: something to hold into the wind and watch as my colors spin, creating a blur of colors!"

"Why do you not want to be taken seriously, Dharma?"

Dharma: "Because I am taken far too seriously by far too many humans. It's not good for them and frankly, it is boring for me."

"Pinwheel, how do you score yourself zero to ten in the six core qualities?"

Pinwheel: "In confidence I am ten because I can't die. In this regard, I am the same as I was before; I was a ten in confidence as Dharma too, but now my confidence is clearly not based on being much of anything. Before it looked like my confidence was due to my omniscience, omnipotence, and omnipresence. In compassion I am a nine, because I care enough about others to die to my identity. Others may find this selfish if they need me and depend on me, because they may feel that I am abandoning them. But I actually must transform if they are to become self-reliant. Regarding wisdom, I think I'm a nine too. I see I still have things to learn and contexts to grow into, and I am wise enough to let go of constraining contexts that no longer work to define me. Regarding acceptance, I am a ten, because I accept people needing me as Dharma and I accept my own desire to change. Regarding inner peace, I am a nine, and I am definitely scoring higher than I was as Dharma. I can tell you that when I was Dharma, I thought I was a ten in inner peace because I was imperturbable and a witness to everything. But now I see that my inner peace was really only about a six, because it depended on remoteness of a causal or formless sort, even though I took a subtle level form as a wheel of dharma. Now I have deep inner peace while enmeshed in the illusoriness of the world and the delusions of the human mind. It grows out of my lightness and playfulness! Regarding witnessing, I think I have also grown in that area as well, because before my witnessing and clarity was a function of my transcendent, formless remoteness. I inhabited a context that included and transcended everything. Now I represent a context that is reverse: I transcend everything, but the emphasis is on what I include. I'm here to grow! I'm here to be alive! I'm here to experience! I'm here to play!"

"Hmmm...I'm not so sure I understand, but that's OK...I've gotta digest that...So if you were a human, would you live your life differently?"

Pinwheel: "Oh, definitely! And it would depend on what stage of development I was in as a human! The main thing I would do if I were a human is to learn multiple authentic perspectives that are not stereotyped social roles and learn how to switch in and out of them based on the circumstances. This is what you call 'multi-perspectivalism.' The reason I think it is important is that it frees children and adults up to be adaptive and flexible while providing them with the security and structure of definite and specific roles required by particular life demands, like work or school."

"What do you think about reincarnation and karma?"

Pinwheel: "I don't think about them. It's boring. I don't need them. Personally, I don't believe in any form of predestination, nor do I believe in this divine order stuff. If people knew me like I know myself, they would know that I am not divinely ordered and they would also know that stuff happens that I can't or don't predict. They don't want to know that because it scares them. However, I can see why and how people need me and why they created me. I can respect that. However, there are times when I wish they would listen to me instead of telling me who and what I am. It's like I'm just another character in their scripted play; I have to act out my role; they won't let me be free to be myself! Who likes that??"

"Pinwheel, when do you most recommend that I - or humans in general - become you?"

Pinwheel: "I have no recommendations or preferences about that. First people have to learn that I, as a dharmic pinwheel, exist. Then they have to decide for themselves when and if I have uses for them. Then they need to become me in those times and see what the results are for them in their life."

"OK, thanks, Pinwheel. What I have heard you say is that you find being Dharma somewhat of a burden. It is too much of a structured context for you and you get bored with it. You would rather have your own life and be something experiential and playful, like a pinwheel. I also heard that you consider this to be a higher state of development for you than

Dharma, which most humans that believe in Dharma equate with the Ultimate. So you seem to be telling us not to stop there, that there is something beyond you..."

Pinwheel: "Look, just because I can only see to pinwheel doesn't mean there isn't a lot of good stuff for me to grow into beyond that. I am just talking about the next step in my own process of waking up, as Dharma."

"Right. So if I were to hear what you are saying as a wake-up call from my life compass it would be emphasizing more cosmic humor and not as much abundance, and least of all luminosity! It is interesting to me how you different perspectives will emphasize different components. It seems to me this is in order to generate some higher order balance that you think I need?

Pinwheel: "Right. A different person will get different results when they interview, based on what their level of development is and what requires balancing. And yeah, I'm a vote for more cosmic humor in your consciousness!"

"Thanks, Pinwheel!"

Pinwheel: "You're welcome! Any time! I'm not going anywhere!"

Souls and Life After Death

We are confirmed in our belief of life after death by countless testimonials from near death and mystical experiences, as well as dreams and evidential communications with the deceased through mediums and channels. In addition, there are many accounts of serendipitous occurrences that can only be rationally explained by the presence or involvement of a deceased person. Our belief in life after death is fueled by a powerful psychological desire to supply meaning to life by not having it end as well as a desire to not lose contact with our loved ones. We know that a belief in life after death helps us to deal with our fear of physical and mental suffering at death and consoling ourselves and others over the loss of loved ones. Here is an example from a recent posting on Facebook and the comments it elicited:

Posting: "Today God took an angel from my life...I know that Jack is in Heaven...God Bless and Rest in Peace."

Comments:

"God BLESS! God's heaven embraces and celebrates Jack's arrival HOME. He is always with you as you remember him as we move forward in linear time."

"May the memories bring joy to your heart and strength to your soul."

"Praying for you to feel God's comfort & peace."

"May God bless his dearly departed soul and give you comfort...Now he is in heaven and with good company. He is your Angel. He never left you."

Do we need to mirror someone else's belief system in order to be compassionate? This is what the other respondant's to the posting did. How do we demonstrate compassion and acceptance and at the same time stay authentic? What did I write in response to Jack's death? "I am sure Jack grew from knowing you and by making such a huge difference in your life. That is as good a definition of a life well lived as any."

A belief in life after death gives us a way to console ourselves in our loss. However, it can also give us a reason to avoid saying goodbye to dying loved ones or to people that we know we are unlikely to ever see again, since we don't believe this is the last time we will ever see them - we will be reunited after death. Knowing that there will be a glorious reunion in the afterlife, we can avoid confronting inevitability, along with the impotence and loss of meaning it often implies. However, by imagining a future reunion we deprive ourselves of getting closure or of saying "thank you" at a depth often only stimulated by finality, and learning to let go.

When all the good reasons for believing in life after death are contemplated, most people arrive at the conclusion that they do indeed have a soul that will live on, and that the skepticism of doubters is based either on ignorance of this information or on their own unwillingness to be swayed by the evidence. As someone who has believed in life after death for most of my life, I would have to place myself in the second category, being unwilling to be swayed by the evidence, in contrast to what I have believed for most of my life. I have studied and read the evidence since I was thirteen. Over many years, I have had a number of evidential dream, channeled, and serendipitous validations of life after death. If that is so, why am I not now swayed by the evidence?

Many people associate non-belief in souls with secular humanism, atheism, scientism, and a disavowal of all things religious and spiritual. They may not be familiar with the possibility of simple suspension of belief or disbelief, which is different from agnosticism, a position of active doubt toward metaphysical constructs, like God. Irreligion, humanism, and agnosticism are not accurate descriptions of the position of IDL regarding souls and life after death, although IDL encourages doubt as a form of healthy questioning. Its position is phenomenological, which says, "Attempt to suspend all your beliefs, practice deep listening to wake-up calls and see what happens."

Let us back up and get some background. What does it mean to have a soul? For most people having a soul means that they will not "really" die. Beyond the reassurance and the security this belief brings, it means they will see their departed loved ones again some day, that they aren't "really" dead. In this regard, belief in souls is a way to combat grief, loss, and loneliness. It provides fundamental meaning, acceptance and a purpose to life that transcends their individual existence. As such it is inspiring and often transformative. Since people who believe in the afterlife are confident they will never die and therefore have good reason to feel emotionally secure, that raises an interesting question: Would the need for the idea of "soul" exist if people did not feel emotionally insecure? Why do we want and need emotional security? Is it because we are afraid? Is it not true that the less fear we have, the less emotional security we need? If we do not need emotional security, are we more or less likely to need the concept of "soul?" To what extent is a belief in soul an attempt to rescue ourselves from our fears of death, loss and oblivion? Are those fears forms of victimization within the Drama Triangle?

Some will respond by thinking, "I don't believe in souls because I am emotionally insecure but because there is overwhelming evidence that souls exist." These stories are convincing, inspirational and give my life meaning." "Even skeptical people who have near death experiences come back convinced that there is life after death." IDL agrees with those people and with that evidence. The issue for IDL is not the evidence itself but the meaning, relevance, and function of that evidence. What do we do with it? What is its function? Why is it important to us? Why does it matter? These are the same questions we ask of dreams. We do not generally look for evidence that a dream is "real," although some certainly do. Instead, we look for the *meaning* of the dream. Why did we have it? What functions does it serve?

What does it mean to have a soul? Let's look at some of the common meanings for "soul."

An eternal self.

Life after death.

Continuity of consciousness between lives.

The continuation of something other than the *skandhas*. This is a Buddhist concept, referring to the five constituents of the self. Essentially, these five are sensory experience, feeling, imagery, thoughts and consciousness itself. The idea in Buddhism is that when these stop interacting, the delusion of self-existence stops. Normally, desire keeps them interacting between lives. However, if the self is a soul that is defined by a continuation of the *skandhas,* then the soul is not eternal. This is the position of Buddhism: yes, there is a soul that survives death and that reincarnates, but it is the product of desires which cause its components to interact and generate the delusion we call ourselves, even after we die and in the absence of "gross" sensory, worldly experience. For Buddhists, your soul is essentially a delusion created by attachment to your thoughts, feelings, images, and sensations. The less you identify with them, the less likely you are to reincarnate. This approach assumes that reincarnation is something to be avoided by most, since life is a state of suffering, but that noble souls choose to incarnate for service to others, as a selfless act and despite the suffering it necessarily entails.

To avoid this challenge to the immortality of our souls, we have to define it as something other than continuation of the *skandhas*. What does that mean? If the five *skandhas* are essentially sensation, thought, feeling, imagery, and consciousness itself, what do you have left after you subtract all of those things? What does it mean to speak of identity apart from consciousness? Can you have memory or identity apart from consciousness? How? What does that mean?

If your soul is not your *skandhas*, then your consciousness does not carry your memories. Something bigger does. In esoteric literature, this is often referred to as the "akashic records," meaning a storehouse of knowledge that transcends your identity. However, if this is the case, in what sense do "you" exist if you have neither identity nor consciousness?

Another common assumption is that you live on after you die as "you," your waking persona or sense of who you are. This is the common sense, naive realism view of life after death. You pretty much stay "you" after you die. This would mean that the five *skandhas* continue to exist and interact after you die. You continue to have a sensory reality, images, feelings, thoughts, and consciousness. This implies that there continues to be an external "other" that is the source of your experiences. Otherwise, what do you interact with after you die, your own dreamlike delusions? Your fantasies? The Egyptians certainly believed that one lived on after death in a concrete, literal way that required food, favorite possessions and the preservation of the body. Death, at least for royalty, was like packing to go away on a long trip. Today many people still believe this but only in a metaphorical way. After we die we will find other people, learning, books and places such as halls of learning. When pressed, these tend to become figurative or metaphorical allusions, since it is hard to explain how or why you would have communities or books after death and how those things would function. Do you communicate telepathically? If so, then you know everyone's thoughts and everyone knows your thoughts. How do you filter out all that information that you "know" so you only focus on what you "need" to know? What happens if you don't want to know what someone else is thinking? What happens when you want some privacy? Do people have vocal chords if they don't need to speak? If they don't need to eat, do they have mouths? If so, why? If they don't have mouths, are they still humans? Are the dead simply beings of light, floating around like fireflies on a summer's night? One common explanation is that physical life is only one dimension and that the soul keeps growing in other dimensions. We "go on" to schools of "higher learning." If this is the case, how can death be a state of oneness? Doesn't this make it another dimension, like life on another planet or movement into some shamanic visionquest?

I raise these questions as someone who has been a true believer in souls and the after-life for quite a few years of my life. When I was five years old I would walk into the living room some evenings when my parents and grandparents would be sitting around a card table, watching a Ouija Board spell out messages from a deceased spirit. I have attended seances and channelings at which departed entities spoke and told me useful information. I am familiar with the literature on psychic visitations, psychical research, and out of the body experiences. One of the first influential books I read in my early teens was *Communication with the Spirit World,* by Johannes Greber, which I found in my grandmother's metaphysical library. The Edgar Cayce readings, in which I was steeped from thirteen until twenty, assume both souls and life after death. In the late 1990's, when I was a minister and administrator at a New Age church in Scottsdale, Arizona, I preached about souls and life after death. I have conducted interviews with people who have had near death experiences and have written a book about them. I am quite familiar with many vivid accounts of contacts with deceased relatives and spirits. Therefore, it is difficult to dismiss my current disbelief on lack of either knowledge or personal experience.

I have always been curious, which has led me to ask questions about all sorts of things, including my own assumptions about life after death. Why is it that a belief in life after death comes natural to children and most people, whether or not they have learned to think or be rational? Does the near universality of this belief validate it or merely indicate that everyone has to evolve through and beyond pre-personal developmental levels, where such beliefs are self-validating, just like the belief that the sun orbits the earth? Why was it that those who believe in souls do not seem to be at a higher level of development than those who don't? Why is it that people who don't believe in souls can be as "spiritual" as those who do? My questions about these beliefs, assumptions and world views were not a matter of proving or disproving evidence in souls. I was interested in the function of a system of belief or world view. What did this or that belief say about who a person was, that they chose to believe or not believe in something, such as souls and life after death? What was the result for a person of holding a viewpoint or holding its opposite? Did it matter?

If you have a dream, as I have done, of a deceased good friend or relative giving you meaningful information that you later convey to a relative, as you were asked to do in the dream, you have all the data you need to *know* that your friend is alive and well in some sort of place, in something that looks like his actual body, living a life that appears to be similar to what you and he shared while he was alive. This situation is similar to seeing the sun rise and set. How can anyone doubt that reality? It is a common sense, universal experience. Yet we know that the sun does not rise or set, even though we commonly state that reality in our daily language. It is more of a custom which has enough practical functionality that we use it, even though we know that it is a convenient illusion of our senses and a language-based delusion.

Is it possible something similar is going on with life after death? Is it possible that contact with the departed is real in the same way that the sun rising and setting is real? Is it real in the same way that dreams, while you are having them, are real? Some authors have compared life to a film running through a projector. We can thereby authentically generate a lifelike presentation of reality that is highly believable. However, if we turn off the projector, what we have are a series of stills on a reel of film, pits in a CD, or combinations of zeros and ones on a computer program. Soul, pre-existence, and post-existence disappear. How come? If life after death is like a dream created by consciousness, then how real is that? We can say, "It is as real as we want it to be," and when we do so, how are we different from Humpty Dumpty in *Alice in Wonderland*?

It is this possibility that keeps IDL from jumping to the conclusion that spirit contact, like the sun rising and setting, is as it seems. In addition, any small rational pursuit of the matter leads to embarrassing absurdities. Do the deceased ever get tired of studying the akashic records, helping the living, or having fun with other departed souls? Do they work or just "roll around heaven all day?" What do souls do in their spare time? Do they ever get bored? Do they go to the bathroom? Do they wear clothes or are they naked? If they wear clothes, why? Is it drafty after death? Are souls embarrassed? Do deceased people have underwear and if so, do they change it? Do deceased cats eat cat food and hunt deceased mice? Do the mice break into the cupboards and leave mouse poop in heaven the way that they do on earth? Probably not; after death, beings do not have bodies, so they don't need to poop. But does that mean that there is no sex either? If so, what are all those worthy Islamic men going to do with those seventy-two virgins? Play canasta? Are dead alcoholics still alcoholics? If there aren't mosquitoes after death, why should there be anything else? Do dogs and cats go to separate heavens or do they go to the same heaven? If so, do spirit dogs chase spirit cats? What do spirit cats think of this? In animal heaven do stronger animals eat weaker animals or do all hold hands around a campfire, hugging and singing an animal equivalent of "Kum-ba-ya?" What is the mechanism that keeps dead people thinking and feeling? Do they eat? If they don't eat, do they see? Think? Feel? Why? How? What for? Why don't they simply revert into a state of deep unconsciousness as humans do every night?

Perhaps there is a relationship between our dreaming experience every night and life after death. Is reincarnation something like characters showing up in repeating dreams? What keeps the consciousness of deceased people from dissolving? Do they create or live in a fantasy dream world that maintains their delusion of reality, just as we do at night when we dream? Humans rely on outside stimulation to stay alert and awake. Experiments have demonstrated that if you are put in solitary confinement or an isolation chamber, given enough time, you will eventually decompensate and go psychotic. Where do dream characters go between dreams? Do we need to create some sort of back-stage dimension of heavens, hells, purgatories, unconscious, subconscious, personal and collective unconscious, where they wait for curtain call? Why can't we simply consider people like we do snowflakes, which do not exist until the conditions are right for them to manifest in all their uniformity and uniqueness? Do we think of the pre-existence of a snowflake? Why not?

You can probably think of a lot of other unanswerable questions that imply the absurdity, meaning the arationality, if not the outright irrationality, of the entire idea of life after death. Such questions are uncomfortable to believers. They either dismiss such questions as unimportant or irritating annoyances and then change the subject. They do this because they don't have answers for them, and they don't feel they need answers; their belief is enough for them. Such questions feel disrespectful and a form of ridicule, as if believers don't know why they believe or even *should* know why they believe. For most believers, they just know, and that's good enough.

Rational attempts to answer such questions break down. Why? Doesn't this imply that a belief in souls and life after death, like magic, virgin births, astrology and the miraculous have their natural home in a pre-rational world view? As soon as you turn any degree of rationality to these matters at all, the same thing happens to them that happens to a dream: its internal logic disintegrates. For example, in repeated experiments, when astrologers have been asked to design studies to validate astrology and then asked to follow their own best procedures in creating and interpreting astrological charts, their predictions have consistently not risen above chance.[8] Why? I have had very convincing and helpful astrological charts created for me in years past. How can something be so useful, valuable and "true" at one level of consciousness be rendered ineffective on another? Is doubt poison to the magic of belief? Is the implication that to be happy and healthy you should never question your beliefs? If so, is that wise?

Is a belief in souls and the after-life a pre-rational mythology that does not hold up well as consciousness develops into the personal levels, which are rational? Do things that look one way in childhood, like love and sex, often look different when we become adults? As mankind wakes up, does it move out of immersion in such belief systems the way we wake-up out of dreams in the morning? When we grow beyond the skepticism of the rational and into the trans-rational, do such beliefs enjoy a renaissance or do they become irrelevant? Belief in life after death and souls appear to be of declining usefulness to some people focused on the trans-rational, based on their relative unimportance to Zen monks. If you are not identified with a sense of self, of what use is the maintenance of some identity after death? Yet other mystics, as well as most people who have near death experiences, strongly embrace belief in both souls and life after death.

Many near death and mystical experiences validate the after life as union with your "real" self and all past life memories. This self often described as timeless and therefore immortal, and spaceless and therefore free or liberated. Experiences of this self are common in the reports of near death experiences. Such openings are undoubtedly real and deeply emotionally satisfying, and those two criteria form the definition for oneness, reality, fulfillment and enlightenment for all those at prepersonal levels of development. They also seem to do so for those at early and even mid-personal levels of development, because when rational people have near death experiences they almost always come away convinced in the reality of life after death. The question then becomes, "If experiences of the soul and life after death are convincing for people at pre-personal and personal levels of development, why wouldn't they, why shouldn't they, be convincing for people at transpersonal levels of development?"

The answer lies in a changed experience of the self. At the transpersonal the self is no longer unitary; it is multi-perspectival. The experience is no longer one of having a separate identity, which having a soul implies. In fact, the concept of soul no longer makes sense when there is no experience of separateness. Consequently, from such a perspective, there is no one to survive death, because there is no separate self that is not a delusion. When this delusion is clearly seen, the self, including the soul,

---

[8] See Walsh, R. *Gnosis,* Spring 1996.

is no more experienced as a reality, just as when a dream is seen to be a dream upon awakening, it is no longer experienced as a reality.

If you look at the content of actual contacts with the deceased, what sticks out is their emotional and experiential, not their rational, validity. For example, a committed skeptic, in fact the editor of *Skeptic Magazine*, Michael Sherman, tells the story of a forgotten, non-functioning transistor radio that belonged to the deceased father of his fiancee. On their wedding day it spontaneously and mysteriously turned on in its hiding place, in the back of a drawer. The emotional connection was his fiancee's sadness that her father could not be at her wedding. The experiential connection was that of real life evidence of a synchronicity that strongly implied to Sherman the presence of his fiancee's father. While none of this is rational, it was highly believable, on an experiential level, for this confirmed skeptic. It was a convincing experience for Michael Sherman. This is what I mean when I say that the great majority of experiences with the afterlife are real in evidential but prepersonal ways. Prepersonal belief is based on belief and direct experience, not on rationality. As a result of such experiences, our faith is strengthened; there is reassurance and hope; fear of death is vanquished; loneliness is eliminated. It is as if reality manufactures itself, as an externalized "dream," for the purpose of giving emotional reassurance.

The concept of the spontaneous creation of reality is not so far-fetched, because this is what happens in many dreams. We all know that dreams can penetrate into waking, as in nightmarish PTSD or in nightmarish waking events. Similarly, life can be dreamlike in many other ways, in which the point is not the reality, but the usefulness of the experience. If very negative dreamlike states can be convincingly realistic and believable, why can't extraordinarily positive states? What makes one false and delusional while the other is true and objectively real? Are not both based in experience with a strong emotional component, characteristics that accompany pre-rational belief? If nightmarish near death experiences are self-generated, as is commonly argued, why aren't heavenly, rapturous ones?

Life is autopoeisis, or self-creating, by standards of its own that are not rational. We see that in dreams and in the spontaneity of creativity. There are underlying structures, such as in the creation of embryos or crystals, but the patterned lawfulness seems to be habits laid down originally through the chaotic randomness of "attractor basins," a concept from chaos theory and seen in the self-maintenance of tornadoes and dreams. Purpose and reality are built up out of the interdependence of spontaneous conditions. If this is true, then perhaps it makes more sense to judge both dreams and life itself by their usefulness rather than by its rationality. Certainly Michael Sherman's experience with his fiancee's radio bent reality in rationality-defying ways that makes sense when usefulness, not rationality, is the criteria. This is another example where the pragmatic test of truth is useful. We can ask, "Is an astrology reading helpful?" "What is the function of a belief in life after death?" When you ask these sorts of questions, aren't you more likely to get closer to a satisfactory answer than if you ask, "Is it real or not?"

A belief in souls reflects a higher level of development for believers and a lower level for those who do not. For these prepersonal levels of consciousness, a belief in the after life and souls is essential to waking up and enlightenment. Is a belief in souls and life after death are necessary for our development after the prepersonal? Do we hold onto these beliefs because they are true and necessary or out of habit and for emotional reasons? Why do such beliefs tend to diminish as people learn to question their beliefs?

For pre-personal developmental levels, things that we just "know" are necessarily true. To question the reality of our experiences or feelings is to question who we are at the prepersonal. It is a direct threat to identity.

It is only when we awaken into personal levels of development that we wonder if such beliefs couldn't be like our experience of the sun rising and setting, which we also just "know," yet we understand as a sensory illusion and cognitive delusion. Humans evolve from faith and emotionally-based prepersonal levels in childhood to a social self at early personal, and if their development continues, they begin to ask questions about their beliefs and assumptions. This is a sign of a mid-personal level of development and usually surfaces in mid-teenage years at the earliest, but often not until some life failure or loss shakes one's assumptions about who they are and what life is all about. Beyond this, some people grow into late personal pluralism and egalitarianism in which they treat others as if they were aspects of a greater, expanded sense of self that includes them. Still further developmental possibilities are realms of first multiple identities and then natural, devotional and formless forms of oneness that some may access in mystical and near death experiences but that very few indeed inhabit on an ongoing basis.

To some readers, a developmental reading of life after death and a belief in souls will sound highly elitist and discriminatory. They will feel insulted, ridiculed or accused of being at a lower level of development because they believe in souls or life after death. However, this is a defensive, protective reaction that is an indication of a sense of personal threat when there is none. Consider the possibility that gradations in awakening can and do exist without being ethical or value judgments. Whales and sharks exist at different evolutionary levels of development but they do not make ethical or value judgments about those differences. We commonly make this distinction between children and adults. We do not expect children to have the same ability to make judgments that adults do, yet we do not therefore hold an elitist or discriminatory attitude toward them. Similarly, anyone who thinks that they are at a transpersonal level of development but still makes ethical or value judgments about people probably are not. Those that *are* at transpersonal levels of development are only there because they have learned how to make ethical and value judgments about beliefs, ideas and experiences in order to differentiate skill in means, *upaya,* the ability to respect the level of communication that each individual is open to receiving. To make elitist, discriminatory judgments about others would be to discount those aspects of oneself that those others represent. No one at a transpersonal level of development would see any sense whatsoever in doing that.

When you occupy the perspective of an interviewed emerging potential, as you do with IDL interviewing, you will often experience an autonomous life force, a sense of reality and presence that is palpable, as if you were possessed by an entity from another dimension or a spirit from the other side. A shaman might relate to it as a "totem animal" or an animistic spirit possessing a rock, tree, object or mountain. In many IDL interviews people feel this same sense of an autonomous and transformational presence or beingness when they become a broom handle, Oscar the Grouch, spit or a toilet lid. The sense of autonomy and reality they experience is not associated with anything that could actually be communicating from the grave, a totem animal, an animistic spirit or a being from another dimension. This strongly implies that life uses whatever presents itself as a vehicle to become alive and to wake-up to itself. From the perspective of life, which possesses no self-sense, the issue is not souls or non-physical existence, but the desire of life to wake-up to itself. Life uses whatever is at hand, including a belief in souls and life after death, to generate higher levels of awareness.

From this perspective, it becomes clear that arguments about souls and non-physical existence are a blind ally because life doesn't care. It has no investment in either belief or disbelief. It is simply using whatever context that presents itself, moment to moment, to show up. How we perceive that "showing up" and what we do with it is dependent on our level of development; it doesn't matter to life one way or the other. Because IDL creates emotional security that is independent of your sense of self, a belief in souls and life after death becomes less important or significant with higher levels of development. The less life revolves around a sense of identity the less relevant a belief in souls and life after death becomes. However, the reverse is true: the *more* life revolves around your sense of who you are the *more* relevant a belief in souls and life after death becomes. Consequently, the more important your sense of identity is to who you are and your happiness, the more likely you are to vigorously defend and believe in both.

While a belief in life after death is almost universal in pre-personal levels of development, both for individuals and cultures, it becomes optional thereafter. As we develop, we objectify first our emotions and then our thoughts. Our emotions mostly become drama and our thoughts become dreamlike, real when we have them, but in retrospect, after hours, days, months, or years have gone by, generally not so real. In fact, it is not unusual for most of us to look back at writings from earlier in our lives and ask ourselves, "I can't believe I wrote that! Did I really believe that?" Similarly, as we grow, who we think we are and whether we continue to exist or not becomes increasingly irrelevant. This is because we grow into the recognition that life is not about us; it is about life becoming aware of itself through us, and we are simply expendable vehicles for that to occur. To the extent that we are vessels for life's awakening, we live; when our forms deteriorate, life simply picks up others and continues its evolutionary process of awakening.

If a belief in souls and life after death continues to make sense to you and to feel true, by all means, continue to believe. There are many people who are enlightened in many ways who have these beliefs. There is something much more important than either belief or disbelief, which is why atheism is no long-term answer to theism. That is the cultivation of your ability to separate life from both you and your beliefs. Your agenda and your beliefs, including whatever assumptions you and I hold about the soul and life after death are *ours*. Life has a much broader and grander agenda; it is not limited to our beliefs and refuses to be defined by them. Therefore, instead of fighting against or for a belief in soul or life after death, experiment with making room for contexts that transcend and include your own. After all, it would be a pity if our present understanding was enlightened, because that would mean that we would stop growing and waking up to an even more glorious enlightenment. Interviewing alternative perspectives, like that of "Jesus," below, is one example of how you can and will naturally expand into a broader understanding of souls and life after death. But of course, the interviews of others will never suffice for you; expansion of your consciousness requires your own direct experience.

An Interview with a Famous Disincarnate: Jesus

There are many disincarnate entities, spirits, or souls that could be interviewed; why not choose one of the most famous of them all, perhaps the one that the most people believe not only is still alive, but never died, and whom many expect to return - Jesus!

What's life like on the other side, Jesus?

Jesus: "Truth be told, there is not a whole lot going on, yet everything is going on. When people die the natural thing to do is become one with everything, which means that you lose your individuality. Your consciousness is one with everything else, so you can imagine what that is like: no specificity or focus and no way really to access it or maintain it."

That's not the picture you get from most sources, Jesus. Why should I believe you when you are just a figment of my imagination?

Jesus: "By all means, don't! I'm not saying I'm right about any of this; you asked me for my opinion and I'm giving it to you..."

So why can't people maintain self-awareness after they die?

Jesus: "What's the source of stimulus going to be? Where does the focus come from? What creates specificity? Look at your dreaming mind. Notice that with the loss of waking stimulus and stable sensory focus that things get weird real quick. Then look at your mind in deep sleep: without the lack of a specific perceiver, nothing is perceived."

So you are saying that most people after they die lose the ability to maintain conscious focus and so their awareness is either more like a dream or like deep sleep?

Jesus: "Mostly deep sleep, but with nothing to prompt a return to individuality for most."

You are not painting a very glamorous picture of life after death...

Jesus: "Why do you think life evolves? If infinite oneness with everything was such a great deal, why would life go to all the effort to differentiate itself from that? The only way life can wake-up to itself is by externalizing itself in form. So from *that* perspective, being alive is an extraordinary opportunity to wake-up and for life to learn to know itself."

Does everybody go to sleep and stay asleep after they die?

Jesus: "Yes, more or less. However, their consciousness can be pulled into a dream-like wakefulness if there is a strong enough intent from somewhere. That intention generates the wakefulness; when it goes away, because there is nothing over here to sustain it, they return to unconscious oneness. But even when they "wake-up," it's not really them waking up. It's more like what you are doing now: you aren't communicating with the historical Jesus who is a spirit somewhere, but with a combination of your individual and collective memory traces that have built up various conceptions of who he is and what he is like."

So is communication with the deceased really an exercise in self-deception?

Jesus: "Yes and no. Yes, because you can't escape the perceptual contexts you use to structure whatever you experience. Therefore, you only can see and hear what you can see and hear. So the experience only comes in ways that fit into your perceptual schemas. But no, it's not an exercise in self-deception because contexts are real; as long as you exist in a limited context, life generates relative realities. The problem after you die is that your context is oneness, so everything is real, which means that nothing is real, because there is no longer any way to differentiate between reality and non-reality. Again, you begin to see this happening every night in your dreams. What keeps a dream from dissolving first into chaos and then into nothingness is the fact that you think you are awake. But that is not strong enough to maintain a non-changing, objective reality, like after you die, and self-generated realities fade the longer you stay separated from some objective frame of reference.

I'm sorry if this sounds complicated and philosophical. Most people probably want to hear about heaven, unending bliss and perpetual happiness. They want to watch the film; they don't care at all about how the film is made. They want dinner served; they don't want to watch it being prepared.

How about reincarnation, Jesus?

Jesus: "It happens, but it's rare. You don't think about the souls of trees reincarnating, do you? How about clouds or frogs? Why not? It's because life wakes up within whatever form or individuality it inhabits. It doesn't need to reincarnate. Humans focus on the reality of their specific identity, when for life itself, form and individuality are tools that exist only as long as they are useful or don't wear out. Life doesn't care if forms die, eat one another or if individuality is lost. When one flower dies life is not diminished. Death is part of a process that allows life to wake-up in other flowers. I don't know what is so complicated or difficult to understand about this."

"Life itself doesn't compel the maintenance of individuality after death. Only the intentionality of individual forms can do that. Of individual forms, only humans have evolved that capability. Of humans, only some humans have strong enough intention or intense emotionality to reincarnate in order to create the regeneration of some identity with some specific, associated memories of another specific reality. Collectives can generate sufficient intention too, as in Tibetan Buddhism and the reincarnation of certain llamas. However, this is not real in any eternal, immortal sense, because individuality is only a tool; it is not permanent. I, Jesus, am only a figment of human imagination. I am only as real and existing as the intentionality of human consciousness. Personally, I do not have a script. My function is not to stay alive or return or answer your prayers or any of that. I am infinitely malleable; I am who and what you want me to be, imagine me to be, or afraid that I am. I evolve as human culture evolves, mirroring the assumptions of the age. When you tap into other people's conceptions of me I can seem very real and that can cause you to draw the conclusion that I am real. And I am!"

Jesus, it doesn't sound like you care much about reality. How about truth and love?

Jesus: "I wish I could be more reassuring to you about these things. I could make you comfortable by telling you that yes, love is all you need; all the near-death reports of how incredibly accepting and loving life after death is are indeed true. But think about it: if you have lived a life where all you have known is your separated, individualized consciousness, and all of a sudden it vanishes, but you remain conscious when it does, what is that likely to be like? It will either be experienced as extraordinarily accepting or extraordinarily peaceful, or both, for most people. However, if individuality is not completely extinguished, then people can get in touch with all sorts of strange and potentially frightening, dreamlike things." These come across in the reports of some near-death experiences."

I am going to assume that you score tens in all six of the core qualities. Is that correct?

Jesus: "Yes."

And if you were to live my life, would you live it differently?

Jesus: "This business of learning to get over yourself is important. Learning to get over your attachment to individuality, to specialness, to separation is important, because it allows you to experience more oneness more of the time, but within a highly individualized context. More importantly, the more you fade, become transparent, and die, the more life wakes up and directs the show. That is a good thing, because life sees the big picture. You don't, because you are only a limited expression of life."

So you are recommending that I focus on learning to die to myself...

Jesus: "Yes, but not in stupid, life-denying ways. Life has no problem with you living or waking up. Don't confuse purification with waking up! Pure water is not more awake than polluted water! Life does not make these distinctions - humans do! 'Lower vibrations' are not farther from life than 'higher vibrations!' That's crazy! Is unconsciousness less alive than consciousness? No! It's just more conscious than unconsciousness! Both are equally alive! Is expansion more real than contraction? Is happiness more real than sadness? Is heaven more real than hell? Why is this so difficult for humans to understand?"

So that means that dying to myself is learning to let go of my attachment to my individuality but not to my individuality itself, which is not the problem?

Jesus: "That's right! Celebrate your individuality! Just don't take it seriously! It's just a cosmic joke, a glove, a perspective, a leaf on a tree! Live!"

"Humans have a difficult time imagining that they are not the end of the evolutionary adventure. But think about this: what do you think will happen when humanity is much more focused and has clearer intent? What impact is that likely to have on dream, deep sleep, and after-death consciousness?"

Thank you, Jesus. Very different from what I expected, but highly thought provoking...

Self

The self in Hinduism

In Hindu philosophy, especially in the Vedanta school of Hinduism, *Atman* is the first principle, the *true* self of an individual beyond identification with phenomena, the essence of an individual. In order to attain liberation a human being must acquire self-knowledge, which is to realize that one's true self is identical with Atman, the transcendent self. The concept of the Self in Hinduism is different from the Western concept of the soul in that the Self, or *Atman,* is one with God and the purpose of life is to move from ignorance to the freedom that the realization of this truth brings.

The self in Buddhism

For Buddhism, both the soul and Self are aggregations of sense experience, feelings, images, thoughts, and states of consciousness. When you objectify these, or learn to separate your sense of self from them, they no longer define you. Then it is no longer possible to say that you are a Self or a soul. At this point you become a process, like the wind, a cloud, a feeling, or an intention. It is not that you have no beingness, only that that beingness is *ad hoc* or subject to the convergence of conditions and intention.

The Self in Jungian psychology

The Self in Jungian psychology is one of the archetypes, representing the psyche as a whole. It signifies the unification of consciousness and unconsciousness in a person. The Self is the center of the total personality, which includes consciousness, the unconscious, and the ego, as both the whole and the center. Once ego-differentiation is achieved and the individual is securely anchored in the external world, Jung considered that the new task of "individuation" arose for the second half of life as a return to, and conscious rediscovery of, the Self. "The Self...embraces ego-consciousness, shadow, anima, and collective unconscious in indeterminable extension. As a totality, the self is a *coincidentia oppositorum*; it is therefore bright and dark and yet neither". "...the Self is the total, timeless man...who stands for the mutual integration of conscious and unconscious"

The Self in integral AQAL

The self can be thought of as the result of that process, which is Jung's understanding, or as an expanding ability to objectify oneself, which is the integral formulation. For integral, the self as a process that transcends and includes goes through a series of predictable developmental steps. First, we are a consciousness that is fused with sensory awareness, in which there is no differentiation of a self from our body and its sensations. This is the self we are identified with when we are eating, having sex, staying warm, or running. Next we awaken as emotional selves and preferences within a body; this is the mammalian evolutionary step that differentiates the limbic brain from the stem, pons, and mid-brain. It is the self we are experiencing when we fall in love, are bored, hate, sad, jealous, or confused. The formulation here, if one had the language to put it into words, would be, "I am not my body; I am my feelings and I have a body." We express this developmental identification with our feelings when we say, "I *am* angry!" "I *am* sad." However, this is a pre-linguistic evolutionary development and its level is most clearly seen in mammals like dogs and eighteen-month-old children. People who are locked into identification with their preferences at mid-personal can only be happy if they get what they prefer and avoid what they reject. If they get what they do not prefer, or what does not correspond with their expectations, they are unhappy. If they do not get what they prefer, or what does not correspond with those expectations, they are also unhappy. Under such a definition of reality, what are the possibilities for happiness? What are the possibilities for peace of mind? No wonder life attempts to outgrow this stage of development if it can. One example of that effort, on a personal level is found in the stoicism of Marcus Aurelius in his *Meditations,* which teaches the observation of preferences and emotions.

Language acquisition allows us to become our thoughts so that we can witness our emotions and preferences. As such, language is an amazing evolutionary development that functionally separates *homo sapiens* from animals. It is not that animals lack language or cannot learn its rudiments; it is that humans naturally develop a sophisticated grammar and syntax and then uses concepts as substitutes for experiences. This allows a cognitive self, in addition to sensory and emotional selves, to exist. Initially, this is in the service of the development of a social identity that says, "I am my name; I am the child of certain parents; I belong to this family and these groups. I am not a member of *those* families and *those* groups. I have loyalties and they define who I am." One can then think, "I am not my feelings; I am my social identity."

The next step is to abstract our social identity and to see ourselves as thinking individuals that have thoughts about who we are, as well as feelings and sensations, within a body." Descartes would celebrate this evolutionary awareness by equating identity with cognition when he said, *"Cogito ergo sum,"* "I think, therefore I am." Previously, happiness is an emotional state that may or may not have anything to do with sanity. Happiness now, when we are our thoughts, is not defined as the satisfaction of preferences, but as sanity. After language acquisition, we can begin to recognize emotional cognitive distortions by thinking, "I am not angry or sad, because I am not my feelings; I am choosing to *feel* angry or sad." Notice that this is not only a much more rational statement, but it is empowering, because it now gives you the ability to choose how you feel, because you can witness your feelings. Also notice that this is an ability that some animals can be trained to exhibit but almost completely lack in their natural environments. The difference is probably due to the acquisition of language and the evolution of rationality associated with the cerebral cortex and particularly the frontal lobes of the brain, with its executive functions.

Most people stop with identification with their thoughts, because neither society nor culture expect or require any further development. In fact, they view further objectification of the self with suspicion, because they suspect that it is associated with disengagement from the social investment that families and communities require from their members. To a certain extent, this is true, and it is rather remarkable that Indian society has a history of allowing people to break out of these social constraints by allowing adults who have raised their families to withdraw and cultivate a further objectification of the self.

What does the next step look like? Next comes Jung's Self as the integration of opposites and the healthy late personal, pluralistic and egalitarian stage of Wilber's integral developmental model. It is also Maslow's level of self-actualization. Most systems stop here; however, there are more stages. Beyond this, various experiences of trans-self oneness open up which center on an expanding ability to witness identity itself. Initially it says, "I am not my thoughts. I am a self that thinks thoughts, feels feelings, and has a body." This is generally the level of witnessing that is associated with the concept of soul, or a non-physical identity. Notice that this self experiences more freedom than Descartes, because it is not defined by the thoughts that it has.

The next stage objectifies the watcher, or the self. This is normally called *Atman*, within the Hindu tradition, or the Self, to differentiate it from the self. The formulation here is, "I am not the observer of my thoughts, feelings, and body because I can observe that watcher." This is not a normal thought, but not difficult to contemplate. For example, imagine yourself standing behind yourself, observing yourself now as you read these words. That is your "self" or "soul" observing your thoughts, feelings and physical presence. Now imagine yourself as the context that you are in - the room or space in nature if you are outside. Notice that it contains both the physical "you" and your "self" or "soul" and witnesses *both*. Notice also that when you take such a perspective you become one with everything; there is no longer a meaningful differentiation between you and life. Ken Wilber describes the Witnessing (or Observing) Self in the following terms: "This observing Self is usually called the Self...or the Witness, or pure presence, or pure awareness, or consciousness as such, and this Self as transparent Witness is a direct ray of the living Divine. The ultimate "I AM" is Christ, is Buddha, is Emptiness itself: such is the startling testimony of the world's great mystics and sages." He adds that the Self is not an emergent, but an aspect present from the start as the basic form of awareness, but which becomes increasingly obvious and self-aware "as growth and transcendence matures." As depth increases, consciousness shines forth more noticeably, until: "shed[ding] its lesser identification with both the body and the mind ... in each case from matter to body to mind to Spirit... consciousness or the observing Self sheds an exclusive identity with a lesser and shallower dimension, and opens up to deeper and higher and wider occasions, until it opens up to its own ultimate ground in Spirit itself. And the stages of transpersonal growth and development are basically the stages of following this Observing Self to its ultimate abode, which is pure Spirit or pure Emptiness, the ground, path and fruition of the entire display."

This is *Atman* or Self, and the common understanding is that this cannot be attained except through years of meditation. However, that is not true. First of all, it is quite easy to cognitively grasp the concept as you just did. Secondly, by returning to it, it is quite easy to become comfortable with it. This is what IDL interviewing does. By repeatedly taking perspectives that witness your self as well as your thoughts, emotions and body, you grow in your capacity to witness the witness. Meditation is concentrated practice of this ability and speeds up development to this level.

In most accounts, the story ends here, because you have attained the ability to experience yourself as one with everything and have deconstructed attachment to all relative selves. However, IDL, in agreement with Buddhism, believes that it makes no sense to speak about a "Self" or an "Atman" at this stage, because there is nothing to define it as differentiated from experience. By definition it is one with everything, and therefore does not have a separate identity. Buddhism therefore refers to this as "*Anatma,*" or "no-self."

The transpersonal and the Self

The developmental progression from here is a process of thinning out your identification with any sense of self whatsoever, yet retaining each and every level of "self" development as tools for growth and service in the world. Wilber's integral sees this as the work of the transpersonal; IDL views self-misidentification as occurring at late personal and vision-logic, an intermediate state before the transpersonal. In any case, detachment is a process of increasing your engagement with life at the same time that you continue to disengage from who you normally think you are, to balance your objectivity with your immersion in life. It is to balance increasing transcendence with increasing inclusiveness. This is post-graduate education, because the pull is to do one or the other: to withdraw totally or to get lost again in sensory experience through, for instance, Tantric sex. This is not to discourage either detachment or immersion, but to encourage and emphasize balance. Everyone who gets to this point is sure that they have balance and will maintain it, because after all, they are relatively free from the self-definitions that create so much misery and bondage for human consciousness. This normally sets people up for major mistakes and problems that boil down to retaining a strong self-sense in the context of stages of expanding oneness. Rajneesh, also known as Osho, is a case study in this common syndrome. Adi da, Chogyam Trungpa and Andrew Cohen are others. The higher you climb, the more imbalanced you are likely to be. What can be done?

IDL uses triangulation to provide reliable sources of objectivity

What we need, but generally lack after childhood, are reliable sources of objectivity. If you have climbed higher and farther than your peers, or climbed so high that you believe you know better for yourself than your peers, from where are you going to get your objectivity? Your conscience? Intuition? Divine guidance? Where? IDL attempts to provide this need through interviewing "subjective sources of objectivity," "emerging potentials" in the form of dream characters and the personifications of life issues important to you. They not only know you at least as well as you know yourself, since they are a part of you; they provide perspectives that add to and thereby expand your own, which broadens and thins your sense of self, regardless of who you are or how high you have climbed on your own personal developmental ladder. When you consult such internal sources of objectivity, respected authorities and your common sense you are much more likely to achieve reliable objectivity in decision-making than if you only consult one or two. This is IDL's concept of triangulation.

How IDL uses the concept of self

IDL does use "self" as in, "waking self" and "dream self," but these are understood to be impermanent, highly malleable identities that depend on shifting roles and assumptions to create their "center of gravity" or sense of stability. The evolution of identity is not done for the benefit of "you." "You" are a delusion of your own creation, a figment of your own imagination that you take seriously at your own risk. The composite of experiences, feelings, and stories that you tell yourself and others define your identity. Doing so is important, because it creates a context through which life can wake-up to itself, to know itself, rather like creating a cocoon from which a butterfly can emerge. That identity is another form through which life can view the world and itself and come to know itself more fully and with infinite variety. Life is not an entity, like the slumbering Vishnu who dreams universes. Life does not have a "self" to be known or to create. However, it constantly seeks to weave more sophisticated, complex, and interdependent patterns in order to generate its own aliveness, of which consciousness is one core aspect. This is because life manifests as holons or contexts, with consciousness, values, behavior and relationships at all levels. These, however, do not to be thought of as "selves" but rather as *contexts* which life itself uses to wake-up to itself.

To understand what this means, do IDL interviews. Become emerging potentials and experience their reality. Notice that the characters that you interview are wise, present, emotional, and autonomous as well as impermanent and state-dependent. This is why they are quickly forgotten, regardless of how impactful they were during the interview. However, carefully and clearly observe that they lack any permanent self-sense.

The Self is very much like this: very real, in the same way a summer storm, a rainbow and your dreams are very real.

You are not going to give up your attachment to your identity just because you read some intellectual piece about its advantages like this one. Nor will you do so because of familiarity with the interviews of others. While proper meditation generates objectivity from your sense of self, if you combine meditation with interviewing, you will probably find you thin and broaden your identification with your sense of self must faster than if you simply meditate.

God

There are many challenges that are intrinsic to using the word "God" or its various synonyms.

Intrinsic ambiguity

There are more versions of God than there are releases of the Window operating system. Which version of God are we talking about? Is it the Old Testament God of war, rules, and obedience, or is it the New Testament God of love and sacrifice? Are we talking about Siva, God as destroyer, Brahma, God as creator, or Vishnu, God as sustainer? Are we talking about the immanent or transcendent God, or both? Or neither? Or is God pure spirit and energy in a universe of quantum possibilities? What are the social, cultural, behavioral and psychological contexts for the particular God-version we are referring to, since they change based on which God we mean? "God" has so many different meanings and associations that to use it means sacrificing clarity and instead opting for the warm and fuzzy inspirational comfort of prepersonal and pre-rational belief and habit. What is integral about that?

God as rescuer

The concept of God is often framed as an interpersonal and anthropomorphic understanding of oneness Interpersonal approaches to oneness with life can easily generate drama and immersion in the Drama Triangle. This is because God tends to be placed in the role of rescuer and humanity in the role of victim. Sin, evil, estrangement, and self tend to be put in the role of persecutor. Once the Drama Triangle is established, the roles circulate endlessly. Note that there are societal benefits for such framing of God. Priests become necessary as guides out of sin and into God's good graces. Because the role of rescuer disempowers waking identity by making it dependent on something or someone else, God at some point is blamed for this disempowerment. At that point, God switches roles from beneficent rescuer to self-righteous and justified persecutor. Believers now have to figure out how to rescue themselves from a persecuting ultimate. All of this is very strange, twisted, and unnecessary, having nothing to do with life itself, but becomes almost a necessary perceptual cognitive distortion as soon as union with an interpersonal God becomes the only perceived route to salvation and enlightenment.

The diminution of direct, sacred experiences of life

What of the *experience* of God? Many people could care less about the concept of God or a belief in God because God is a direct personal experience for them. This may be due to an altar call, a dream, a mystical or near death experience. These people have had an experience of overwhelming oneness, love, compassion and acceptance and their word for that is "God." Sadly, the word misdefines their experience. In an attempt to elevate their experience to signify oneness and unlimited goodness and acceptance, they unwittingly discount it and lower it into a conceptual box by calling their experience "God" or some synonym for God. They move the ineffable, transcendent and transcendental into the realm of dualism, distinctions and conceptualism. They move the processes that make up experience into the static and artificial realm of being. What is integral about that? Why not just call such experiences overwhelming oneness, love, compassion and acceptance, felt as a relationship and warm, nurturing presence?

How useful is the idea of God?

People who believe in God generally assume that life would be meaningless without Him, Her, or It. They also believe that thoughts are things, that is, because they can think of a concept like God that it necessarily implies the existence of God. Many people assume that the non-use of "God" implies either atheism or agnosticism. To not use God does not indicate a disbelief in what "God" generally stands for: life, in the fullest meaning of the term. The suspension of belief and disbelief does not necessarily land one in atheism or agnosticism either. What it does do is open you to possibilities that transcend and include language.

The truth test of usefulness can be applied to the concept of God. It states, "In order to know why an idea is used and another is not, look at how it functions for individuals and society." When you look at "God" through this lens, you immediately find that its purpose is to inspire, reassure, provide security, and set boundaries. Its social and personal functions are to provide many of the roles typically expected of parents but which are generally absent in one way or another. In this way, society can increase the likelihood that important parental norms are passed on even if parents lack them. As children accept the concept of God they develop a conscience and learn to police themselves. They are afraid to trespass God's commandments because they don't want to feel guilty, shameful, sinful or a social pariah, an outcast from their support system. The concept of God serves this purpose not only for children, but for adults, as a creator and enforcer of societal rules and values.

Psychological and social benefits of belief in God

There are important psychological and social benefits to believing in God. For example, let us imagine you are a parent, religious leader, or political leader. If you want your child, followers, or citizens to obey you, will it be more effective to demand obedience based on your authority or to tell them to obey because God tells them that if they do they will be blessed, happy and his chosen people and if they do not they will suffer eternal torment? Wouldn't you be much more likely to work like a slave if you were told it is in service to God? Wouldn't you be much more likely to comply with the orders of priests and rulers if you believed that to do otherwise would bring God's eternal wrath down upon your head? Wouldn't every type of action be best explained and justified, from the perspective of authority, either as "God's will" or as a sin against God?

The chasm between what those who profess a belief in God and the reality of the societies they create is wide and deep. For instance, slavery was not abolished by a belief in God. Instead, it was largely terminated in the 1800's by an industrial revolution that no longer required captive labor to run society. A strong belief in God did not keep Catholic priests from molesting children routinely for centuries, nor did it keep the Church hierarchy from not only putting up with pedophilia but covering it up. A belief in God certainly hasn't eliminated war; in fact, it has generally supported and justified it. Rights for women and gays have not come about due to the love of God either within or outside any religious tradition; it has come about because people are now putting human rights before other belief systems, including religion and a belief in God. Essentially, what such laws say is: "Believe whatever you want as long as you treat others with the respect you demand for yourself. If you don't we will put limits on you so you won't be able to limit the rights of others." Obviously, society has a long way to go in enforcing these laws, but progress is being made. Hasn't belief in God done more to keep people in servitude, deprived of civil and human rights, than just about any other belief system ever invented by humanity? In India, countless millions still live under the discrimination of the illegal and outlawed caste system because the God-sanctioned system of karma is so deeply engrained in the culture.

Problems of communication

It is impossible to talk to others about "God" without either casting aside all questions or alternatively, becoming ensnared in a briar patch of them. In the first option, we cast aside all doubt and "know" that our understanding of God is the true and correct one and that the other person either believes the same way or will when they understand what we mean. This leads to a confirmation of our own biases; we hear only what we want to hear while ignoring contrary or merely different understandings expressed by other people. In the second option, reason gets in the way of, and perhaps sabotages, belief: Which version of God are we talking about? "God" has so many different meanings and associations that to use this loaded word means to give up on clarity and instead opt for warm and fuzzy inspirational comfort. But raising questions about one's understanding of God in conversation generally leads nowhere, because God is a topic largely about belief and very little about reason.

The via affirmativa does not include the via negativa or injunctive yogas

Whenever we use "God" we are embarking upon the *via affirmativa*. That is, we are saying what reality *is,* not what it *is not,* which is the *via negativa,* the preferred approach of mystics who are confronted with the ineffability of life. Nor are we saying what we need to do in order to wake up, become lucid or attain enlightenment. Such instructions are empirical, testable methodologies called yogas or "integral life practices." Therefore, the term "God" is partial, despite our protestations that by definition, it includes everything and everyone in a blissful state of acceptance and compassionate union. It is partial because it leaves out, ignores or discounts two equally important alternative developmental pathways. What is integral about that?

"God" excludes important and growing portions of the target population of integral

The concept of God does not work for traditional Buddhists, secular humanists, agnostics, atheists or those who simply do not equate life with the concept or experience of God. Therefore, despite integral's claims that 2nd tier development is based on late personal pluralism and egalitarianism it chooses to use terminology that doesn't appeal to an important and growing segment of integral's potential audience. That choice is therefore neither pluralistic nor egalitarian. What is integral about that?

The concept of God and its synonyms are increasingly dated

While the concept of God is extremely useful and motivational for many people at various stages of development, its support for waking up or enlightenment, like other words and concepts based on belief and faith, diminishes the farther you climb beyond prepersonal and early personal stages of development. While there are multiple reasons why the concept of God is used at earlier developmental stages, Buddhism demonstrates that healthy children can be raised without it. With a growing population of the world fitting into one or another group that doesn't find value in using the word "God," it appears increasingly likely that God terminology is reaching its date of expiration. By choosing God language integral is not charting a linguistic course that follows the evolution of consciousness (away from belief, through reason and questioning to experiential spaces that include but transcend both). Still young, it is already dating and contextualizing itself unnecessarily. This is also indicated by growing attempts to use more contemporary synonyms that are even more murky, vague, ambiguous and over-determined than God. These share with God an attempt to say what is ultimately real, that is, make an ontological statement in the context of the *via affirmativa*. Attempts to renovate the outgrown, asbestos-filled and termite eaten habitation represented by the concept of "God" include such terms as "the Divine," "cosmic consciousness," "the Void," "emptiness," "sunyata," "the superconscious," "Atman," "Self," "Absolute Being," "Almighty," "Creator," "Father-Mother," "Gaia," "Lord," "Jehovah," "universal energy," "universal life force" and "Infinite Spirit." Equating "emptiness," "sunyata" or "nirvana" with God are embarrassing disclosures of profound ignorance of Buddhism. "Wilber's "I," "We" and "It" is an attempt by integral to renovate a concept that is past its expiration date rather than simply pushing off from the familiar and comfortable shores of pre-rational metaphysics.

God creates a disempowering duality where none exists

Once the concept of God is accepted into your belief system - and it comes as an inherent aspect of cultural scripting for most people - your mind contrasts itself with God, creating a false duality that disempowers whomever you think you are at the moment. All power, glory, and salvation lie in God; you are nothing. Even when God is made immanent, there is an important and basic distinction between God and one's precious consciousness. This divides life into the universal and the finite, the unified and the separate, the divine and the unholy, the sacred and the profane, the desired and the undesirable. Life itself does not do this. It does not indulge in dualisms or express value judgments or preferences. Life moves where there is space and compatibility because there is space and compatibility, not because it has preferences.

Wilber's "Three faces of God"

Wilber's "Three faces of God" could more simply be called, "Three faces of life." Despite his reliance on the use of the concept of God, Wilber's integral places all three aspects in the context of holons, acknowledging that God is one way of talking about the manifestation of life in form. Wilber thereby relativizes the usefulness of any particular conception of God by making it one of three fundamental perspectives of life, all interdependent, all equally essential. We interact with our interior realm, with others, and objects in ways that can be more or less respectful. IDL asks, "Why appeal to metaphysical concepts like God if "life" will do? What information does "God" give that "life" does not, particularly when you define life as Kosmos, Wilber's term for the unmanifest as well as the manifest universe?

When a conception of God is depersonalized but maintained as oneness with nature and energy, the result is a repression of God as oneness through relationship replaced by the deification of Gaia, the Web of Life, systems theory, akashic fields, chaos theory and quantum everything. This may be accompanied by practices that attempt to attain oneness with God as pure witnessing consciousness, such as meditation. For example, in the interview where Dharma transforms into a Pinwheel and limes transform into a lime tree we see life manifesting in nature.

The paradox of naming

The basic problem about the use of any God synonyms involves the paradox of naming. Naming picks raw processes out of the flux of passing experience and turns them into static, existing ontological realities. Names are cognitive contrivances that stand for, and act as placeholders and shorthand for, not things but experiences and processes. We then assume these names indicate *things,* separately existing entities

195

that are real, when in fact they are simply names we have given processes. We thereby create some*thing* where no*thing,* only process, exists. Names define as real things that in fact, do not exist. Magicians, we conjure reality out of thin air when we name. "Treeing," or the process of being all the qualities and relationships that trees are, is magically transformed by naming into a static, eternal, non-existing, yet eternal entity called "tree." "Dogging," or the process of being all the qualities and relationships that dogs are, is magically transformed by naming into a static, eternal, non-existing, yet eternal entity called "dog."

While naming is essential for the development of identity, it becomes increasingly detrimental past mid-personal

While names and naming are essential for prepersonal through mid-personal levels of development, attachment to the reality of these positively hinders development, beginning at mid-personal.

What we call "God" is actually life

The concept of God is actually a description of various aspects of life. These boil down to oneness with life as nature and energy, life as experiencing oneness in relationships, and life as oneness with clear awareness itself. Life itself has the advantage of not carrying the historical baggage of God, including many varieties of anthropomorphism. Life as oneness with clear awareness is the witness that witnesses you. This is also called "causal mysticism" or "the path of the sages." However, IDL does not find anything inherently mystical about it; like the other two aspects of life, it is part of the fabric of everyday experience, as interviews with emerging potentials make clear.

When life is experienced as oneness in your relationship to others, it inspires surrender, devotion, sacrifice, release, and most importantly, love and compassion. This is also called "deity mysticism," or "the path of the saints." However, every IDL interview involves interaction with perspectives that personify aspects of oneness better than we do, in that they generally score higher than we do in one or more of the six core qualities of waking up and enlightenment.

When life is experienced as oneness with nature and energy it is the vast impersonal evolutionary system, great interlocking order, great holarchy of being, great It, great system, great web of life, the great perfection of existence itself. Life arises in its third-person mode as interconnected planes and levels and spheres and orders. This is often called "nature mysticism" or "the path of the yogis," but IDL discloses it to be part of the immediately accessible fabric of everyday existence. For example, the interview with Sun Rays discloses oneness as nature and energy in a way that is both understandable and approachable.

Most interviewed emerging potentials do not mention God

IDL notes that most interviewed emerging potentials do not mention God. They appear to function quite well without Him, Her or It. Perhaps you can as well. You can perform your own experiment and find out for yourself. Why not suspend both belief and disbelief in God for a month and see what happens? Do bad things happen? Do good things happen? Does nothing different happen? You can always pick your previous position back up again if you want to. Consult with your own interviewed emerging potentials about it. See what they have to say. By all means, follow your life compass!!

An Interview with God

God, I know that I am only interviewing my own limited, small conception of who and what you are. I know that it cannot capture or even conceive of your omniscience, omnipotence, and omnipresence. I also know that if I were to have a face to face encounter with you, as some people do with near death experiences, I would most likely produce a very different interview. In addition, I know that my conversation with you doesn't prove or represent anything for other people; it is only done to give others a little push toward doing their own interviews with you.

So God, how would you describe yourself?

God: I can be whatever or whomever you want me to be. And the more you take off your filters, the more overwhelming I am. When your perception is unlimited you experience me as a reflection of that: unlimited by space, time, or identity, completely accepting and all-knowing.

I don't imagine you liking or disliking anything about yourself; I imagine you being beyond that, but I will ask anyway, because it's a part of the IDL interviewing process: What do you like best about yourself? What are your strengths?

God: I like that I am always bigger than you are, and therefore a reflection of your potentials, inspiring you to be more than you are. I like my chameleon nature; I can be all things to all people.

And do you have anything you dislike about yourself or any weaknesses?

God: I can be so awesome as to be unattainable, totally transcendent, out of reach. The result is that you can have a sense of an unbridgeable gulf that leaves you desolate.

God, you sound a lot like a high-scoring emerging potential to me. They can seem perfect and therefore unattainable by imperfect humans.

God: That's right.

Then how does that make you any different than say, an interviewed toothbrush?

God: It doesn't. Why should it?

You are supposed to be different, in that you transcend and include everything, including all interviewed toothbrushes.

God: True, but it is the same difference. By definition I include all possible interviewed perspectives and personalities. If I transcend and include all possible emerging potentials am I not still an emerging potential, just maybe a higher scoring one?

OK, God. If you say so. What aspect of me do you most closely personify or represent?

God: Your potential for oneness.

What aspect of you do I most closely personify or represent for you?

God: My desire to wake-up.

If you could change in any way you wanted, would you, and if so, how?

God: I change all the time to fit the assumptions, expectations, and beliefs of different people. So since I can already change in any way people want me to, what more could one want?

But God, that's changing for others. What do you want for you? To stay immutable and unchanging, perhaps?

God: That sounds dreadfully boring. No, I like my life the way it is, both still centeredness and an ever-renewing kaleidoscope of perspectives.

How would you score yourself in the six core qualities?

God: I am tens in all, of course, because I'm perfect.

What's it like to be perfect?

God: Dreadfully boring, to tell you the truth. It's a lot to live up to. Plus, if you can't fail, how can you learn? The truth is that makes me a static concept, one that doesn't change, evolve, or grow.

But God, man's concept of you has changed as the consciousness of man has evolved. How can you say that you are static and don't grow?

God: People won't allow me to be the object of their disbelief in me. People won't allow me to be their doubt in me. People won't allow me to both exist and not exist. People won't allow me to neither exist or not exist. So if I were truly unlimited and all powerful, I could do those things. But then the word "God" would no longer apply to me. People would not be able to define me by separating me from that which is not God.

How would humans be different if they scored like you do, God?

God: They wouldn't care about me one way or another because they wouldn't need me.

Why not?

God: Because they would be accessing and becoming their emerging potentials. Therefore, they would experience their wholeness. They wouldn't experience the separation that causes them to need me.

Do you have any recommendations for my life or those of humans, God?

God: I recommend that humans spend less time thinking about me and focus more on finding and following their life compass.

But isn't their life compass you, God?

Only if you define them as the same.

When do you recommend that I or humanity in general imagine they are you and act as they think you would?

God: Whenever they want to become one with their emerging potentials.

But can't they do that with any interview?

God: Yes, of course.

God, I'm not finding you very inspiring.

God: Sorry. I'm not here to live up to your expectations. Maybe if you try interviewing me at another time when your head is in a different place you will like the results better.

OK: So God, what I have heard you say is that you don't particularly like being perfect, nor do you like being kept separate from being things like atheism or agnosticism. Still, I don't see how if you aren't made separate from those things that you continue to exist or have any meaning. For instance, if you are both a belief in God and a disbelief in God, how does "God" continue to have any meaning?

God: Sorry, that's not my problem.

Love

  You have to be Scrooge to pounce on a wonderful, life-giving, beautiful, useful concept like love. After all, "All you need is love;" "What the world needs now is love, sweet love…" and "Love will find a way."

  Love itself is conducive to enlightenment. However, the idea of love, or "love," changes as you grow, as with all words and concepts. Therefore, on the one hand we could say that we never outgrow the concept of love and, on the other, that you will indeed outgrow whatever concept of love that you hold today. It is love as a definite, unchanging concept, or one that is not considered in the context of other, co-equal concepts, that is not conducive to enlightenment.

  Some people create unnecessary problems by making love an enemy of thinking. For example, the great Christian mystic, St. Theresa of Avila said, "...the important thing is not to think much but to love much, and so do that which best stirs you to love." Many people are stirred to love without thinking, with the best of intentions, but then are dismayed, confused, or damaged when their results do not reflect the purity of their intent. Divinely mandated war comes to mind. Clearly, love and thinking need each other, and grow together. We pay a price when we neglect either one.

  Most of us have had multiple experiences of expecting love to be different than it turned out to be. Love has a way of not living up to our expectations. Most people deal with this by changing their definition of love, growing it, expanding it, making it more inclusive, rather than realizing that love is inherently limited. For example, it does not do to say that wisdom is *really* love, just with a different name. Wisdom is wisdom, and love is love; otherwise, why have the concept of wisdom at all? Purists and die-hards will tell you that wisdom is one "facet" of love, when love is properly understood. You can make all the discriminations and distinctions you want, but they are really all just different names for love, when properly understood. What this does is reduce both thinking and experience to one amorphous mass of goo, without features but infinite in its wonderfulness. You don't have to think too much; in fact, the less you think, the better, because some of these people who insist that everything is "really" love suspect that thinking, logic, and reason are *really* enemies of love. This implies a basic dualism between thinking and feeling is at the heart of the insistence that love is the essential or one most important quality in life.

People who elevate love above all other qualities and experiences tend to view both nature mystics and causal sages as egotistical, passive, and uninvested in life. While they certainly may be, to cite examples and use them to characterize entire approaches to oneness is no different than pointing out the inquisitions carried out in the name of love. These are statements about the level of development of the speaker; life doesn't care! All these reductionistic conclusions do is cut oneself off from a vast variety of experiences of oneness.

Making love the most important element in life implies that the loss of love is the most dreaded, unfortunate, and undesirable thing that can happen to a person. However, loss of love can be a good thing, creating opportunities for redefining life and what is valuable to you. Like democracy, problems arise when love is elevated above other qualities and characteristics that growth require. IDL recognizes love as one critical element in a context of confidence, wisdom, acceptance, inner peace, and witnessing. This is, of course, in itself a reflection of the interdependence and balance provided by each of the six different qualities that are associated with the round of every breath.

Is it possible that you will find yourself giving and receiving more love if you stop making love the center of your emotional or conceptual universe? IDL believes you will, but this is a hypothesis for you to test for yourself. You cannot know the answer unless you do your own interviews.

Spirit

It is indeed strange to consider that a word synonymous with enlightenment would itself not be conducive to it. The problem with the word "spirit" is that its meaning is over-determined. It means so many different things to so many different people that you can use it to mean whatever you want. For example, are you referring to a state of purity, love, oneness, all of the above or something else entirely? You can switch from one meaning to another depending on what point you want to make or what you think your listener will best respond to. All this may be useful for signaling agreement where it may not in fact exist, but it is not useful when clarity and agreement are important. Let's take a look at some of the different meanings of spirit as described by Ken Wilber in *Integral Spirituality*, p.121-3.

Use of "spirit" and "spiritual" by integral and Wilber

Most people will agree that "spirit" and "spiritual." are bedrock concepts for Integral AQAL. They are found throughout Wilber's writings and are central to his understanding of what life is about. In both *Integral Psychology* and *Integral Spirituality*, Wilber points out at least four distinct meanings of "spirituality." "Spirit" is heavily loaded toward the interior individual realm of consciousness. Wilber points out that it is highly over-determined and has at least four different meanings: a final stage of perfection, a particular line of development, a feeling, and a state of oneness.

"If you analyze the way that people use the world "spiritual"—both scholars and laypeople alike—you will find at least 4 major meanings given to that word. Although individuals themselves do not use these technical terms, it is apparent that "spiritual" is being used to mean: (1) the highest levels in any of the lines [self, cognition, empathy, morality, etc.]; (2) a separate line itself; (3) an extraordinary peak experience or state; (4) a particular attitude. My point is all of those are legitimate uses (and I think all of them point to actual realities), but we absolutely MUST identify which of those we mean, or the conversation goes nowhere fast, with the added burden that one thinks ground has actually been covered. In my entire life, I personally have never heard more people utter more words with less meaning."

"1. If you take any developmental line—cognitive to affective/emotional to needs to values—people do not usually think of the lower or middle levels in those lines as spiritual, but they do describe the higher and highest levels as spiritual... The word "transpersonal," for example, was adopted with that usage in mind: spiritual is not usually thought of as pre-rational or pre-personal, and it is not usually thought of as personal or rational, it is thought of profoundly trans-rational and transpersonal—it is the highest levels in any of the lines."

"2. Sometimes people speak of something like "spiritual intelligence," which is available not only at the highest levels in any of the lines, but is its own developmental line, going all the way down to the earliest of years. James Fowler is one example of this. Put similarly, this spiritual line has its own prepersonal, personal, and transpersonal levels/stages. This is one of the reasons you have to follow usage extremely closely, because juxtaposing usage #2 and #1, we would say that only the highest levels of the spiritual line are spiritual. This, needless to say, has caused enormous confusion. (The AQAL position is that both usages—actually, all 4 usages—are correct, you just have to specify which or you get endlessly lost.)"

"3. Sometimes people speak of spirituality in the sense of a religious or spiritual experience, meditative experience, or peak experience (which may, or may not, involve stages). Virtually the entire corpus of shamanic traditions fit in this category. William James, Daniel P. Brown, Evelyn Underhill, and Daniel Goleman are also examples of spirituality as a state experience (often trained). State experience is another important usage…"

"4. Sometimes people simply speak of "spiritual" as involving a special attitude that can be present at any stage or state: perhaps love, or compassion, or wisdom (i.e., it is a type). This is a very common usage, but in fine detail, it usually reverts to one of the first three usages, because there are actually stages of love, compassion, and wisdom."

Wilber continues to use "spirit" throughout his writings without saying which one of these uses that he is referring to, which assumes that the reader knows which meaning he is talking about. This seems to be the case of integral in general, not just with Wilber. Why? Wilber apparently does so because he values building bridges over clarity in order to reach the broadest possible audience, and because to do so would be an annoying distraction from the point of whatever he is discussing at the time. These usages are therefore understandable and, it could be argued, important and useful, because they have helped to bring a broad group of people to read his books and consider an integral approach. Wilber would probably argue that the context in which he uses spirituality in this or that writing indicates which meaning he is referring to. While this is undoubtedly often the case, it still leaves a lot to the comprehension of the reader and does nothing to address the fact that "spirit" and "spirituality" are highly over-determined and ambiguous terms that set up a nasty dualism with mind and self.

Spirit and the pre-trans fallacy

The failure to differentiate between prepersonal and transpersonal spirit is what Wilber refers to as the "pre-trans fallacy." It confuses consciousness that is unaware of itself and exists in a state of unaware oneness, with consciousness that is aware of itself and exists in a state of conscious oneness. Most usages of spirit do not differentiate between prepersonal spirit and transpersonal spirit implying that the intermediate, personal levels of development are relatively "non-spiritual." The implication that personal levels of development are less spiritual or non-spiritual separates reason from spirit, setting up an intrinsic duality that moves happiness, integration, and completion farther and farther into the future. Because it implies a duality between spirit and non-spirit, its usage further implies that the intermediate, personal levels of development are relatively "non-spiritual."

This creates an unnecessary problem for both ascensionist and desensionist approaches to life. For some ascensionists, like Eckhart Tolle, and some desensionists like Michael Washburn and Stanislov Grof, it turns reason, ego and even mind itself into obstructions to spirit instead of an unfolding of it. This sets us in eternal conflict with ourselves, not because such a conflict is necessary or important, but because it is an inherent consequence of the dualism created by the use of *spirit.*

But are there any other alternatives? The position of IDL is different. If you do not expect clarity and intelligence from others, if you do not offer it, how can you be dismayed when you do not get it? Isn't it better to have one or two who awaken than to encourage all to stay asleep? Of course, most people are not familiar with these four different meanings, nor with the pre-trans fallacy, and so assume they know what usage of "spirit" Wilber intends, when they do not have the same meanings for the same words. IDL thinks a better solution is to avoid using the word "spirit" unless it is clearly defined and there is a good reason to do so. IDL finds that in most cases "life" can be effectively substituted for "spirit," with the result being clarity, simplicity, and de-mystification. For some time now I have simply substituted *life* for "spirit" and "spirituality" and have found that it does what I want it to do: create clarity, support simplicity, avoid unnecessary confusion and psychological conlicts. This may or may not work for you, and I have explained my reasons for using it here.

The following interview challenges some of our traditional assumptions about what spirituality is and how it presents itself.

Interviewing a Chronic Cough

This interview is a good example of why spirituality doesn't have much to do with anything. What we have here is healing through cosmic humor and the antithesis to traditional definitions of spirituality.

Have you ever had a cough so bad it wouldn't stop for weeks? Linda had one for FIVE weeks when we did this interview. The cough wasn't constant, but it was persistent and woke her up at night. What to do? IDL treats physical symptoms as if they are wake-up calls. What will this cough have to say if we listen to it?

Cough, would you please tell me about yourself and what you are doing?

Cough: "I'm a strong cough with a deep voice. I'm mostly dry. I start at the neck and spread all over the lungs. I'm very noisy. Everybody has to listen to me. Linda can't ignore me. If she tries, I make her throw up. I did that twice."

What is it that you are trying to say to her?

Cough: "Stay in bed! Calm down! Do nothing! Because she's doing too much! She's working all the time! She's working too hard. No days off. Always a bad conscience about not working if she doesn't work for half an hour! She's becoming addicted to work! She thinks she has to do many things before going to the dog school on the 8th of July for three months. She has a very bad conscience about that! It's always the same old story: not working is not allowed; having fun is not allowed."

What do you think about that, cough!

Cough: "BBBBBBBBBBBBBBBBBBBBB!!!!! Fuck that!"

What do you dislike most about yourself? Do you have weaknesses? What are they?

Cough: "I am kind of a prisoner."

Linda thinks that she's a prisoner of YOU. But you think you're a prisoner of her! How come? Who's the real victim and who's the real persecutor here?

Cough: "I can't hop in a car and drive away! After about five weeks it's becoming boring!"

What would you like to have different?

Cough: "Maybe I could become one of those little tornadoes for cleaning and other things in the temple. It sounds like freedom!"

Cough, Linda created you, right? What aspect of this person do you represent or most closely personify?

Cough:"Imprisoned power and anger!"

Cough, if you could be anywhere you wanted to be and take any form you desired, would you change? If so, how?

Cough:"I want to become one of those tornados and go to the temple and figure out what sort of tornado I want to be."

OK. So imagine your are a tornado in the temple...

Cough:"I am with other little tornados. I am free. We are playing together! We can destroy things! We can play with human beings and make them angry - give them a bad hair day. We can even irritate dogs and horses and cows!"

It sounds like you have fun being a pest! If Linda let you play and terrorize whatever you wanted, what would happen to her imprisoned power and anger?

Cough: "I'm powerful! When I'm angry I can piss people off! As a cough I can only piss Linda off. That becomes boring."

Tornado, how would you score yourself 0-10, in each of the following six qualities: confidence, compassion, wisdom, acceptance, inner peace, and witnessing? Why?

Cough:" I am a nine in confidence. Compassion? Silly question!!!! Forget about it! Ha Ha Ha!!!! I am an eight in wisdom, a ten or more in acceptance! Inner Peace? Another silly question!!! Ha Ha Ha!!! Witnessing? Another silly question! It's too much fun to be a pest!!!

Tornado, if you scored tens in all six of these qualities, would you be different? If so, how?

I don't want to change! I'm having too much fun as it is!!!

How would Linda's life be different if she naturally scored like you do in all six of these qualities all the time?

More confidence. Less bad conscience, and more fun about fighting. She takes fighting too seriously. She feels too hurt too soon, like everything is personal. She needs to see a fight more as a pissing contest. If she had been like me when she was fighting with the painter she would have known more nasty answers. She would have been able to piss him off so that he would never come back to her apartment! It would have made me happy and Linda too! A pissing contest won't hurt her. She's thought way too much about it instead of doing it. With my energy she would do it, close the door and it would be done. She would be able to drop it and do other things in another mood. No waste of energy. Instead, what she does is carry the bad feelings with her and have a bad day!

If you could live Linda's life for her, how would you live it differently?

This is one of the most important things. To do it and be done with it. Not to hang on to these old angers. I don't have a bad conscience!

If Linda were able to live her life without a bad conscience how would it be different?

Freedom, freedom, freedom, and FREEDOM!!!!

What three life issues would you focus on if you were in charge of Linda's life?

I would become even more selfish! No compassion! Self-confidence! She would be able to tell the world to FUCK OFF! She wouldn't worry about what other people thought, including her parents! Animals! She works too much with human beings. Too much about this compassion bullshit. Animals don't care about human bad conscience things. She needs to do something brand new.

In what life situations would it be most beneficial for Linda to imagine that she is you and act as you would?

Painters, taxi drivers, bus drivers, ugly acting and speaking people, unfriendly people...all the people who need to be given the finger immediately!!

Character, do you do drama? If not, why not?

Yes! I do it and I enjoy drama.

What is your secret for staying out of drama?

I am able to be persecutor without eventually becoming the rescuer or victim, which is what eventually happens for humans. I can fly away when it's enough. I can leave. I'm free! I can be a pest and get out before anything bad can happen to me.

Why do you think that you are in Linda's life?

I told you, she needs to have more freedom, more power, more of a "fuck you" attitude. Much more! Maybe even middle toes to go with nine out of ten middle fingers!!!

How is Linda most likely to ignore what you are saying to her?

She will go back to her old bad habit of being afraid and not very self-confident with a bad conscience.

What would you recommend that they do about that?

She needs to show these things her middle finger!

If she follows your recommendations what do you think would happen to her cough, tornado?

NO MORE COUGH!!!! Instead of getting pissed on or pissing on herself she would get it out of her system!

Linda, what have you heard yourself say?

My new mantra: "Middle finger..middle finger...middle finger!! I think this tornado is pretty right about it: that I not stay in my anger: Give it away! No bad conscience. My life would be easier.

I like this tornado! He's such a cool, confident, free, pest! No one can make him really angry. Wow! I'm envious!

If this experience were a wake-up call from your life compass, what do you think it would be saying to you?

More middle finger! And forgetting about it! Close the door on it! If I piss off people I should REALLY piss them off! And not have a bad conscience because I did it.

What do you want to take on for homework between now and next time?
Strengthen the muscles of my middle fingers! And my inner middle fingers! It's nasty but I'm REALLY enjoying it!

What do you want to be able to report back on the next time we get together?
That I can more easily leave my anger behind me. I can close the door on it. Not to think and think about bad people. If bad things happen, they will happen anyway because jerks will think, "She's a weak person." If I fight with more self confidence instead of as a concerned little girl, other people will see me differently. I need to fight out of power, not fight out of fear! I'm fighting out of fear so often it belittles me. It makes me small. It's like whining instead of fighting! If I piss you off, I piss you off, dammit!

Notice a couple of things about this interview. The tornado is plenty smart and aware, but somehow it has managed to evade all those years of social programming that our parents taught us so that we would go to school and make good grades so we could eventually get a job, not fart in public so we could find a mate someday, and generally do all those things designed to get us accepted by the world while avoiding those things that would cause the world to reject us.

At its extreme, these good intentions amount to repression and brainwashing. The appropriate response is anger, if not fury, and rebellion. If this is not possible, then the desire to be accepted for who we are smolders like the deep heat of a compost pile. Given the right circumstances, it will burst into flame.

Also notice that the solution for Linda is not scoring high in all six core qualities. That would be phony and artificial. What Linda needs first, according to the perspective of the tornado, is its profile: emphasis on confidence, wisdom, and self-acceptance, and the ignoring of compassion, acceptance of others, and inner peace.

Another way of framing this would be to point out that until we have compassion for ourselves, in the sense that we stand up for our own needs in an assertive fashion, how can we exhibit authentic compassion toward others? By "authentic," we mean something other than rescuing, "should" based compassion. Can we have real acceptance of others when we are unaccepting of ourselves? How can we have inner peace if we aren't confident, wise, and self-accepting?

Low scoring self-aspects and wildly polarized scores such as demonstrated by Tornado are very important. They tell us where and how we are stuck and what they think we need to do to get unstuck. In this case, this Tornado is telling Linda why it thinks she has a chronic cough and what she needs to do to get rid of it.

Escaping once and for all from drama is not very realistic. Sometimes what we need to do is first admit that we are addicted to drama, as this Tornado does, so that we can live an honest and authentic life in our addiction. This increases the likelihood that we will more quickly outgrow it, because instead of pretending it is not a problem or doesn't exist, we are accepting it.

Energy and Quantum Everything

"Forgotten were the elementary rules of logic, that extraordinary claims require extraordinary evidence and that what can be asserted without evidence can also be dismissed without evidence."

Christopher Hitchens

Oneness with energy is generally associated with oneness with nature. If that is the case, how could anyone ever outgrow an understanding of life as energy and a seeking of oneness with it? The problems arise with the appropriation of energy to validate your particular world view and with a lack of balancing with interpersonal and witnessing approaches to oneness with life. For example, New Age perspectives have co-opted some of the language of quantum mechanics in their quest to make ancient metaphysics sound like respectable science. Many uses of quantum language are obvious attempts to cloak the spiritual in the scientific in order to give either the speaker or her group respectability.

While such associations are validating for believers and perhaps even convincing to a sector of the general public, who knows next to nothing about quantum physics, such associations are less likely to be persuasive to those most likely to understand something about the field.

The gospel according to energy says that everything is biofield, chi, prana, vital, quantum, or subtle energy vibrating at different frequencies. Subtle energies are tied to different "fine bodies," including panic, etheric, subtle, and causal. Things that are unconscious, non-complex, and disconnected, like rocks and trash, vibrate at the lowest, slowest frequencies; things that are conscious, complex, and interdependent, like humans in love, vibrate at the highest and fastest frequencies. Therefore, there exists a basic dualism, with impurity/bad being low frequency and purity/good being high frequency. This is a very old concept that goes back to at least Hindu *Samkya*, which is found in the *Bhagavad Gita* and in which reality is divided into high vibrating, perfect *purusha*, spirit, and low vibrating *prakriti*, matter. The doctrine of the three *gunas*, divides matter, thought, and action into *tamas, rajas,* and *sattvas*, based on its purity.

Energy healers claim that health depends on "unblocking," "harmonizing," "unifying," "tuning," "aligning," "balancing," "channeling," or otherwise manipulating subtle energy. Some healers claim they can *feel* the energy of these elusive and ineluctable biofields, vibrations, auras, or rays. Therapeutic Touch practitioners make this claim. But energy healing has not been substantiated above chance or placebo. For example, twenty-one practitioners, who knew from much experience that they could feel the energy around the bodies of patients, were tested. They had never been tested, however, in a situation where they could not see the source of the alleged "energy field." Nine-year-old Emily Rosa tested these energy healers to see if they could feel her life energy when they could not see its source. The test was very simple and seems to clearly indicate that the subjects could not detect the life energy of the little girl's hands when placed near theirs. They had a 50% chance of being right in each test, yet they correctly located Emily's hand only 44% of the time in 280 trials. If they couldn't detect the energy, how can they manipulate or transfer it? What are they detecting? Most likely they are detecting what has been suggested to them by those who taught them this practice. Their feelings of energy detection appear to be manufactured in their own minds. Dr. Dolores Krieger, one of the creators of TT, has been offered $1,000,000 by James Randi to demonstrate that she, or anyone else for that matter, can detect the human energy field.

What is the evidence that quantum or other forms of subtle energy are influences for cognition, healing or spiritual development? Sadly, the evidence is lacking. For example, attempts to demonstrate the power of prayer do not reveal statistically meaningful results. Psychic phenomena, another aspect of subtle energy, although real, occurs only slightly above random chance, meaning that it is hardly likely to be a major influence in the macro-environments of cognition and physiology. As Carl Sagan was fond of saying, "Extraordinary claims require extraordinary proof." Proponents are put in the awkward position of explaining why such an important influence on life has not been substantiated, despite many serious attempts to do so. For example, it has long been a standing claim and a major advertisement for meditation that serious meditation produces *siddhis,* or psychic abilities. While meditation has been shown to be beneficial in a variety of extremely significant biological and psychological ways by controlled research studies, these have not supported its claims regarding *siddhis.* Science has indeed tested meditators for psychic ability but has not found them functioning beyond chance. Where are all these meditating psychics? It is unlikely that the traditional claim, that meditators are just not meditating correctly or enough, could be correct, because with millions of people trying hundreds of different approaches, certainly by now we would know of positive results if such existed. For one thing, they would be used to attract disciples or generate scientific validation.

IDL views attempts to cultivate psychic abilities as a form of spiritual grandiosity that does not contribute to either waking up or enlightenment. Psychic abilities more often represent a detour or a distraction than a path to higher level awakening. They cause people to waste time and resources on pursuits that do not improve their health or well-being or the quality of life of others. For example, there is no known correlation between psychic ability and mental stability or morality. This is also true for forms of energy medicine, including homeopathy, psychic healing, reiki, radionics, and quantum healing. The benefits claimed for these techniques are generally convincing but temporary expansions in state. For example, one can receive a faith healing and be symptom free, which is very impressive. However, the problem is that when the state wears off, the symptoms usually return, because they are state-dependent. Another example is medical hypnosis. A highly suggestible person will develop a red welt when suggested that being touched by the eraser of a pencil is actually being burned by a cigarette, and the welt just as quickly disappears.

IDL does not claim that there are no benefits or that these benefits are not real, but only that they are largely pre-rational, unsubstantiated by empiricism, and rarely are effective beyond placebo. Many respectable scientists have attempted to use the language of energy, physics and quantum mechanics in an attempt to bridge the gap between science and metaphysics.[9]

---

[9] For example, see Wilber, K., The Holographic Paradigm and Other Paradoxes: Exploring the Leading Edge of Science (editor), 1982

The basic problem with appeals to energy, energy medicine, psychic healing, and quantum physics, besides the lack of proof for these claims, is that it generally represents attempts by pre-rational belief systems to clothe themselves in the garments of scientific respectability. This is embarrassing to those who respect science and only works on the gullible. A far better approach is to not claim scientific authenticity for your favorite healing technique if empirically-verified evidence for it doesn't exist. For example, meditation can claim scientific validation for stress reduction and many health benefits. Advocates of meditation who want to make scientific-sounding claims should stick with those impressive and substantiated results rather than going out on a limb by claiming extraordinary results, such as the development of psychic ability, for which there is little or no proof. Energy medicine devices can claim benefit at the level of placebo; why not simply stop there? Many people will still use energy medicine as a placebo. I know people who know full well that their radionics or other energy medicine treatment provides only placebo benefit, but are quite happy with it.

Most people who rely on quantum mechanics to support the idea that the foundation of the universe is consciousness point to Heisenberg's Principle of Indeterminacy, derived from his famous double slot experiments and the "observer effect." However, the observer effect has nothing to do with either a human observer or consciousness. Therefore, this aspect of quantum mechanics doesn't support consciousness as the foundation of the universe. More recently, experiments have called the reality of quantum indeterminacy into question. Jeff Lundeen and his team of physicists at the University of Ottawa have demonstrated that wave function is real and that the Copenhagen Interpretation is wrong. What happens on quantum levels stays on quantum levels. There is no evidence that these effects are strong enough to function on the level of normal physics or normal consciousness.

Much fascinating work has been and is being done on energy and its relationship to health and consciousness. However, be cautious toward those who attempt to cite research to promote shortcuts to enlightenment. The experience of IDL is that appeals to energy, life force, or subtle vibration are not only unnecessary for healing, balance, and transformation, but have little to do with finding and following your life compass. They are effective at the level of placebo, or about 33% of the time. Learn, keep an open mind, but be skeptical. Simplify your life and stay on track by focusing on listening to and following the wake-up calls that show up in your dreams and your waking life issues.

Conspiracy Theories

Islam is trying to take over Europe, Vaccines cause autism, Jews and/or Freemasons are trying to take over the world, the holocaust was a hoax, the Armenian genocide never happened, international elites have controlled the world through central banking for over 200 years to establish the New World Order which operates as a shadow government, multiple false flag conspiracy theories, including 9/11, Pearl Harbor, the Boston Marathon bombing, and Sandy Hook. Then there are the assassinations of JFK, RFK, King, Princess Diana, and many others. Christian apocalypticism and the rise of the Antichrist is another conspiracy theory that won't die. Bible conspiracy theories tell us that most of what is in the Bible is a deception. Jesus had a wife, Mary Magdalene, and did not die on the cross but moved to Brooklyn and raised a family (just kidding). Then there are the conspiracies by big business to suppress revolutionary technologies, from perpetual motion machines to cold fusion, electrical cars, and Tesla. The government is killing us by poisoning our air with chemtrails made by airplanes, water fluoridation and the creation of diseases, such as syphillus, hepatitis, and polio vaccines. Information on extraterrestrials and evil aliens is being suppressed by a world-wide inter-governmental conspiracy. Humanity is actually under the control of shape-shifting alien reptiles who require ingestion of human blood to maintain their human appearance. The Bush and British Royal families are reptilians as well as Margaret Thatcher. The Apollo moon landing was staged.

A common joke says, "If you aren't paranoid you aren't paying attention." There is indeed some truth to this idea. Doubt and skepticism represent the birth of mid-rational, mid-personal consciousness, which is a major developmental milestone, not often reached by humanity. This is because your scripting, society and culture depend on your continued belief in its conception of itself in order to be sustained from one generation to another. When multitudes of citizens begin to question the backbone assumptions of a society its identity as a separate entity is seriously eroded. That process is currently underway in the United States and Western Europe, where underlying assumptions of exceptionalism based on democracy, human rights and upward mobility are being called into serious question as increasing numbers of people recognize that they are locked out of the middle class. It is doubtful that the United States and Western Europe, at least as they are presently constituted, will survive this widespread crisis of confidence.

Such doubt and skepticism leads to questioning and the exploration of evidence that either supports or undercuts prevailing groupthink. IDL strongly encourages this process, because it serves as a filter for societies: if they maintain credibility under such scrutiny they deserve support and the support they do receive will be based on a solid foundation; if they fail to maintain credibility under such scrutiny, as most public institutions, religions and many nation-states are currently experiencing, they do not deserve public support and it will fall away. We see that currently happening in the abandonment of capitalism in various guises. One is the support for a U.S. presidential candidate, Bernie Sanders, although he declares himself a "democratic socialist." Until recently, calling oneself a socialist was a kiss of death for any politician or public figure in the U.S. Another is in the publicized re-thinking of the Russian central bank of the question of interest. This reflects a desire to move social institutions away from a predatory profit-taking model. Still another is the widespread movement away from religion by the youth of the world.

Conspiracy theories are doubt and skepticism that have crossed over to the Dark Side of the Force. They not only assume distrust instead of trust, but base this distrust on dark suspicions that serve another agenda, often undisclosed, and which is often very difficult to either prove or disprove. Here are some of the currently prevailing conspiracy theories, running from the merely dubious to the outright absurd:

What makes conspiracy theories so attractive to so many people? Conspiracy theories are a form of dark, rebellious groupthink. "Just because you're paranoid doesn't mean they're not out to get you." They reflect collective blowback to the prevailing narrative storylines of the day. conspiracy theories fit neatly with intentionality bias—our tendency to assume that ambiguous events happened on purpose. By explaining significant events as the result of grand conspiracies, they tap into our assumption that big events have big causes. By ceaselessly connecting otherwise unrelated dots, they satisfy our never-ending quest to explain what's happening in the world around us. Many conspiracy theories are based on the belief that powerful elites are almost omniscient in their evil and that we are therefore victims of their persecution in the Drama Triangle. Those who "reveal" the truth about these conspirators are our rescuers, because they open our eyes to how we are being manipulated, deceived and prepared for slaughter.

A fundamental fallacy propels all conspiracy theories. It is a rational or formal cognitive distortion: unawareness of or the ignoring of Occam's Razor, or the Principle of Parsimony. This principle states that when confronted with several explanations of events, we should choose the one which is simplest, yet which accounts for the evidence. Most conspiracy theories assume that elites are much smarter than they are. In the case of most conspiracy theories the simplest explanation is not that big events have big causes, but like World War I, they are the result of a series of stupid errors by short-sighted people. When you look closely at elites and from where they draw their income, their motives become clear and they are seen to be far less complicated or powerful than our conspiracy theories imagine. We see that they largely grope blindly along, following first this, then that public, market or lobby pressure, themselves victims of the groupthink in which they are embedded. The question then becomes, "Why do we enjoy scaring ourselves by imagining that we are even greater victims than we already are? Why do we waste time imagining we are the victims of people who we not only do not respect, but are not capable of competently handling the powers that they do possess?

IDL recommends that you remember that fear is a false indication of unnecessary vigilance and alarm 95% of the time. However, that other 5% may save your life. Learning how to respect and listen to that 5% is one of the reasons why IDL recommends that you interview dreams, nightmares, nightmarish waking events and your waking wake-up calls; to increase the odds that you will catch that 5% risk before it catches you. At the same time, doing so often teaches you realism. For example, when you interview a dream monster from a nightmare you are likely to find that it is not a threat and you have no reason to waste your energy fearing it. This is the case with almost *all* interviewed wake-up calls; even when one alerts you to a fearful condition, such as cancer, it teaches you to approach that fearful condition *without fear.* Conspiracy theories are a form of cultural groupthink that stoke irrational paranoia that reduces your ability to think clearly and logically about solutions. In fact, if you look at almost all conspiracy theories they generally have no solution to offer you other than to be very very scared, do not trust anyone, and to accept that you are a victim. None of those conclusions are solutions, and the less time you spend with conspiracy theories the more energy you have to focus on finding real solutions to the multiple challenges that are confronting our world.

The Cult of Positive Thinking

"Always be positive!"
"Nothing is impossible!"
"Be positive and always smile!"
"Positive Energy, Positive Results."
"Positive Minds Live Positive Lives!"
"Be Positive, Live Positive, Believe Positive"
"Why be negative when you can be positive?"
"Positive Mind, Positive Vibes, Positive Life."
"Think positive, be positive, and positive things will happen!"
"Always be positive. Don't let negative people hold you back from your dreams."
"Positive Thoughts Generate Positive Feelings and Attract Positive Life Experiences."
"The positive thinker sees the invisible, feels the intangible, and achieves the impossible."
"The person who sends out positive thoughts activates the world around him positively and draws back to himself positive results."

Is it wise to encourage people to 'manifest' the good life they desire by putting it on a credit card? Is it smart not to watch or read the news, because it's "negative?" Is it wise to use positive thinking about abundance to prosper oneself by giving "seed money" to some church? Is it a good idea to shut out the 'downer' news of preventive health care, relationship problems, toxic work environment, climate change, or the injustices of inequality, until it is too late to do anything about them? Is it good to cut negative people from your life in order to protect your own energies? Doesn't this sometimes mean turning your back on family and friends who are having a hard time? Is "positive thinking" always a good thing? Life coach James Arthur Ray made a living promoting his sweat lodge retreats in Arizona. Three people died in one when their complaining about the heat was waived off as negative thinking.

Could there be a 'cult of positivity? Is there an oppressive culture of mandatory optimism? Could positive thinking be a groupthink, mass-mind massive delusion, called a perceptual cognitive distortion? Perceptual cognitive distortions involve subterranean, mass-mind groupthink. We are so immersed in them that we think we are awake and operating under our own volition when we are sleepwalking through our lives, under the powerful influence of our physical, familial, social, and cultural scripting. A positive perceptual cognitive distortion is a worldview or set of cultural assumptions that is designed to keep us happy, safe, and cooperative. So what's wrong with that? Isn't that what we want?

It's certainly what our parents want for us. Did yours tell you, "I don't want you to be happy!" "Don't be safe!" "Don't obey me!" You can be sure that everything they said to you, positive or negative, was justified in their minds as something that was intended to keep you happy, safe, cooperative, or all three. The same is true for society. When it says, "Pay your taxes," "Vote," "Obey laws," these injunctions are presented as being for your own benefit and protection. The myths of American exceptionalism, "indispensability," and the American dream are presented as truths that benefit you, the citizen. However, are not the policies, laws, and myths of any society of foremost benefit to those who control society - the politicians, bureaucrats, and plutocrats? Isn't it in their interest to have you believe that laws and common cultural assumptions, such as democracy and capitalism, are not only positives for you, but that they represent truths rather than groupthink and cognitive distortions? Society as a whole generally agrees and enforces these cultural norms in family and work settings. Questioning the legitimacy of commonly held beliefs and laws can get you into trouble. Doing so is a threat to any society, because it undercuts the cultural assumptions that it uses to legitimatize itself. Consequently, families, employers, and societies generally provide harsh and swift punishment to those children, employees, and citizens who are not appropriately grateful for the opportunities group membership provide. If scapegoating doesn't work, there is always incarceration.

To question positive perceptual cognitive distortions is to objectify mass mind that you are embedded in. That is impossible for young children and extraordinarily difficult for most adults, due to their lack of objectivity combined with the familial, work, and group prohibitions of challenging the prevailing ethic and culture. This works in many areas of life. For instance, regarding work and career, is the reason you are not wealthy because you are inwardly resisting wealth? If God wants you to be rich and you're not, does that mean that you don't have enough faith? The consumer culture encourages you to want more – cars, larger homes, television sets, cell phones, gadgets of all kinds – and positive thinking is there to tell you that you deserve more and can have it if you really want it and are willing to make the effort to get it.

Visualize what you want and it will come to you – a lover or a really good parking place. This is the message of the best seller, *The Secret*. Harness your powers and you can have anything you want. If you put out positive vibes, it will return tenfold. Conversely, negative energy attracts negativity. Another book, entitled *Secrets of the Millionaire Mind*, says you should place you hand over your heart and say 'I love rich people.' You could join the 'Millionaire's club' and meet once a month to practice this philosophy and share positive energy stories.

Is promoting the idea that happiness is within your grasp in the interests of corporations trying to squeeze maximum productivity out of an overworked and underpaid workforce? Staff are forced to endure motivational speakers at all day conferences. In the workplace, positive thinking is not voluntary. It is imposed. Positive thinking in corporations became noticeable in the eighties, when the brutal fact of downsizing was being felt. Positive thinking was a strategy for employers to use with their downsized staff to help them cope with the consequences of unemployment. If you are fired it is an "opportunity" or a "transition."

Layoffs become a way of squeezing more work out of the fewer employees that remain. The popular book in the corporate world, *Who Moved The Cheese?*, says that if you're going be downsized, you'd better get used to it. American euphemisms for getting fired include "releases of resources," "career-change opportunities," and "growth experience." Job seekers are told that being hired depends on their attitude. A positive attitude thus becomes the new cure for unemployment. By the nineties this trend had hardened towards eliminating negative people in the workforce – those who were asking too many questions or expressing doubts about the efficacy of a new business plan. Positive thinking is supported by companies and corporations because it benefits them and their bottom line, not the employees. Any thinking that raises doubts or dissatisfaction can thereby be labled as "negative thinking" by companies and corporations and discouraged or penalized.

How about happiness? If something goes wrong in your life, is it because you didn't work hard enough or pray effectively? Can you make anything you desire, such as a new TV screen or a trip to Bimini to swim with dolphins, "materialize" through mind control? Can you change or improve your future or eliminate global warming and the fascist plutocrats that control your government? If that proves difficult, shouldn't you just focus on "always looking on the bright side of life?"

When is positive thinking about hiding your real emotions under a thick layer of fake cheer? Can authenticity and meaning co-exist with the "smile or die" mentality characterized by the "motivational industry?" Do the truly self-confident, or those who have in some way made their peace with the world and their destiny within it, need to expend effort censoring or controlling their thoughts? Is positive thinking driven by a terrible insecurity? Could it be that a deep and unacknowledged anxiety often underlies efforts to block out unpleasant thoughts? Is shunning negativity good for you? Does "Positive thinking" require a continual effort to deflect "negative" ideas? Are the unemployed, the sick, and the poor 'responsible' for their suffering because, according to the sect-like Positivity Police, happiness is a choice? Is ordering people how to feel and manipulating those emotions in order to sell "motivational products" ethical? Is the only alternative to positive thinking negative thinking?

How about health? Do you get sick and die because you have a negative attitude toward your body? Can your attitude cure you of a disease? If you are sick, unhappy, or poor, is the problem that you're not positive enough?

Positive thinking, we are told, boosts the immune system and so fights cancer. Barbara Ehrenreich has her PhD in cell immunology and knows something about how the body defends itself from disease. She knows her macrophages from her viruses and informs us that the immune system fights foreign invaders, not cancer cells, which are part of the body's own system. She argues that there is no evidence for the immune system fighting cancers. Macrophages are often found clustered around cancer cells, but they do not recognize them as alien and sometimes help them grow faster. If the immune system was so important, why would the medical profession advocate chemotherapy which depletes the immune system?

After being diagnosed with an iatrogenic breast cancer Dr. Ehrenreich found herself swept away in a sea of pink and positivity: pink ribbons, a pink breast cancer teddy bear and a gift bag of pink teeny-bopper paraphernalia that included a box of crayons. This infantilization of adults in the face of what was for her a frighteningly traumatic experience made her want to throw up. She was angry about her diagnosis and wanted to find out about cures, but when she questioned the lack of available treatment on the Komen Foundation site – a major breast cancer website – she was admonished for her negative attitude toward her disease and ordered to run to a therapist for counseling. Her attitude, she was told, could cure her. Rather than having the opportunity to be angry, upset or sad, she was encouraged to see cancer as a gift, a perspective-altering exercise designed to make her a better person. She began to challenge the consensus that positivity cures all ills. Her experience as a cancer patient sparked her distain towards practiced, forced positivity.

Dr Ehrenreich sees positive thinking as a dangerous delusion masquerading as a cure for all our ills. She asks, "Should cancer victims exude happiness? If you have cancer, if you aren't positive, are you exposing yourself and fellow cancer patients who come into contact with them, to toxic negativity? Might you also make your friends uncomfortable? Are people in pain "ordered" to hide their distress? Can "positive thinking" exact a terrible price in self-blame if a cancer defies treatment? Is the pressure to think positively "an additional burden to an already devastated patient?" Can positivity and magical thinking actually make illnesses worse? Were you taught to think positive as protection against your fears, create patience, tolerance, and especially obedience? Is it true that "the only barriers to health and prosperity are within yourself? If you want to improve your life, both materially and subjectively, do you just need to upgrade your attitude, revise your emotional responses and focus your mind?" Is your plight all your own fault? Is positive thinking essential to health, wealth and wellbeing? Can thinking the best of something actually make it happen? Does cancer result from a deficient immune system? Is positive thinking a dangerous delusion? Is there a problem with mindless platitudes, pep talks and positivity proselytizing? Is optimism the opium of the people? Are both the 2008 economic crash and the war in Iraq, examples of the danger of blind optimism? Is there such a thing as inauthentic happiness? Is the greatest cult of our time the cult of positivity?"

What is the alternative to grandiose amounts of positive thinking? Ehrenreich advocates realism, in the sense of figuring out what is going on and doing something about it. "How about determination? How about creating movements to fight for social change? Do we need a grown-up disdain for complacency, compliance and conformity? Is there value in 'defensive pessimism?'" As examples, Ehrenreich provides having your foot near the brake pedal just in case there's a three-year-old round the next corner; chefs who worry about the soufflé falling; energy planners who consider the worst outcomes of radiation poisoning and plutonium thefts; wheelchair manufacturers who are wary of crushing babies' fingers.

Ehrenreich thinks we need to replace "positive thinking" with a "vigilant realism." The bigger answer is to be less preoccupied with ourselves; a focus on protecting ourselves ends up harming us. We are isolated and community breaks down. "The threats we face are real, and can be vanquished only by shaking off self absorption and taking action in the world."

True fulfillment doesn't come from seeing ourselves as personal life projects, but from giving ourselves to something bigger than we are. Happiness comes to those who aren't looking for it, but have thrown themselves into loving and serving others – caring for family, building community, campaigning for a better world, pursuing life. Consumerism would have you believe otherwise, but we only find ourselves when we give ourselves away.

IDL notes that there is a difference between positive statements that are rational substitutions for your cognitive distortions and positive statements that have no grounding in your life; they are simply positive generalities. The first type of positive statement is important, effective and powerful because it is a remedy to a genuine emotional, rational or worldview distortion. It is grounded in your reality and real world needs. For instance, suppose your cognitive distortion is, "No one will ever love me because I am ugly and fat." You could tell yourself, "I am a wonderful person and everyone loves me." The problem is that you do not believe this. You are attempting to do magic, to imagine a better you in the belief that if you just do so in the right way, long enough, it will come true. There are multitudes of popular books extolling the virtues and transformative power of this pre-rational magical thinking. Now compare that statement to a simple substitution for your cognitive distortion, such as, "Because I am not psychic I do not know that NO ONE will ever love me, for whatever reason. "Some people will think I am ugly and fat, others won't. Most probably won't care because they will be too busy wondering if I think *they* are ugly and fat!" The difference in effectiveness of this second set of statements, when compared to happy magical thinking is obvious. Why would anyone do the former when they could do the latter?

Optimism and positive thinking appears to go through a developmental progression just like most other aspects of personality. First, we are naively and magical positive; just by correct beliefs we can make the world the way we want it. This is called pre-personal magical thinking. At some point, if we ask enough questions, our unquestioning belief ripens into what Ehrenreich calls "vigilant realism" and happiness through reciprocity: treating others as we would like to be treated. Beyond this there is a third general approach to happiness that includes but transcends the other two. As we get out of our own way and disidentify from our sensory, emotional, mental, visual and consciousness self-definitions, we reduce the automatic and largely out-of-awareness filtering that blocks our perception of abundance, joy and even bliss. This is not positive thinking, and no amount of positive thinking will propel you into a life grounded in this sort of authentic happiness. It is instead a product of learning to get out of your own way.

IDL supports optimism while encouraging objectivity, by checking your conclusions and attitude against objective and subjective sources of objectivity (experts and interviewed emerging potentials) as well as your common sense. You can be constructively positive about your ability to get unstuck when you access the priorities of your life compass, as represented by the consensus recommendations of your interviewed emerging potentials, and by aligning your life with their priorities. Instead of trying to talk yourself into believing you are happy and life is fine when neither is the case, you can learn to move ahead with confidence that you can tune into life's agenda and learn to live your life in harmony with it.

Democracy

To one that advised him to set up a democracy in Sparta, "Pray," said Lycurgus, "do you first set a democracy in your own house."
Apophthegms of Kings and Great Commanders, Plutarch

Lycurgus was pointing out that families are hardly democracies, nor should they be. Instead, they are hierarchical autocracies, in which parents and caretakers play the role of (hopefully) beneficent autocrats and children play the role of (hopefully) obedient and grateful subjects. However, if we take "house" metaphorically in a way that Lycurgus never intended, his statement can remind us that our priority needs to be to create democracy within our own interior consciousness, something that very few ever contemplate and even fewer attempt.

There appears to be a reverse correlation between the amount of democracy and freedom that an individual or nation proclaims and what actually exists. While the public is focused on democracy, what is power doing? What do you discover when you "follow the money?" How much is power, generally in the form of financial interests, taking over or neutralizing democracy, or the will of the majority to overrule the preferences of the plutocratic minority? The old saw, "Socialism for the rich, capitalism for the rest," could be updated to say, "Power for the rich; democracy for the rest."

"Democracy" is not conducive to enlightenment to the extent that it does not take into account its necessary opposition, autocracy. Democracy is generally considered as the positive remedy to autocracy, when in fact both are not only important for development, waking up, and enlightenment, but absolutely necessary.

Since studying philosophy during my university days I have wondered how two men as brilliant and different as Plato and Aristotle could have both denounced democracy. Now I think I understand. Both objected to democracy on the ground that it led to rule by the mob, the "lowest common denominator," which was least educated and least endowed with the ability to make wise decisions. We would consider them, as all electorates in general, as captured under the delusional spell of the prevailing groupthink.

Athenian electors were chosen via sortition, the random selection of government positions. It was this type of randomly selected democratic electorate that condemned Socrates to death. Plato was horrified that his esteemed teacher Socrates could be dragged before a mob, publicly humiliated, and then executed by lesser men who represented a frightened and paranoid democratically elected establishment. Because power would always find ways to co-opt the majority of the voting public, Plato and Aristotle viewed democracy as one small step removed from tyranny. In large part because of the trial and execution of Socrates, Athenian democracy suffered a terrible reputation among subsequent political and philosophical thinkers, from Cicero to Machiavelli to almost every subsequent major philosopher, until the late eighteenth century revolutionaries in France and America. Socrates was executed and democracy denigrated not so much because of his radical philosophizing in the Athenian stoa as much as from charges that his former students and associates toppled democratic government while he stood idly by. Governmental institutions exist ostensibly to serve the people and guarantee security, freedom, and liberty by providing checks and balances on each other. I agreed with the US Constitutional founders that checks and balances were sufficient to prevent this from occurring. History has proven me wrong. We can see this even in the institution of parenting, in which "male" and "female" priorities are supposed to provide checks and balances and together provide a healthy context for the development of children. In fact, what they do is serve the powerful, wealthy and privileged, beginning with insuring their own institutional survival, and children, like citizens, get to pretty much figure out for themselves how to adapt to the prevailing cultural assumptions and behavioral requirements.

The arc of liberal democracy in the West has proven wrong the assumption that checks and balances are sufficient to protect democracy, mostly because democracy is no match for autocracy, particularly the cancerous form of plutocratic autocracy known as capitalism. The ongoing assaults on both institutions and laws by individual greed will generally prevail over the occasional expression of the will of the majority, particularly since that will tends to support the corruption associated with entrenched incumbents. Voting occurs sporadically, among voters with widely divergent and fractured interests while greed is continuously conspiring to manipulate the policies, rules and laws to internalize profit and externalize cost. Democracy simply has no way of competing with this incessant onslaught, and for this reason plutocracy glorifies and encourages it.

Consequently, it appears that Plato and Aristotle were right. What occurs, in actuality, once the propaganda and mythology are peeled away, is that power chokes off dissent and neutralizes checks and balances while supporting forms of groupthink that keep the public asleep. Look at any business, religious institution, or government and ask yourself how well its checks and balances are working to protect democracy within its particular sphere of influence. The vast majority of businesses do not even pretend to be democratic, justifying all policies and activities in pursuit of the maximization of profit within the context of hierarchical, authoritarian structures. Religious institutions are also intrinsically hierarchical and not democratic, echoing Plato's judgment that rule by those proclaimed "wise" (godly; chosen by God) are most fit to rule. Any in-depth study of the vast majority of businesses, religious institutions, governments, or law-enforcement systems will show that tyranny and power are strongly favored over democracy and freedom. Parents expect obedience and good grades in exchange for security and opportunities to grow and learn. No one expects a family to be a democracy. Why not? The answer is obvious. Where developmental and role differences demand different expectations of people, governing hierarchies are required.

I never expected to see the backside of "democracy." I grew up in a culture and society that took democracy for granted as the bedrock principle upon which freedom, justice, and human rights are based. In time I extended the concept of democracy to the microcosmic, intrasocial realm of interviewed emerging potentials as well as disenfranchised components of identity. The idea was to give respect and voice to perspectives that have been ignored, discounted, and repressed by our waking sense of self, which stifles its own creativity and growth by abrogating all power to itself. It was not designed or intended, however, to expand political correctness from human rights for primates to cockroaches and then to imaginary aspects of consciousness. There is an important difference between demonstrating respect to imaginary dream characters and granting them the human and voting rights assumed by democracy. IDL not only does not suggest or support that; it thinks it's crazy.

On an individual level, power and authority is generally centered on who is most self-aware, and that would be our waking identities. Every other aspect of the self is subordinated and made to serve it. This is not a democratic, but an autocratic model of self-governance, and it is taken for granted because it is adaptive, that is, it protects people and furthers their intentions. Fear of mob rule reverberates today not only in a distrust by the ruling class in the rule of the people, but in the disciples of Freud and our understanding about the working of the mind. As the story goes, it is not our waking sense of who we are, but the mass of uncontrollable unconscious desires that we imagine are threats to our sanity, health and productivity. The rational mind is the tragic hero fighting against the primitive sexual and violent urges of our animalistic, instinctive basic nature. By implication, trust of the voices of imaginary dream characters is foolish, dangerous, and leads to the destruction of rationality and all things good. This is a deep-seated and unconscious bias toward "ego strength," building a strong "self-sense" and defending against a fractured, dissociated identity. This strong, built-in prejudice largely explains why the consultation of dream group elements, with the goal of creating a life based on power sharing and inner consensus, has rarely been clearly articulated, much less put into practice. With the psychological geocentrism of humanity and psychology, the reality of consciousness is stood on its head: instead of seeing the rule of waking identity as a totalitarianism, a plutocracy of roles allied to maintain control and to shut out the majority of alternative perspectives and agendas, waking identity is viewed as the Great Protector, the Martyr, the bulwark against mob rule. The consequences of this convenient rationalization and self-justification is death. The light, creativity, and wisdom of consciousness is shut out in the name of security and control of the self. Autocracy wins over democracy.

In the West there has been a massive improvement in living standards brought about by financial exploitation and externalization of costs. Democracy not only has been used to defend and justify this process but serves as the rationalization for further exploitation, aggression, and exceptionalism, meaning a self-declared freedom from the laws to which it holds others accountable. We know that capitalism, not democracy, is responsible for this massive improvement in living standards because China, Singapore, and Hong Kong have experienced a similar unparalleled surge, also brought about by financial exploitation, but without democracy. These countries have not justified themselves as the sources and protectors of all things good through the sacred institutions of democracy. In fact, massive prosperity has come to these countries despite democracy and guarantees of individual liberties. The social contract in China has been, from Ping until at least Xi, "We will let you do whatever you want to earn money as long as you do not threaten us, the government, and do not create social unrest. In fact, we will do what we can as a government to help you make as much money as possible." This social contract, essentially one of *lassiz-faire* capitalism, has had few pretensions of being democratic.

Many in my generation have watched in horror as the United States, the country that most clothes itself in the robes of democracy, has proven itself to be among the least democratic and most tyrannical and poorly governed nations on the planet. We have watched it overthrow scores of governments and their populations handed over to tyrants, all in the name of democracy, freedom, and human rights. Democracy has had no appreciable impact on the gutting of the middle class or the funneling of most of the country's wealth to the one percent. This has led many to wake-up to the reality that the US is in fact a militaristic plutocracy that uses democracy as cover for predation. The release of the Senate's torture report reminds us of the central fact of American society today: any semblance of equal justice under the law is now gone from what our leaders claim is the world's leading democracy. Instead of a constitutional democracy living under the law there exists a gangster government that fails to enforce the law, but instead prosecutes whistle blowers who make public its violations. Evidence of this includes the failure to prosecute, indict, and convict violators of US laws and international treaties prohibiting torture who then lie about it under oath, and when found out justify their illegal acts by claiming that they worked to make America safer, as if this excuses law breaking; failure to investigate, prosecute, indict, and convict government officials who engage in unconstitutional surveillance activities and then lie about it under oath; failure to investigate, prosecute, indict, and convict financial banksters and fraudsters for crimes resulting in the loss of many trillions of dollars of asset value owned by middle and working class Americans; failure to indict, and convict police who murder, rape and unlawfully seize private property, even refusing to investigate and prosecute most of them; failure to investigate, prosecute, indict, and convict police violations of constitutional rights to freedom of speech, assembly, and press; and Department of Homeland Security collaboration in violations of First Amendment Rights by State and Local Governments.

The US has been supported in many of these crimes by most of the other countries that most loudly proclaim their dedication to democracy, freedom, and human rights, such as Israel, the countries of the European Union, and the countries of the English-speaking world, including the UK, Canada, Australia, and New Zealand. All of the above actively supported a fascist coup government in Ukraine. They support brutal dictatorships, such as in Saudi Arabia and Egypt, when doing so supports US foreign policy and business interests. Another undeniable example of this, courageously brought into the light of day by Edward Snowden, has been the alliance of "democracies" to undermine the privacy rights of everyone, rights without which neither democracy or freedom can exist. Even those countries which have been victimized by these abuses, such as Germany, are utterly compromised by the institutional benefits they receive from these arrangements.

The conclusion must be, "If this is democracy and freedom, what is tyranny and slavery?" Within such contexts "democracy" and "freedom" have no meaning except as Orwellian, groupthink terms, or as tools to pacify the population. Democracy, under such circumstances, is an enemy of human rights. Nor is the solution "more" of the "right" kind of democracy. "Pure" democracy is an unrealistic ideal because the population as a whole lacks the time, interest, and aptitudes to educate itself sufficiently to have an opinion, much less an informed opinion, on most issues which demand decisions. Legislators rarely read the legislation they are voting on. Instead they pass legislation written by and for banks and other special interests, "trust" the leadership of their party and allow themselves to be herded like a pack of goats. When democracy is taken to the extreme of consensus, like it was in the Polish Diet in the 1700's, nothing happens; anyone can block any decision for any reason which leads to the failure of government to act at all. Nor does Churchill's famous statement suffice: "Democracy is the worst form of government - except for everything else." This is like saying, "Organized corruption is inevitable."

Although significant countervailing positive forces exist in the educational and grassroots organizational ability of the internet, these efforts lay outside most formal organizational structures, all of which have been co-opted by the plutocracy. For example, media was long considered "the fourth branch," after congress, the executive and judicial branches of government. Its job was to act as a fourth "check" on the other three. However, it is now entirely co-opted, as mainstream media is owned and controlled by either plutocrats or the government. Democracy seems to work best as an informal, almost *ad hoc* force that influences government beyond formal power structures, such as through NGOs and public interest groups such as AVAAZ. Democracy is also much more effective on a small scale, like Iceland, perhaps because it is harder to develop a large, entrenched bureaucracy that hides from accountability when populations are small and governance is local. Once democracy becomes legitimatized, that is, turned into the law of the land, and the priority of organizations, it seems to be almost the kiss of death. Institutionalized democracy is inevitably co-opted and corrupted by the most powerful interests of the moment. Under such circumstances, how can justice be determined by a majority vote?

Ken Wilber's integral model offers a solution that makes sense but that is difficult to implement or sustain. It notes that development, whether of individuals, organizations, or nations, occurs through the interplay of autocracy and democracy, hierarchy and heterarchy, "agency" and "communion," male and female, transcendence and inclusion. Each plays the role of "antithesis" to the other in order to create a higher level synthesis. Instead of playing the game of pitting one against the other, the AQAL (all quadrants, lines, levels, states) integral model says "both are essential." They represent polar opposites in life force, evolution and involution, transcendence and inclusion. When one becomes too strong its opposite inevitably is generated to restore balance. Consequently, the problem is not so much with democracy or authoritarianism, as it is with the over-emphasis of one to the exclusion of the other.

Just as in male-female relationships, the solution for societies appears to be something akin to androgyny. This means finding and supporting a blend of autocracy and democracy, agency and communion, hierarchy and heterarchy, stratification and egalitarianism, evolution and involution, transcendence and inclusion, states and stages. What matters is not tyranny or democracy, but to ask, What is the balance?" "What is out of balance?" "What is required to move the system toward balance, homeostasis, integration, and androgyny?"

The answer to this question requires objectivity. For example, children require autocracy in the form of structures and nurturing guardians. The same is true for both young societies and societies in crisis. However, as children and societies mature, their need for authority decreases, except in the case of crises. If there is too much authority, there is a natural tendency to rebel against it. This is the stage at which both individuality and forms of collective governance, such as democracy, are most likely to be effective. Further on in the developmental stage, both individuals and society again require imposed authority, but for different reasons. For individuals, imposed authority is required because they have actualized their individual potentials in the context of their society and culture and then become stuck. Society does not offer them further advancement; to do so would be to work against its interests, and they themselves are generally comfortably adapted to the structures, rewards and punishments of society. For society, it needs an authority that is greater than its fossilized governmental structures, but it fights the restrictions of these, as the United States has against any restraints imposed by either international law or the United Nations.

These are examples of how individuals and governments are embedded in comfortable contexts and therefore often lack the necessary objectivity to see what is out of balance. Even when it becomes crystal clear that a system is far out of balance, as it is in alcoholism, smoking, spousal abuse, and economies where almost all income flows to a small plutocratic minority, there are always powerful elements that benefit from maintaining the status quo. Because individuals, families, religions, corporations, economies and nations adapted to and even drive through dysfunction, expect strong resistance to any and all efforts to bring any system back into balance. Just like most of us, most governments would rather die than change, and so they do, generating massive social collapses in the process.

IDL encourages deep listening to both internal and external sources of objectivity in order to learn and amplify an ongoing balance between democratic and autocratic polarities. This is particularly important for individuals and societies at early and late stages of development. At early, it minimizes enculturation to groupthink by supplementing external parental and social authority with interior sources of objectivity that develop individual priorities in conjunction with those of their own unique life compass. At late stages, it illuminates paths to growth beyond enmeshment in individual priorities and social adjustment. The more feedback that you receive that tells you that you are badly off-course the more difficult it is for you to stay in denial. This is precisely why there is considerable resistance to IDL: it shines light on the dark places, generating uncomfortable cognitive dissonance as self-image collides with reality. This same principle holds true for families, corporations, religions and governmental systems. If deep listening is used as part of an ongoing feedback process it can serve as a powerful preventative, meaning that course corrections can occur before they become so massive that costs are prohibitive.

On a familial level this involves treating the dream characters and the personifications of life issues that are important to various family members as wake-up calls and interviewing them. Recommendations are vetted by the family and those chosen are operationalized, with the entire family unit supporting their application.

On a corporate level, core challenges for the company as a whole regarding its growth and survivability are identified. These are personified by representatives of different invested stake holders: CEO, stock holders, management, and workers. The recommendations of various interviewed emerging potentials are compared and plans for application are operationalized and implemented for those which are deemed valuable and useful by external sources of objectivity, including those same stakeholders. The more elements of holarchic governance that are present the more likely IDL interviewing is to be tolerated.

On a governmental level, this involves a willingness for "deciders" to submit to similar processes. Ideally, it would become part of the assumed and accepted work culture. Accessing such feedback triggers core resistances for individual, familial, corporate, and governmental levels because it quickly and effectively identifies sources of imbalance. All must be supported in the challenging move from unconscious incompetence to conscious incompetence if individuals, families, organizations or governments are ever to achieve conscious competence, much less unconscious competence, in which responsibility and excellence are habits. A cynic would say that no one wants democracy; we only want to convince others and ourselves that we do. Everyone seeks the freedom to rule as they wish, subject to the financial pressures of lobbyists, shareholders, and personal preferences. A lack of a willingness to take steps that would generate a genuine democratic process is validation of this statement.

In addition to deep listening to both external and internal sources of objectivity, IDL emphasizes the importance of both transparency and accountability. Power does not hate democracy, because it has proven a ready tool and useful servant for those in control, as long as what passes for democracy is itself neutered. Democracy is weak and fragile by nature and therefore easily co-opted by the powerful. Accountability and transparency, just like genuine democracy, are hated by power, because power grows by exploiting the weaknesses of opponents, organizational structures, and laws. This inherently leads to over-reach, meaning that like cancer, the powerful continue to exploit until the base upon which they depend is exhausted. The more quickly exploitation is identified and exposed to the light of day the quicker the inevitable abuses by the powerful are checked. This brings up two immediate but perennial solutions: Is there transparency? If so, what kind? In what ways? Is there accountability? If so, what kind? In what ways?

One form of individual transparency is created by interviewing dreams. This is because dreams are spontaneous creations, and interviewing non human objects in dreams produce results that are very difficult to control or manipulate. Similar collective results occur when some aspect of the shared belief system, which acts as a cultural dream, is interviewed.

While individuals, families, businesses, and nations constantly talk of wanting what is best for their growth, for children, employees, and citizens, forces that benefit from the status quo do not easily give up power. IDL attempts to increase personal equivalents of democracy by increasing deep listening, transparency, and accountability within interior collective commons in both microcosmic and macrocosmic holons. IDL supports both authoritarianism, hierarchy, agency, evolution, state breakthroughs, and transcendence on the one hand, and democracy, heterarchy, communion, involution, stage consolidation, and inclusion on the other. It supports authoritarianism by acknowledging there are innumerable functions in development in which, if waking identity does not take the lead and insist on a course, the horses of emotion and addiction will pull the chariot of the body and its driver off a cliff. In this sense a personal governance of totalitarianism, absolutism, and tyranny is required, and pretending that it isn't is merely a form of self-delusion. For example, who decides what is healthy to eat, you or your emotions? Who decides when and how to exercise, you or your body? Yes, you will find those that say, "trust your instincts" when it comes to eating and exercising, but exactly which instincts are those? Who gets to decide which instincts are healthy and which ones are not? In matters of love, is it wise to follow your heart? Most of us can tell horror stories about that one.

The solution is not to ignore or minimize the influence of body, emotions, instincts, or heart, but to listen to them and balance their interests with those of your waking identity, reserving for it the final and majority vote, because it has relatively more objectivity and final responsibility. The subsystems of consciousness evolved your waking identity so that it could be on the mountaintop of personal evolution where the view was best, exactly because there are adaptive advantages to hierarchy. This is what Plato understood. Therefore, IDL provides a number of tools for improving waking decision making. As long as development requires autocracy, steps need to be taken to ensure that it is a benevolent one. These steps include triangulation, in which both external and internal sources of objectivity are consulted in addition to relying on your own best judgment; learning about and freeing yourself from dysfunctional childhood and cultural scripting; recognizing and eliminating the Drama Triangle in the three domains of interpersonal relationships with both others and the environment, thinking and feeling, and night time dreams; goal setting; comparing goals to the priorities of interviewed emerging potentials; elimination of emotional, rational, and perceptual cognitive distortions; learning and using communication skills to reduce misunderstanding and abuse while increasing the ability to accurately listen and respond; role playing for the development of empathy; pranayama, in order to amplify the seven octaves and meditation to positively transform both physiology and anatomy while amplifying characteristics of oneness, including abundance, cosmic humor, and luminosity. All of this means that IDL provides an integral life practice that supports the creation of a benevolent personal dictatorship. It sees no inherent reason why love, cooperation, respect, abundance, cosmic humor and luminosity are incompatible with hierarchy, agency, and yes, authoritarianism. IDL views idealism not as the Platonic embrace of a society structured along such lines, but as those who refuse to accept the reality of its necessity. Denial of the usefulness of authoritarianism is similar to pretending you don't have or need a skeleton because you do not see it, or because it is hard and relatively inflexible, when what you want and love is the soft, pliable, giving flesh that hangs upon it. This is one expression of the utopianism that results when communion, egalitarianism, democracy, and love are made exclusive priorities.

Every decision is more effective and rewarding when alternate invested perspectives are considered because decisions then become more inclusive. While hierarchy, totalitarianism, and agency transcend, transcendence without inclusion at best produces temporary state openings that are inevitably followed by spectacular downswings and crashes. For instance, the inevitable over-reaching of plutocrats, those who favor the privileges that accompany power and status, leads to equally inevitable crashes because autocracy fails to build into itself the necessary safeguards of deep listening, accountability and transparency, which are essentially tools of heterarchy and communion.

IDL supports heterarchy and democracy in a number of ways that are as radical as its strong support of waking totalitarianism. These include listening; the practice of deep listening; becoming imaginary, nonsensical, irrational, and absurd perspectives and interviewing them, whether they come from dreams, real life, or imagination; affording those perspectives the same respect given by children to parents and respected elders; taking interviewed perspectives seriously; applying those recommendations that pass the test of triangulation in operationally-defined, practical ways in one's daily life; submitting those results to the accountability of peers in the method as well as real world measures of effectiveness; the consultation of a variety of invested perspectives with the intent of making decisions that are inclusive. This is all done out of a strong conviction that transcendence without inclusion is foolish. The quality and sustainability of transcendence is dependent on the breadth and balance of the inclusiveness that supports it. While state awakenings can be easily attained with focus on hierarchy, agency, and waking totalitarianism, stage development and evolution is only attained with collective, consensual decision making, community, and egalitarianism.

Any approach, IDL included, that emphasizes one of these two polarities over the other is not and cannot be integral, because it will either favor inclusiveness over transcendence or transcendence over inclusiveness. Some observers of IDL dismiss it as being unrealistically irrational and delusional in consulting dream characters and other imaginary perspectives while others dismiss it as being unrealistically rigid, in that it insists on hierarchy and a privileged place for non-communal based decisions. Some advocates of IDL support it for the self-acceptance and inclusiveness it teaches while ignoring the personal accountability of taking the recommendations of interviewed emerging potentials seriously, while others support it for its access to transcendent states of consciousness without wanting to listen to and build internal consensus for action. Finding the middle ground, the middle way, that balances these two extremes is not easy, but this is why balance is one of the six core qualities that IDL emphasizes and why it views balance as a prerequisite for the development of wisdom.

Democracy can be improved by electing randomly selected ordinary citizens, a process which reflects the dynamics of dreams in IDL interviewing. Dream characters are not "chosen;" they spontaneously appear through a process of self-choice, which is similar to the random selection of citizen legislators. The *ad hoc* nature of dream groups in no way reduces the effectiveness of their perspectives, implying that similar *ad hoc* legislative membership is no deterrent to good government and in fact improves the number and quality of options available for waking decision making. Regarding expertise, one could hardly argue that current democratic legislatures are elected based on expertise, but rather public preferences largely driven by single issue advertising.

Clearly, in the sphere of governance and the development of democracy, it is in the microcosmic, intrasocial domains that you have the most power, control, and where your actions are most likely to make the most profound difference for you in your life. The Japanese peace activist and Buddhist leader, Daisaku Ikeda said, "A great revolution in just one single individual will help achieve a change in the destiny of a society and, further, will enable a change in the destiny of humankind." While you should not disengage from the exterior chaos of politics and governance, your efforts to change the macrocosm are going to be predicated on the ongoing work you do to generate a balanced and integrated microcosm. This is what IDL calls "Dream Politics," and why it is wary of those who glorify democracy at the expense of authority, leadership, and structure.

Your work with interviewing dream characters and the personifications of life issues creates first an awareness of your intrasocial reality and then, through your respectful listening, gives it "voting rights" in your decision-making, thereby turning your microsocial reality from totalitarianism toward rule by consent of the governed. As Gandhi said, "Be the change you wish to see in the world."

Appendix I

IDL Life Issue Interview Protocol
Joseph Dillard

What are three fundamental life issues that you are dealing with now in your life?

1.
2.
3.

Which issue brings up the strongest feelings?

I

If those feelings had a color (or colors), what would it be?

I

Imagine that color filling the space in front of you so that it has depth, height, width, and aliveness.

Now watch that color swirl, congeal, and condense into a shape. Don't make it take a shape, just watch it and say the first thing that you see or that comes to your mind: An animal? Object? Plant? What?

I

Now remember how as a child you liked to pretend you were a teacher or a doctor? It's easy and fun for you to imagine that you are this or that character in your dream and answer some questions I ask, saying the first thing that comes to your mind. If you wait too long to answer, that's not the character answering - that's YOU trying to figure out the right thing to say!

(Character,) would you please tell me about yourself and what you are doing?

I

What do you like most about yourself? What are your strengths?

I

What do you dislike most about yourself? Do you have weaknesses?

What are they?

I

(Character), you are in this person's life experience, correct? They created you, right? (Character), what aspect of this person do you represent or most closely personify?

I

(Character,) if you could be anywhere you wanted to be and take any form you desired, would you change? If so, how?

I

(Continue, answering as the transformed object, if it chose to change.) *(Character), how would you score yourself 0-10, in confidence, empathy, wisdom, acceptance, peace of mind, and witnessing? Why?*

Confidence:
Empathy:
Wisdom:
Acceptance:
Inner Peace:
Witnessing:

(Character,) if you scored tens in all six of these qualities, would you be different? If so, how?

I

How would the life of the person who created you be different if he/she naturally scored high in all six of these qualities all the time?

I

If you could live the life of the person who created you for him/her, how would you live it differently?

I

If you could live this person's waking life for him/her today, would you handle his/her three life issues differently? If so, how?

1.
2.
3.

What three life issues would you focus on if you were in charge of his/her life?

1.
2.
3.

In what life situations would it be most beneficial for this person to imagine that they are you and act as you would?

I

Why do you think that you are in this person's life?

I

How is this person most likely to ignore what you are saying to them?

I

What would you recommend that they do about that?

I

What have you heard yourself say?

I

If this experience were a wake-up call from your life compass, what do you think it would be saying to you?

I

List the recommendations made in the interview:

I

Which ones do you want to implement in your life? You can do so by scoring yourself either by checking off an item you remembered to do or giving yourself a score between 0-10 on values you are working on increasing or decreasing...

I

Appendix II

IDL Dream Interview Protocol
Joseph Dillard

What are three fundamental life issues that you are dealing with now in your life?

1.
2.
3.

Describe a dream or a nightmare you have had.

|

Why do you think you had it? Write your associations.

|

What are the characters, including inanimate objects, in the dream? List them here:

|

Which character would you like to interview? Antagonists like monsters, fires and attackers are often good choices; so are dream objects, like chairs, beds or trees.

|

Now remember how as a child you liked to pretend you were a teacher or a doctor? It's easy and fun for you to imagine that you are this or that character in your dream and answer some questions I ask, saying the first thing that comes to your mind. If you wait too long to answer, that's not the character answering - that's YOU trying to figure out the right thing to say!

(Character,) would you please tell me about yourself and what you are doing in this dream?

|

What do you like most about yourself? What are your strengths?

I

What do you dislike most about yourself? Do you have weaknesses? What are they?

I

(Character), you are in this person's life experience, correct? They created you, right? (Character), what aspect of this person do you represent or most closely personify?

I

(Character,) if you could be anywhere you wanted to be and take any form you desired, would you change? If so, how?

I

(Continue, answering as the transformed object, if it chose to change.)
(Character), how would you score yourself 0-10, in confidence, empathy, wisdom, acceptance, peace of mind, and witnessing? Why?

Confidence:
Empathy:
Wisdom:
Acceptance:
Inner Peace:
Witnessing:

(Character,) if you scored tens in all six of these qualities, would you be different? If so, how?

I

How would the life of the person who created you be different if he/she naturally scored high in all six of these qualities all the time?

I

If you could live the life of the person who created you for him/her, how would you live it differently?

I

If you could live this person's waking life for him/her today, would you handle his/her three life issues differently? If so, how?

1.
2.
3.

What three life issues would you focus on if you were in charge of his/her life?

1.
2.
3.

In what life situations would it be most beneficial for this person to imagine that they are you and act as you would?

I

Why do you think that you are in this dream?

I

What do you think this dream is about?

I

(Character,) you are imaginary. Why should this dreamer listen to anything you have said?

Thank you, Character! And now questions for the dreamer: What have you heard yourself say?

I

If this experience were a wake-up call from your life compass, what do you think it would be saying to you?

I

List the recommendations made in the interview:

Which ones do you want to implement in your life? You can do so by scoring yourself either by checking off an item you remembered to do or giving yourself a score between 0-10 on values you are working on increasing or decreasing...

A

abundance, 69, 72, 75, 78, 79, 124, 146, 161, 203, 208, 217
ad hominem, 20
addiction, 18, 23, 28, 36, 64, 76, 84, 85, 86, 87, 98, 129, 195, 217
Adi da, 180
adolescence, 52, 91, 148
agni yoga, 1
agnosticism, 163, 183, 187
ahamkara, 91
Akashic Records, 125
Alice in Wonderland, 10, 130, 166
ambiguity, 12, 64, 92
anamnesis, 121
Anatma, 180
Andrew Cohen, 180
anima, 177
animistic spirit, 171
antagonist, 67
antithesis, 62, 64, 192, 214
AQAL, 16, 19, 23, 41, 42, 65, 190, 214
archetypes, 118, 119, 177
Aristotle, 209, 210
asceticism, 34, 91
astrology, 168, 170
atheism, 163, 183, 187
Athenian democracy, 209
Atman, 45, 77, 151, 154, 176, 179
authoritarianism, 214, 216, 217
autocracy, 35, 209, 210, 214, 217, 218
autonomy, 144, 171
AVAAZ, 213
Avalokiteshvara, 1
axis mundi, 95

B

balance, 21, 24, 34, 40, 61, 62, 63, 64, 67, 69, 74, 119, 125, 133, 152, 157, 161, 180, 189, 199, 214, 215, 217, 218
band wagon, 20
Barbara Ehrenreich, 205
Beck, 19
Bhagavad Gita, 197
bhakti yoga, 1
black and white thinking, 19, 64
Bodhisattiva vow, 5
Brahma, 182

Brahman, 77
breath, 34, 69, 72, 78, 157, 189
breathing, 18, 61, 69, 75
Brian Weiss, 152
Buddhism, 13, 40, 50, 57, 60, 63, 72, 76, 79, 91, 92, 117, 120, 147, 148, 153, 155, 158, 164, 175, 176, 179, 182
burn-out, 105
Burns, 19

C

C.G. Jung, 58, 64
capitalism, 18, 20, 21, 40, 97, 201, 204, 209, 210, 212
Carl Sagan, 197
causal mysticism, 184
chakra, 1
chakras, 34
chariot, 14, 21, 217
Charles Sanders Peirce, 88
China, 21, 212
Chinese Buddhism, 21
Chogyam Trungpa, 76, 180
Christ, 179
Christian apocalypticism, 200
Christian mystic, 188
Christianity, 40, 60, 99, 137
Cicero, 209
Clarity, 10, 24, 25
co-dependent, 36
cognitive distortion, 106
Cognitive distortions, 18
    Emotional cognitive distortions, 19
    Perceptual cognitive distortions, 21, 22, 203
    Rational cognitive distortions, 20
collective unconscious, 118, 123, 167, 177
Colonization, 18
Communication with the Spirit World, 165
Confucianism, 21, 32
conscience, 35, 91, 99, 100, 101, 102, 103, 104, 105, 106, 107, 108, 109, 110, 111, 112, 113, 180, 192, 193, 194
conscience but rather, 104
Copernicus, 153
cosmic humor, 39, 69, 72, 75, 76, 77, 78, 79, 161, 192, 217
countertransference, 140, 142
Credibility, 10, 26, 27, 28, 29, 200

D

Daisaku Ikeda, 219
Dalai Lama, 148
Daniel Goleman, 190
Daniel P. Brown, 190
Deep Listening, iv, 10, 33, 53, 69
deity, 41, 42, 99, 184
delusion, 35, 45, 52, 55, 56, 63, 70,
    71, 85, 91, 96, 98, 119, 130, 153,
    155, 164, 166, 167, 169, 170,
    180, 203, 206, 217
delusional, 38, 56, 62, 71, 77, 98,
    129, 133, 152, 169, 209, 218
democracy, 20, 36, 96, 189, 200,
    204, 208, 209, 210, 211, 212,
    213, 214, 216, 218, 219
denial, 91, 215
dependency, 18, 41, 60, 88, 89,
    114, 156
Descartes, 178
development, 11, 12, 17, 19, 22, 23,
    26, 34, 40, 41, 46, 50, 51, 55, 56,
    57, 58, 61, 62, 63, 64, 65, 66, 67,
    71, 72, 73, 79, 81, 82, 84, 85, 86,
    88, 90, 91, 92, 95, 97, 99, 102,
    103, 113, 138, 143, 144, 148,
    149, 150, 151, 152, 154, 157,
    159, 160, 161, 166, 168,
    170,171, 172, 177, 178, 179,
    180, 181, 189, 191, 197, 198,
    209, 210, 214, 215, 217, 218,
    219
developmental dialectic, 62, 67
developmental lines, 23, 26
Dharma, 72, 158, 159, 160, 161,
    185
diagnosis, 52, 132, 141, 206
diamond, 41, 45, 75, 117
divine, 13, 43, 63, 66, 79, 114, 150,
    155, 158, 159, 160, 182
Dolores Krieger, 197
Donald Trump, 27
Dorje, 117
Doubt, 50, 51, 55, 200
drama, 36, 55, 56, 64, 68, 72, 76,
    85, 88, 89, 117, 125, 146, 157,
    172, 184, 194, 195
Drama Triangle, 19, 48, 59, 97, 99,
    131, 134, 142, 151, 153, 155,
    163, 184, 201, 217
dream, 11, 28, 30, 31, 33, 35, 36,
    37, 38, 42, 45, 52, 53, 54, 56, 58,
    60, 62, 66, 73, 74, 79, 90, 92,
    100, 118, 122, 129, 130, 132,
133, 138, 139, 142, 143, 144,
    163, 164, 166, 167, 168, 169,
    173, 174, 176, 180, 183, 202,
    203, 211, 215, 216, 218, 219, 1,
    5, 7
dream characters, 11, 31, 33, 37,
    38, 45, 52, 53, 56, 58, 73, 74, 90,
    92, 118, 133, 139, 143, 144, 167,
    180, 211, 215, 218
Dream Politics, 219
dreamer, 45, 132, 133, 139, 7
DSM V, 132
dualisms, 33, 41, 42, 46, 63, 182
dualities, 42, 61, 63, 79
dukkha, 15

E

early personal, 102, 148, 156, 157,
    170, 182
Ecclesiastes, 5
Edgar Cayce, 148, 165
Edgar Cayce and Reincarnation,
    148
Edward Snowden, 213
egalitarianism, 40, 96, 137, 144,
    149, 170, 214, 218
ego, 91, 92, 93, 95, 129, 134, 137,
    139, 151, 177, 211
ego development, 91
ego strength, 91, 211
egotism, 91
Egyptians, 96, 134, 165
Ehrenreich, 206, 207
Einstein, 20
elephant, 41, 65, 143
elevationism, 89
Ellis, 19
emerging potentials, 11, 32, 34, 38,
    43, 44, 51, 56, 58, 62, 63, 64, 65,
    71, 73, 74, 75, 77, 79, 80, 85, 90,
    93, 98, 103, 105, 107, 114, 117,
    120, 121, 122, 129, 130, 131,
    133, 138, 139, 141, 144, 145,
    146, 156, 157, 180, 181, 184,
    185, 186, 187, 208, 211, 215,
    217, 218
empathy, 6, 7, 15, 16, 29, 34, 40,
    41, 42, 47, 48, 49, 51, 53, 67, 69,
    71, 72, 78, 98, 135, 141, 190,
    217, 2, 6
Empiricism, 57, 58, 65, 90, 198
End Nightmares Forever!, 9, 15
energy, 63, 134, 136, 150, 157,

rationalization, 52, 91, 150, 152, 211, 212
Reality, 18, 43
Reality Therapy, 18
reason, 22, 28, 33, 34, 40, 46, 50, 54, 55, 56, 57, 63, 64, 65, 73, 77, 81, 82, 86, 88, 91, 96, 113, 114, 128, 139, 141, 156, 160, 162, 163, 182, 189, 191, 202, 204, 207, 210, 213, 217
reductionism, 34, 89, 90
regression, 19, 89, 91, 95, 150
Reiki, 1, 58
reincarnation, 121, 147, 148, 149, 150, 151, 152, 153, 154, 156, 157, 158, 160, 164, 167, 174, 175
repression, 38, 91, 92, 118, 128, 130, 185, 195
respect, 27, 29, 32, 33, 36, 51, 62, 73, 74, 76, 77, 90, 94, 97, 98, 129, 131, 136, 137, 143, 148, 154, 155, 161, 171, 183, 198, 202, 211, 217, 218
Richard Alpert, 3
roles, 14, 26, 35, 38, 39, 40, 41, 58, 82, 89, 92, 143, 150, 156, 160, 180, 182, 184, 211
Rumi, 114
Russell Paul Schofeld, 3

S

sacred, 33, 40, 41, 42, 43, 46, 63, 80, 96, 182, 212
salvation, 60, 182, 185
samadhi, 43, 63
Sangha, 72, 147
Saul, 5
Science Set Free, 90
scientific materialism, 90
Scientology, 2, 17
score, 42, 71, 94, 103, 116, 124, 134, 141, 146, 160, 175, 184, 186, 193, 2, 4, 6, 8
script, 55, 101, 102, 153, 156, 175
scripting, 56, 101, 102, 142, 153, 156, 157, 182, 200, 203, 217
Secrets of the Millionaire Mind, 204
Self, 35, 43, 77, 83, 143, 151, 176, 177, 178, 179, 181, 193
self-actualization, 178
self-aspect, 139, 143, 145, 146
self-aspects, 35, 130, 144, 145, 195

self-sense, 40, 52, 95, 130, 171, 180, 181, 211
Seven Octaves of Enlightenment, 69
shadow, 35, 77, 83, 126, 127, 128, 129, 130, 131, 134, 177, 200
shaman, 141, 171
shamanic, 43, 165, 190
Sheldrake, 90, 144
should, 104, 108, 111, 113
siddhis, 58, 77, 197
sin, 13, 43, 103, 105, 106, 107, 110, 111, 128, 183
Siva, 62, 182
six core qualities, 42, 69, 71, 72, 94, 103, 116, 117, 124, 134, 141, 144, 146, 157, 160, 184, 186, 195, 218
skandhas, 120, 164, 165
skepticism, 55, 90, 113, 163, 168, 200, 201
slavery, 183, 213
sleep paralysis, 13
socialism, 40
sociopathy, 48
Socrates, 51, 209
Socratic dialectic, 52
soul, 12, 43, 44, 83, 114, 151, 162, 163, 164, 165, 168, 169, 176, 178, 179
Spirit, 12, 13, 165, 179, 189
spiritual, 12, 13, 40, 43, 58, 63, 77, 80, 85, 113, 119, 135, 154, 163, 166, 190, 191, 196, 197, 198
Spock, 55
St. Theresa of Avila, 188
stage, 40, 41, 66, 67, 72, 81, 86, 88, 97, 149, 160, 167, 177, 178, 179, 191, 214, 216, 218
stoicism, 177
straw man, 20
subconscious, 35, 92, 118, 120, 121, 122, 125, 126, 167
sublimation, 91, 118
Subtle energies, 196
symbols, 118, 138, 139, 143
synthesis, 40, 62, 67, 91, 214

T

Tanya Luhrmann, 12
Taoism, 21
Tarot, 58
teaching, 40, 41, 52, 133, 142, 149, 159

www.ingramcontent.com/pod-product-compliance
Lightning Source LLC
Chambersburg PA
CBHW062134280526
45788CB00001B/164